Julián Casanova is Professor of History at the University of Zaragoza. His books include *Anarchism, the Republic and Civil War in Spain: 1931–1939* (2005) and *The Spanish Republic and Civil War* (2010).

I.B.TAURIS SHORT HISTORIES

I.B.Tauris Short Histories is an authoritative and elegantly written new series which puts a fresh perspective on the way history is taught and understood in the twenty-first century. Designed to have strong appeal to university students and their teachers, as well as to general readers and history enthusiasts, *I.B.Tauris Short Histories* comprises a novel attempt to bring informed interpretation, as well as factual reportage, to historical debate. Addressing key subjects and topics in the fields of history, the history of ideas, religion, classical studies, politics, philosophy and Middle East studies, the series seeks intentionally to move beyond the bland, neutral 'introduction' that so often serves as the primary undergraduate teaching tool. While always providing students and generalists with the core facts that they need to get to grips with the essentials of any particular subject, *I.B.Tauris Short Histories* goes further. It offers new insights into how a topic has been understood in the past, and what different social and cultural factors might have been at work. It brings original perspectives to bear on manner of its current interpretation. It raises questions and – in its extensive further reading lists – points to further study, even as it suggests answers. Addressing a variety of subjects in a greater degree of depth than is often found in comparable series, yet at the same time in concise and compact handbook form, *I.B.Tauris Short Histories* aims to be 'introductions with an edge'. In combining questioning and searching analysis with informed history writing, it brings history up-to-date for an increasingly complex and globalised digital age.

A Short History of . . .

the American Civil War	Paul Anderson (Clemson University)
the American Revolutionary War	Stephen Conway (University College London)
Ancient Greece	P J Rhodes, FBA (University of Durham)
Ancient Rome	Andrew Wallace-Hadrill (University of Cambridge)
the Anglo-Saxons	Henrietta Leyser (University of Oxford)
the Byzantine Empire	Dionysios Stathakopoulos (King's College London)
the Celts	Alex Woolf (University of St Andrews)
the Crimean War	Trudi Tate (University of Cambridge)
English Renaissance Drama	Helen Hackett (University College London)
the English Revolution and the Civil Wars	David J Appleby (University of Nottingham)
the Etruscans	Corinna Riva (University College London)
Imperial Egypt	Robert Morkot (University of Exeter)
the Korean War	Allan R Millett (University of New Orleans)
Medieval English Mysticism	Vincent Gillespie (University of Oxford)
the Minoans	John Bennet (University of Sheffield)
the Mughal Empire	Michael Fisher (Oberlin College)
Muslim Spain	Alex J Novikoff (Rhodes College, Memphis)
Nineteenth-Century Philosophy	Joel Rasmussen (University of Oxford)
the Normans	Leonie Hicks (University of Southampton)
the Phoenicians	Glenn E Markoe
the Reformation	Helen Parish (University of Reading)
the Renaissance in Northern Europe	Malcolm Vale (University of Oxford)
the Risorgimento	Nick Carter (University of Wales, Newport)
the Spanish Civil War	Julián Casanova (University of Zaragoza)
Transatlantic Slavery	Kenneth Morgan (Brunel University)
Venice and the Venetian Empire	Maria Fusaro (University of Exeter)
the Vikings	Clare Downham (University of Liverpool)
the Wars of the Roses	David Grummitt (University of Kent)
Weimar Germany	Colin Storer (University of Nottingham)

'Julián Casanova is one of the most original and exciting historians currently working on the Spanish Civil War. His books on anarchism, the Catholic Church and the Francoist repression have earned him a glowing international reputation. This short history draws on his own research and combines his trademark reliability and readability in a book that students and general readers alike will find invaluable.'

Paul Preston, Príncipe de Asturias Professor
of Contemporary Spanish History, London School of Economics

'Julián Casanova is one of the most productive of the current generation of Spanish intellectuals who are determined that democracy and human rights, now better established than in any previous period of Spanish history, will become the habitual and accepted framework of Spanish public life. He shows clearly how the political shortcomings of the Republic, the enthusiasm of Mussolini and Hitler to aid General Franco, the Stalinist mixture of military aid with secretive political interference in the life of the Republic, and the failure of the Western democracies to aid the Republic, all combined to assure the military victory and postwar dictatorship of Franco. This is an excellently written and very carefully documented history of the Civil War of 1936–39.'

Gabriel Jackson, Professor Emeritus of History,
University of California, San Diego

'Julián Casanova is one of Spain's leading historians. His innovative and groundbreaking research on the Spanish Civil War and its long aftermath has also garnered him an international reputation, and in this Short History he distils his rich knowledge and insight into a readable synthesis. Casanova explains the deep domestic origins of the Spanish war, while also placing it in its proper European context of convulsive continental change from First to Second World Wars. Students and general readers alike will find his book informative, enlightening and thought-provoking in equal measure.'

Helen Graham, Professor of Modern Spanish History,
Royal Holloway, University of London

A SHORT HISTORY OF THE SPANISH CIVIL WAR

Julián Casanova

I.B. TAURIS

LONDON · NEW YORK

Published in 2013 by I.B.Tauris & Co Ltd
6 Salem Road, London W2 4BU
175 Fifth Avenue, New York NY 10010
www.ibtauris.com

Distributed in the United States and Canada Exclusively by Palgrave
Macmillan, 175 Fifth Avenue, New York NY 10010

ISBN: 978 1 84885 657 8 (hb)
ISBN: 978 1 84885 658 5 (pb)

A full CIP record for this book is available from the British Library
A full CIP record is available from the Library of Congress

Library of Congress Catalog Card Number: available

Typeset in Sabon by Ellipsis Digital Limited, Glasgow
Printed and bound in Great Britain by T.J. International, Padstow,
Cornwall

MIX
Paper from
responsible sources
FSC® C013056

Contents

Acknowledgements

I am grateful to Martin Douch, for his excellent translation; to my editor, Alex Wright, who invited me to write the book for the *I.B. Tauris Short Histories*; to Helen Graham and Paul Preston for their support and friendship; and to Carmen Esteban at Crítica, Víctor Pardo and José Luis Ledesma for their invaluable assistance with the images.

Introduction

THE ROOTS OF THE CONFLICT

In the first few months of 1936, Spanish society was highly fragmented, with uneasiness between factions, and as was happening all over Europe, with the possible exception of Great Britain, rejection of liberal democracy in favour of authoritarianism was rife. None of this need have led to a civil war. The war began because a military uprising against the Republic undermined the ability of the State and the republican government to maintain order. The division of the army and security forces thwarted the victory of the military rebellion, as well as the achieving of their main objective: the rapid seizure of power. But by undermining the government's power to keep order, this *coup d'état* was transformed into the unprecedented open violence employed by the groups that supported and those that opposed it. It was July 1936 and thus began the Spanish Civil War.

The history of Spain in the first third of the twentieth century was not one of secular frustration sliding inevitably into an explosion of collective violence, or of an accumulation of failures and defects in industry, agriculture and the State, that prevented the country from following the road to progress and modernisation.

The history of Spain in those three decades did not run its course independently of the rest of Europe, nor was it any stranger to the social, economic, political and cultural transformations experienced by the rest of the continent. There were many more similarities than

1

differences, particularly with her southern European neighbours. Historians also know that there is no 'normal' model of modernisation with which Spain could be contrasted as being an anomalous exception. Hardly any country in Europe resolved its conflicts of the 1930s and 40s – the century's dividing line – by peaceful means.

Two world wars with a 'twenty-year crisis' in between marked the history of Europe in the twentieth century.[1] It took only three years for Spanish society to undergo a wave of violence and an unprecedented disdain for the lives of others. Despite all that has been said about the violence that preceded the Civil War, in an attempt to justify its outbreak, it is clear that the *coup d'état* of July 1936 marked a watershed in twentieth-century Spanish history. Furthermore, for at least two decades after the end of the Civil War in 1939, there was no positive reconstruction, such as had occurred in other countries in western Europe after 1945.

FROM MONARCHY TO REPUBLIC

At the beginning of the twentieth century, Spain was a debilitated country. She had just lost Cuba, the Philippines and Puerto Rico, and *El Desastre (The Disaster)* of 1898, as the final collapse of the old empire and the loss of the last colonies was called, saw an increase of pessimism among the people, although the debate as to how to 'regenerate' the country also opened new paths towards the democratisation of the political institutions and society.

Upon reaching the age of majority in 1902, Alfonso XIII came to the throne of Spain, after swearing the Constitution, a text that had been in force for 25 years. The political system in Spain at the time was known as the Restoration, a system in which power was held alternately by two parties consisting of distinguished liberals and conservatives, who controlled the administration through a political structure based on *caciquismo*,[2] a network of patronage that also operated at the time in other Southern European countries, such as Italy and Portugal.

The challenge facing Alfonso XIII and the political elite was to embark on a reform of the political system from above, in order to prevent revolution from below – a reform which would broaden the social bases without threatening their control. The political history of Alfonso XIII's reign tells the story of the failure of this venture. The king intervened in politics in an attempt to manipulate internal divisions within the liberals and conservatives, with factions, patrons and *caciques* all struggling for a share of power. Furthermore, along with problems inherited from the nineteenth century, such as clericalism and militarism, there were new ones to contend with, such as the war in Morocco, Catalan nationalism, the appearance of a more radical republicanism and the growth of an organised labour movement.

Between backwardness and modernisation, stagnation and slow but steady progress – these were the paths that Spanish society seemed to be taking during the first three decades of the twentieth century, judging by the accounts of various observers of the time and the latest historical studies. A good many testimonies of the time transmitted a lasting image that Spain, the Spain that had just lost the last vestiges of its colonial past, was a rural and backward society, barely industrialised, with parasitic landlords and a bourgeoisie that was weak and lacking initiative. However, 100 years later, historians have revised this image, comparing it with that of other countries with the same profile, and they have demonstrated, backed up by evidence and figures, that what really occurred were alternate phases of underdevelopment and industrialisation.

Between 1900 and 1930 Spain experienced a period of marked modernisation and economic growth. The principal cities doubled their population. Barcelona and Madrid, with over half a million inhabitants each in 1900, reached 1 million three decades later. Bilbao went from 83,000 to 162,000; Zaragoza from 100,000 to 174,000. Admittedly, these populations are not particularly significant if we compare them to the 2.7 million in Paris in 1900, or the number of European cities, from Birmingham to Moscow, including Berlin and Milan, whose populations were higher than Madrid's or Barcelona's in 1930. But the demographic panorama was undergoing a notable change. The total population of Spain, which was 18.6 million at the beginning of the century, reached almost 24 million in 1930, due mainly to a sharp fall in the death rate.

Up to 1914, this demographic pressure had given rise to a high rate of emigration, but from the First World War (which Spain did not participate in) onwards, it was Spanish cities that experienced mass immigration. In the first three decades of the century, the average life expectancy rose from 35 to 50, and the illiteracy rate fell from 60 to 35 per cent, the result of considerable progress in primary education and the educational and cultural improvements that went with urban growth.

Around 1930, the rural world was still predominant in many areas of Spain, but the agricultural labour force amounted to less than 50 per cent of the total active population. The agricultural sector grew in productivity, area sown and crop diversity, although it was losing ground to the secondary sector. Industry, with a million new workers since the start of the century, doubled its production and the tertiary sector, albeit at a slower rate, showed obvious signs of growth and renovation in the transport system as well as in business and the administration.

In the years between Alfonso XIII's ascension to the throne and the eve of his overthrow, the national income doubled and Spain, while experiencing major regional disparities, in general narrowed the gap between itself and other European countries.

The society that resulted from these changes was also diverse and complex. At the top were the 'good families' of the bourgeoisie who, through the banks, controlled the large industries and influenced the economic policies of the governments during the reign of Alfonso XIII. It was a capitalism that was protected by the State, with high tariffs, corporative and familiar in style, good examples of which were to be found in Catalonia, Asturias, Vizcaya and Madrid. However, the true summit of this society was occupied by the rural oligarchy, a new class of rural landowners, large landholders in the south, who had acquired their land as a result of nineteenth-century confiscations. Most of them did not belong to the nobility, but a good many achieved titles through marriage, which meant that large tracts of land ended up in the hands of just a few families. Landowners who became ennobled and industrialists and bankers who also obtained titles: in short, a convergence of the old and new nobility, producing what the historian Manuel Tuñón de Lara called a 'power block'.[3]

The members of this dominant social block were the heirs of the old privileged classes, the aristocracy and the Catholic Church, as well as the rural and Basque and Catalan industrial oligarchy. And this block provided most of the figures who governed in a political system, Alfonso XIII's monarchy, against which emerged the republican, anarchist and socialist seeds that had been sown in the final decades of the nineteenth century.

The political system presided over by Alfonso XIII was unable to widen its base, or channel through parliament the various interests of these social classes that had originated from industrialisation, modernisation and urban growth. The people, the working classes, with their organisations, collective actions and mobilisations, appeared on the public stage and relentlessly demanded not to be excluded from the political system. What was at first merely a whisper brought about, in April 1931, the collapse of the pinnacle of this system.

Previously, the king and the army had tried to forestall this, with a dictatorship imposed by General Miguel Primo de Rivera in September 1923, but when this dictator fell, on 26 January 1930, abandoned by the king, hostility towards the monarchy spread unchecked through rallies and demonstrations throughout Spain. Many monarchists, some of them distinguished names, abandoned the monarchy, convinced as they were that it was better to defend conservative principles within a Republic, than to leave the way open to the parties of the left and the workers' organisations. Republicanism, which until then had been weak, unable to break the control of *caciquismo* and propose real alternatives, became in just a few months a movement with various political parties, with well-known leaders such as Manuel Azaña, and new social bases.

The call to municipal elections on 12 April 1931, to be followed later by a general election, designed by the authorities to control the process of returning to constitutional normality after Primo de Rivera's dictatorship, caught the traditional conservative and liberal right unprepared and in disarray, and the extreme right, those loyal to the fallen dictator, in a process of reconstruction and as yet unable to mobilise its counter-revolutionary forces.

The elections on 12 April became a referendum to choose between the monarchy or a republic. Up to the very end the monarchists thought that they were going to win, confident of their ability to manipulate the mechanism of government. And this is why they showed their 'consternation' and 'surprise' when they learned very soon of the republicans' victory in 41 of the 50 provincial capitals. The following day, many municipalities proclaimed the Republic. Niceto Alcalá Zamora, a former liberal minister in the monarchy, and chairman of the Revolutionary Committee formed by republicans and socialists, called for the king to leave the country.

'The elections held last Sunday clearly show me that I do not have the love of my people today', wrote King Alfonso XIII in a farewell note to the Spanish people, before leaving the Royal Palace on the night of Tuesday 14 April 1931. When he arrived in Paris he declared that the Republic was 'a storm that will soon blow over'. It was to take longer to blow over than Alfonso XIII thought, or indeed wished. This Republic was to experience over five years of peace, until a military uprising and a war destroyed it by force of arms.[4]

THE REPUBLIC

The Republic was welcomed by celebrations in the streets, amid a holiday atmosphere that combined revolutionary hopes with a desire for reform. The crowds took to the streets, as may be seen in contemporary press reports, in photographs and in the numerous testimonies of those who wanted to put on record this great change that had a touch of magic, that arrived peacefully, without bloodshed. The middle class 'embraced the Republic' as a response to 'the disorientation of conservative elements', wrote José María Gil Robles, the principal architect of the Catholic and landowners' mobilisation against the republican reforms.[5]

The new government of the Republic was headed by Alcalá Zamora, an ex-monarchist, Catholic and man of order, a key piece in ensuring the necessary support for the regime of the more moderate republicans. As well as the Prime Minister, there were eleven ministers, including Alejandro Lerroux, leader of the main republican party, the *Partido Radical*, a centrist party despite its name; and Manuel Azaña, who headed the representation of the leftist republicans, and who became Minister of War. For the first time in Spain's history, socialists also took part in the government of the nation, with three ministers: Fernando de los Ríos, as Minister of Justice; Indalecio Prieto in Finance; and Francisco Largo Caballero, Minister of Labour.

The map laid out for this government included a general election and providing the Republic with a Constitution. Elections with universal suffrage, both male and female, representative governments that answered to parliament, and compliance with the law and the Constitution were the distinguishing features of the democratic systems that were emerging or being consolidated at that time in the main countries of western and central Europe. And this is what the republicans and socialists who governed Spain tried to introduce during the early years of the Second Republic, to a large extent successfully.

The Constitution that emerged from Parliament after heated discussions, and which was passed on 9 December 1931, defined Spain as a 'democratic Republic of workers of all types, which is organised under a regime of liberty and justice'; it declared the secular nature of the State, did away with State financing of the clergy, introduced civil marriage and divorce, and banned religious orders from teaching. Article 36 granted the vote to women, something that was being done in the democratic parliaments of the most enlightened countries in that period. Once the Constitution was passed, Parliament elected Niceto Alcalá Zamora as President of the Republic, and Manuel Azaña, the leading light in the executive power, as Prime Minister and Minister of War.

From the arrival of the Republic in April 1931 until the removal of Azaña in September 1933, the coalition governments of republicans and socialists untertook the reorganisation of the Army, the separation of Church and State, and took radical and far-reaching measures concerning the distribution of agricultural land, the wages of the working classes, employment protection and public education. Never before had Spain experienced such an intense period of change and conflict, democratic advances or social conquests.

In its bid to consolidate itself as a democratic system, the Republic needed to establish the superiority of civil power over the Army and the Catholic Church, the two bureaucracies that exercised tight control over Spanish society. The Army that the Republic inherited in 1931 had a history that abounded with interventions in politics, occupied a privileged position within the State and society, lacked modern armaments and was top-heavy with officers, many more than were necessary.

The reforms undertaken by Manuel Azaña in the Ministry of War, aimed at making a more modern and more effective army under the control of constitutional political power, was strongly resisted by a sector of the officer class, conservative politicians and the military media. There had already been a rattling of sabres in the summer of 1931, although the first attempts at conspiracy were neutralised by the government. A more serious matter was the military uprising in August 1932 led by General Sanjurjo, a hero of the Morocco campaign in the 1920s, which failed because he was unable to attract any major military garrison to his cause, except the one in Seville.

Sanjurjo was sentenced to death by a court-martial, although he was later pardoned; he went to live in Portugal, and from there, he led another *coup d'état* against the Republic, this time with fatal consequences, in July 1936. Many of the officers who accompanied him in this second uprising had been affected by the policy of reforms and promotions implemented by Azaña, who became the *bête noire* of a large sector of the army.

Similarly, establishing the supremacy of civil power called for a broad secularisation of society, and this brought the Republic into conflict with the Catholic Church. Article 26 of the Constitution stated that Church property was to be declared as belonging to the State, and barred religious orders from taking part in industrial and trading activities, as well as teaching. Although the implementation of this law banning teaching activities by religious orders was suspended when the socialists and leftist republicans lost the election in November 1933, republican legislation in religious matters reinforced still further the traditional identification in Spain of social order with religion.

As well as religion, land became one of the main centres of conflict during the Republic, in a country in which, despite industrial development and urban growth, agriculture still accounted for over half the economic output. There were very few medium-sized farms in Spain, but plenty of smallholdings and small estates in the north, and a predominance of large properties, with hundreds of thousands of impoverished labourers in the south. Agricultural reform that would distribute land more fairly, while necessary, was perceived by the owners as an expropriatory revolution.[6]

Most of the laws drawn up by the republican-socialist coalition government and passed by Parliament during the early years of the Republic were moderate in practice, and in many cases unworkable, but they were threatening in principle. And those who did feel threatened by them very soon organised themselves to fight the Republic.

Against the republican reforms, anti-democratic postures and counter-revolution were advancing rapidly, and not only among the most influential sectors of society, such as businessmen, industrialists, landowners, the Church and the Army. After the first few months of disorganisation among the right, political Catholicism burst onto the republican scene like a whirlwind. The close link between religion and land ownership could be seen in the mobilisation of hundreds of thousands of Catholic farmworkers, poor and 'extremely poor' landowners, and the almost total control wielded by landowners over organisations that were supposedly set up to improve the lot of these farmworkers. And here, money and the pulpit worked wonders: the former served to finance, among other things, an influential local and provincial press network; from the latter, the clergy took it upon itself to unite, more than ever, the defence of religion with that of order and ownership.

Dominated by large landowners and urban professionals, the *Confederación Española de Derechas Autónomas* (Spanish Confederation of the Autonomous Right – CEDA), the first mass party in the history of the Spanish right, set itself up in February 1933 to defend 'Christian civilisation', combat the 'sectarian' legislation of the Republic and 'revise' the Constitution. It was the party that received the most votes in the election in November that year, and it governed with Alejandro Lerroux's centrist republicans between October 1934 and December the following year. During that time, the CEDA was unable to meet its goal of halting the march of reform and revising the Republic on a corporative basis. Victory in the February 1936 election, the third and last held during the Republic, went to the leftist *Frente Popular* coalition, and because of this defeat, the Catholic right and the Fascists, unable as they were to win power by parliamentary means, agreed to consider the use of force as a response to the government and the Republic.

The Republic was also under threat from below, because there was a powerful anarcho-syndicalist movement in Spain, organised around the *Confederación Nacional de Trabajo* (National Labour Confederation – CNT), founded in 1910, which preferred revolution as an alternative to parliamentary government.[7] Some of the most hardline and radical groups of this movement initiated insurrections in January 1932 and January and December 1933, as a means of coercion against the established republican authority. Underlying these attempts at revolution, which were easily put down by the forces of order, was a rejection of the representative institutional system and the belief that force was the only way to eliminate class privilege and power abuse.

However, the history of the Republic shows that the use of force against the parliamentary regime was not limited to the anarchists; the democratic ideal did not seem to be deeply-rooted among certain republican politicians or socialists, and they mounted their first insurrection in October 1934, after being removed from power as a result of the general election the previous year. That revolution, which kept the republican authorities fully occupied for ten days in the mining region of Asturias, was put down leaving approximately 1,000 dead among those who supported the insurrection, some 2,000 wounded and 300 dead among the police and the army.

With this rebellion, the socialists who supported it showed the same condemnation of the representation system as the most radical anarchist groups had done in previous years. After their defeat in the November 1933 elections, the socialists broke with the democratic process and the parliamentary system as a means of rechannelling politics towards the reform projects of the first two years. The movement's leaders, at the instigation of the younger members, who formed militias and developed a taste for a military framework, tried to copy the Bolshevik model in Spain.

The police and Civil Guard,[8] as well as the army, were loyal to the government in all these attempts at insurrection by the left and there was no chance of them joining the revolutionaries or refusing to repress them. Against a State that kept its armed forces intact and united, a revolutionary strategy based on scattered support could never spark widespread disruption and it ended up being easily put down. After the Russian example of 1917, where the army suffered tens of thousands of desertions following heavy defeats in the First World War, there were no successful workers' revolutions in Europe, except for the one led by Bela Kun in Hungary for a few months in 1919.

These revolts against the Spanish Republic, serious disruptions to public order that were put down amid a great deal of blood-shed by the armed forces of the State, made the Republic and its parliamentary system's survival much more difficult, but they did not bring down the Republic, let alone cause a civil war. After October 1934, the socialist movement tried to become democrat-ically and politically active again, and win seats at the polls; this they did in February 1936, together with the republicans and other leftist parties who had joined forces to form the *Frente Popular*. In the months that followed these elections, the people of order felt more threatened than ever by the new thrust from the trade union organisations and social conflicts. A significant sector of the Army plotted against them and did not stop until the republican regime was overthrown. February 1936 saw free democratic elections; July 1936, a *coup d'état.*

WHY WAS THERE A CIVIL WAR IN SPAIN?

Between 1910 and 1931 various Republics, democratic regimes, or regimes with democratic aspirations, emerged in Europe, which replaced hereditary monarchies that had been established for centuries. Most of them, significantly those such as the German, Austrian and Czech republics, had been established as a result of their defeat in the First World War. The sequence had begun in Portugal, with the overthrow of the monarchy in 1910, and the Spanish Republic was the last to be proclaimed. The only example that survived as a democracy during those years until the outbreak of the Second World War was the Irish Republic, created in 1922. All the others were overthrown by counter-revolutionary military uprisings, authoritarian movements or Fascists. But the *coup d'état* of July

1936 was the only one that led to a civil war. And this difference needs to be explained.

Let us start with an obvious observation. Had it not been for the military uprising in July 1936, there would not have been a civil war in Spain. In view of the history of Europe during those years, and that of the other Republics that were unable to survive as democratic regimes, the Spanish Republic probably could not have survived either. But we shall never know for certain, because in this case the military uprising caused a split within the Army and the security forces. And by doing so, it meant that different armed groups competed to maintain power or conquer it.

The civil war came about because the military *coup d'état* failed to achieve its basic objective at the outset, which was to seize power and overthrow the republican regime, and because, unlike the events in other republics of the time, there was comprehensive resistance, both military and civil, to counter any attempt at imposing an authoritarian system. Had it not been for this combination of *coup d'état*, division of the armed forces and resistance, there would never have been a civil war.

Thus the civil war came about as a result of a military uprising, not unusual in view of the Army's tradition of intervening in politics and its privileged position within the State; this circumstance had been challenged by republican legislation, and the Army responded. This *coup d'état* met resistance because the Spanish society of 1936 was not the same as that of 1923, when the uprising in September of that year led by General Miguel Primo de Rivera was favoured by the general abstention of the Army, the weakness of the government, the apathy of public opinion and above all, the consent of King Alfonso XIII.

In 1936 there was a Republic in Spain, whose laws and measures had given it the historical opportunity to solve insurmountable problems, but it had also come across, and caused, major factors of instability, against which successive governments could not provide the proper resources to counteract. Against such a broad level of political and social mobilisation such as had been set up by the republican regime, the *coup d'état* could not end, as had occurred so many times in Spain's history, in a mere return to the old order, based on traditional values. To overthrow the Republic, what was needed was a new, violent, anti-democratic and anti-socialist order, such as had previously been established elsewhere in Europe, to end the crisis and repair all the fissures that had been opened, or widened, by the republican regime.

Up to the beginning of the Second Republic in April 1931, the Spanish society seemed to have managed to avoid the problems and troubles that had beset most European countries since 1914. Spain had not taken part in the First World War, and therefore had not undergone the upreaval that this war had caused, with the fall of empires and their subjects, the demobbing of millions of ex-combatants and massive debt caused by the vast spending on the war effort.

In Europe, after the First World War, the fall of monarchies, the economic crisis, the spectre of revolution and the spread of political rights to the masses caused a major sector of the property-owning class to perceive democracy as opening the door to government by the proletariat and the poorer classes. As Mark Mazower states, universal suffrage threatened the liberals with a marginal political role as opposed to the movements of the left and the Catholic, nationalist and newly formed parties. Fearful of communism, they leaned towards authoritarian solutions, a direction which brought together 'business managers and technocrats, who wanted scientific, apolitical solutions to society's ills and were impatient with the instability and incompetence of parliamentary rule'.[9]

It also happened that from the start these new parliamentary, constitutional regimes had to face a fragmentation of party loyalties of a nationalist, linguistic, religious, ethnic or class-related nature, which gave rise to a political system with a great many parties, all of them very weak. Forming a government became more and more difficult, with unstable coalitions that were constantly changing. In Germany no party ever achieved a solid majority under the proportional representation system laid down in the Weimar Constitution, but the same may be said of Bulgaria, Austria, Czechoslovakia, Poland and Spain during the later stages of the Republic. Rarely would the oppostion accept the results of elections, and faith in parliamentary politics was shaken, beset as they were during those years by instability and conflict, leading broad sectors of these societies to seek political alternatives to democracy.

A great deal of this reaction revolved around Catholicism, the defence of national order and ownership. The Russian revolution, the rise of socialism and the secularisation processes that accompanied political modernisation intensified the struggle between the Catholic Church and its anticlerical opponents of the political left.

The dictatorship option in much of Europe restored some of the traditional structures of authority that had been present before 1914, but it also had to look for new ways of organising society, industry and politics. This was the case with fascism in Italy, and this was the solution seized upon in the 1930s by the parties and forces of the Spanish right: how to control social change and put a brake on revolution at a time of an emerging politics of the masses.

Fascism and communism, the two main movements that emerged from the First World War and were to play two of the leading roles 20 years later in the Second, had very little presence in Spanish society during the years of the Republic and only began to gain a real foothold in Spain once the Civil War was under way.

Fascism appeared in Spain later than in other countries, particularly in comparison to Italy and Germany, and was very low-key as a political movement until spring 1936. During the early years of the Republic, it was barely noticed on a stage occupied by the extreme monarchist right and the moving to the right of political Catholicism. Hitler's ascendancy in Germany, however, attracted the interest of many extreme rightwingers who, while still knowing little about fascism, saw in the Nazis a good example to follow in their attempts to overthrow the Republic. What was to be the main fascist party in Spain, *Falange Española*, was founded by José Antonio Primo de Rivera, the son of the dictator, on 29 October 1933.[10]

Also absent from Spanish society in those years was communism, the other major ideology and political movement to emerge from the First World War. The Communist Party of Spain (PCE), founded at the beginning of the 1920s in line with the essential principals of the Communist International, came to the Republic while still in its infancy, compared to Socialism and Anarchism, and was an organisation that brought together several hundred militants. In the first two elections, in June 1931 and November 1933, it failed to return a single member, and it began to make its presence felt in Spanish society for the first time in 1934 when the Comintern changed its 'class against class' policy, criticising bourgeois democracy, for one that advocated the formation of anti-fascist fronts. In the February 1936 elections, as part of the *Frente Popular* coalition, the PCE won 17 seats (of the 470 in the Spanish parliament). It was not yet a party of the masses, but it had come out of isolation.

In short, and only owing to a civil war, communism, like fascism, ended up by exerting a marked influence on politics and Spanish society in the 1930s. Before the military uprising in July 1936, neither the fascists nor the communists had the resources to destabilise the Republic. In the spring of that year, after the *Frente Popular* victory in the elections, violence made its presence felt, with asassination attempts against prominent figures, and armed clashes between political groups of the left and right, occasionally with bloodshed, served to give practical expression to the verbal excesses and aggression of certain leaders. And neither of the two leading parties in parliament, the socialists and the CEDA, contributed during those months to the political stability of the democracy and the Republic. Spanish politics and society displayed unequivocal signs of crisis, although this did not necessarily mean that the only solution was a civil war.

In conclusion, there is no simple answer as to why the climate of euphoria and hope in 1931 was transformed into the cruel, all-destructive war of 1936–1939. The threat to social order and the subverting of class relations were perceived with greater intensity in 1936 than in the first few years of the Republic. The political stability of the regime was also under greater threat. The language of class, with its talk of social divisions and incitements to malign one's opponents, had gradually permeated the atmosphere in Spain. The Republic had tried to change too many things at once: land, the Church, the Army, education and labour relations. It raised major expectations that could not be met, and it soon made many powerful enemies for itself.

While the armed forces defended the Republic and obeyed their governments, it was possible to maintain order and check any military/right-wing or revolutionary attempts to subvert it, even if, as in the case of the rebellion in Asturias in October 1934, the cost in lives was high. The death blow to the Republic was dealt from within, from the very heart of its defence mechanisms, the military factions that broke their oath of loyalty to this regime in July 1936.

In charge of the organisation of the plot were various right-wing officers, including some from the *Unión Militar Española* (UME), a semi-clandestine, anti-leftist organisation consisting of several hundred officers. A group of generals, including Francisco Franco, met on March 8 in Madrid, and decided to mount 'an uprising to re-establish order in the interior as well as Spain's international prestige'.[11] General José Sanjurjo, who had led the first attempt at military rebellion against the Republic in August 1922, and who was living in Portugal after his pardon in April 1934, was appointed head of the uprising, although the leading role was played by General Emilio Mola, who coordinated the entire conspiracy.

The assassination of José Calvo Sotelo, the rightwing monarchist leader who defended an authoritarian and corporative State, committed at dawn on 13 July 1936 by members of the Republic's police force, convinced the plotters of the urgent need to intervene and brought into the fold many of the undecided, who were waiting for things to become clearer before agreeing to participate in the coup and risk their salaries and lives. Among them was General Franco, stationed in the Canary Islands, who took command of the garrisons that rose up in Spanish Morocco on the evening of 17 July 1936. In the early hours of 18 July, Franco declared a state of war and pronounced himself in opposition to the government of the Republic. On 19 July he arrived at Tetuán. Meanwhile, many other military garrisons in the Peninsula joined the coup. Peace was over in the Republic.[12]

Timeline

1931

12 April	Municipal elections. Republican victory.
14 April	Proclamation of the Republic. King Alfonso XIII goes into exile.

1936

16 February	Elections won by the *Frente Popular*.
19 February	Manuel Azaña, Prime Minister.
10 May	Manuel Azaña, President of the Republic.
12 May	The republican Santiago Casares Quiroga is appointed prime minister.
17–20 July	Military rising in Morocco and the Peninsula.

Civil War

20 July	The republican José Giral forms a government; the government appeals to France; Franco sends emissaries to Italy and Germany.
28–30 July	Italian and German aircraft arrive in Morocco and Seville.
8 August	Closing of the French border; unilateral declaration of Non-Intervention.
4 September	The socialist Largo Caballero leads a government with republicans, socialists and communists.
9 September	First meeting of the Non-Intervention Committee in London.

1 October	The republican *Cortes* pass the Basque Statute; in the other camp, Franco is designated *Generalísimo* and supreme head of the military rebels.
6 October	The Soviets declare that they will feel no more bound by Non-Intervention than Germany, Italy and Portugal do.
24 October	First Russian tanks in action; Russian officers arrive in Madrid; German and Italian aircraft bomb the capital.
4 November	The anarchists, in a historic move, join Largo Caballero's government.
6 November	Worried that the Nationalists will take Madrid, the republican government transfers to Valencia.
8 November	General attack against Madrid; arrival of the International Brigades.
18 November	Attack on Madrid suspended; Germany and Italy recognise Franco's government in Burgos.

1937

10 February	The Nationalists take Malaga.
6–15 February	Battle of Jarama.
8–18 March	Battle of Guadalajara.
19 April	Franco orders the merging of the *Falange* and *Carlists*, giving rise to the single party, FET-JONS.
26 April	Bombing of Guernica.
3–8 May	Barricades and political fighting, with several hundred deaths, in Barcelona.
17 May	Dismissal of Largo Caballero; a new government under the socialist, Juan Negrín.
16 June	Arrest of POUM leaders, accused of provoking the events of May in Barcelona. Disappearance of its leader, Andreu Nin.
19 June	The Nationalists take Bilbao.
1 July	Collective letter by the Spanish bishops supporting the civil war as a religious Crusade.
7–26 July	Battle of Brunete.

24 August–	
15 September	Battles of Belchite and Quinto.
26 August	The Nationalists take Santander.
19 October	The Nationalists seize Gijón.
31 October	The Negrín government transfers to Barcelona.
14 December	The beginning of the Teruel offensive, which the republicans take, the only provincial capital they were able to seize during the war.

1938

22 February	The Nationalists recapture Teruel.
9 March	Beginning of the Nationalist offensive in Aragón.
15 April	The Nationalists arrive at the Mediterranean.
24 July	Start of the Battle of the Ebro.
15 November	Retreat from the Ebro; farewell parade to the International Brigades.
23 December	Nationalist offensive in Catalonia.

1939

15 January	The Nationalists seize Tarragona.
26 January	Occupation of Barcelona.
4 February	Occupation of Gerona and mass withdrawal to the French border; the Nationalists end their occupation of Catalonia.
9 February	The Political Responsibilities Act, the principal repressive law of Franco's dictatorship.
27 February	France and Great Britain recognise the Burgos government; Azaña resigns.
7–11 March	Revolt in Madrid against Negrín's government, which hastens the end of the Republic.
28 March	The Nationalists enter Madrid.
1 April	Total surrender of the republican army. Official end of the civil war.

1

SPAIN SPLIT IN HALF

The military coup was unable to bring about a rapid seizure of power. Confidence in the swift success of the uprising was dispelled when the rebels were defeated in most of the big cities. It took less than a week for the situation to become clear. The uprising, by bringing about a deep divide in the army and security forces, weakened the republican State and set the stage for armed struggle, military rebellion and popular revolution wherever the rebels failed to meet their objectives. Spain was split into two. It was to remain so during a war that lasted a thousand days.

COUP D'ÉTAT

The leading role in the preparation of the rebellion was played by General Emilio Mola. His plan was for the military leaders in different parts of Spain to join the uprising and declare a state of war in order to place civil authority in military hands and thus control or eradicate potential adversaries. General Mola had been the last Director General of Security in Alfonso XII's monarchy. Having been expelled from the army by the Republic, he was pardoned in 1934 and the centre right government, with Gil Robles as minister of War, sent him to Morocco in 1935 as Commander-in-Chief of the army in Morocco. After the February 1936 elections, the government led by Manuel Azaña transferred him a few weeks later to Pamplona,

General Emilio Mola (private collection, Zaragoza).

thereby distancing him from the significant Africa army, and from that northern city, under the pseudonym of '*El Director*', he issued the secret reports and instructions for those who were to lead the uprising.

On hearing of the beginning of the military uprising in Morocco, Prime Minister Santiago Casares Quiroga,[1] fearful of revolution and the popular unrest that might break out, ordered the civil governors not to distribute arms to the workers' organisations. He also refused to accept the importance of what was happening. The government issued a decree suspending the rebel military personnel, dissolved the rebel units and demobbed its soldiers. As Gabriel Cardona points out, 'it was a futile mistake, because the rebels ignored the decrees and refused to allow any of its men to leave. On the other hand, the troops in many of the government units abandoned their posts when they were most needed'.[2]

Casares Quiroga, unable to cope with events, resigned on the night of 18 July. The following morning the difficult task of forming a government was taken on by José Giral, another friend and confidant of Manuel Azaña. This government consisted of leftist republicans only, practically the same faces as had previously served under Casares Quiroga, with the addition of two army officers: General Sebastián Pozas as Interior Minister and General Luís Castelló in the War Ministry. It was Giral who decided to authorise the arming of the most politically committed militant workers and republicans, and they took to the streets to fight the rebels wherever the loyalty of certain military commanders, or the indecision of others, permitted. This was the case in Madrid, Barcelona, Valencia and San Sebastián.

In Madrid, General Joaquín Fanjul, who had been relieved of his command by the government for his proven anti-republicanism, revolted, even though he had not been designated for this role in Mola's plans, and he secured himself in the La Montaña barracks, along with over 2,000 troops and 500 Falangist civilians to whom he had issued arms. Hours later, groups of armed workers and troops loyal to the republic attacked the barracks and killed on the spot over 100 rebel troops and Falangists after they had surrendered. Fanjul survived a few days before he was tried and shot.

The coup also failed in Barcelona, Spain's second city, the bastion of the anarchists, soon to become the symbol of popular resistance and revolution. Barcelona had a large garrison made up of soldiers who supported the Republic and others who were involved in the plot. The general who, at the last minute, was charged with command of the rebellion, Manuel Goded, the general commander of the Balearic Islands, arrived late when another general, Álvaro Fernández Burriel, had already revolted without any definite plans.

There was little Goded could do because a sector of the Civil Guard, the forces of public order of the Generalitat, Catalonia's autonomous government, and the most radical anarchists, who had seized hundreds of rifles, were already in control of the situation. By the time the last rebel troops in Barcelona had surrendered on 20 July, and General Manuel Goded, holed up in the old *Capitanía General* (regional army headquarters) had announced their defeat and surrender on the radio, the fighting in the Catalan capital had left a balance of 450 deaths. And the war and the revolution had not even started yet.

The uprising failed in Spain's two most important cities, but was successful in other strategically important cities, from where vast tracts of territory could be controlled. Seville, the most important city in Andalusia, quickly fell to General Gonzalo Queipo de Llano, who in a very short time had gone from being one of the Republic's most loyal officers to its bitterest enemy. And another supposedly republican general, Miguel Cabanellas, a mason, was responsible for the uprising succeeding in Zaragoza, the capital of Aragón, which also had a powerful, well-supported anarcho-syndicalist movement. It was vital that the uprising be successful in Zaragoza, in order to control the large area of the Ebro basin, march on Madrid and stop any armed groups that might come from Barcelona.

It needs to be emphasised, in order to understand why a civil war started, that it was not the army 'en masse' that rose against the Republic, nor was it a 'rebellion of the generals', as the propaganda would subsequently have it. Of the 18 generals controlling the major intervention units, only four rebelled: Cabanellas, Queipo de Llano, Goded and Franco. Furthermore, the military rebels brooked no indecision or resistance from their colleagues, and anyone who tried paid the price, beginning with several commanders and officers who were summarily sent to face the firing squad in Spanish Morocco. This is what happened in Melilla to General Manuel Romerales, arrested at gunpoint in his office by some of his subordinates. Miguel Campins, the military governor of Granada, who opposed the uprising, was detained by various officers and driven to Seville, where he was shot on 16 August accused of 'rebellion'. The same fate befell General Miguel Núñez de Prado, the director general of Aviation, who went to Zaragoza to try and persuade Cabanellas not to revolt.

The most active role in the uprising was played by the officer corps. The rebels initially had some 120,000 armed men, of the 254,000 in the peninsula, the islands and Africa at that time, including the forces of public order. But above all, from the very beginning, they had the Africa Army, including almost all its 1,600 officers and junior officers and the 40,000 men in their command. Its best-known and best-trained troops were the *Tercio de Extranjeros*, the Legion, founded by José Millán Astray and Francisco Franco in 1920, and made up of deserters, criminals, outcasts and fugitives, who were trained to venerate virility and violence. Alongside the Legion were the *Fuerzas Regulares Indígenas*, made up of Moroccan mercenaries and some Spaniards.

The rebel commanders believed that the Republic had given them a long list of grievances that needed to be redressed. Some of these officers had been affected by the review of promotions granted for war service by Primo de Rivera's dictatorship and annulled by Manuel Azaña's government by decree in January 1933. Such was the case with Generals Aranda, Orgaz and Varela, who were to play a significant role in Franco's army, although other officers such as Asensio Torrado, Romerales and Hidalgo de Cisneros, while in the same situation, remained loyal to the republican government.

The review of promotions, Azaña's Military Reform Act and the sacking of some of the officers who were most closely committed to Primo de Rivera's dictatorship stimulated the hostility of many officers against the Republic. The reasons they claimed for rebelling, in July 1936, judging from the declarations of the state of war that they issued, were the 'total absence of Public Power' and the need to maintain order and the unity of the Fatherland. And although they did not say so explicitly, another important reason was the list of grievances against the politicians whom they despised and detested as being leftist and Bolshevik lackeys.

General Sanjurjo had been appointed head of the rebellion by his coup partners, but he died on 20 July when trying to take off in the light aircraft that was due to take him to Spain from his exile in Portugal. The Falangist aviator, Juan Antonio Ansaldo was sent to fetch him by General Mola. The aircraft, a flimsy two-seater Puss Moth, crashed immediately after taking off and burst into flames near the aerodrome at Cascais. Ansaldo escaped unhurt from the accident.

Sanjurjo's accidental death forced the rebels to rethink their plans. Four days later, acting on a suggestion by Mola, they set up the *Junta de Defensa Nacional* in Burgos, presided over by General Cabanellas. This was the first military coordinating body in the rebel zone and was to last throughout the summer until 1 October, when General Franco was invested by his military colleagues as the sole political and military leader.

This occurred because Franco, with Sanjurjo dead, used his privileged position as commander of the Morocco garrison to prepare the ground for what Paul Preston, his best biographer, termed as 'the Making of a Generalísimo'.[3] The problem facing Franco was how to move these troops from Africa to the Peninsula, in view of the fact that the Strait of Gibraltar was controlled by the crews of the republican fleet that had mutinied against their rebel officers.

Franco thus asked Adolf Hitler and Benito Mussolini for help. To reach the leader of Nazi Germany, he used a German businessman living in Spanish Morocco, Joahnnes Bernhardt, who met the Führer on 25 July and told him of the events in Spain and of the right-wing and anti-Bolshevik leanings of the rebellion. Hitler decided to back this cause, starting with the dispatch of 20 Junkers Ju 52 transport aircraft, six Heinkel 51 fighters, 20 anti-aircraft guns, munitions and flight and ground crew, which began to arrive in Spanish Morocco on 29 July, barely ten days after the start of the military rebellion against the Republic.

Mussolini decided to do the same, after receiving constant requests for aid from Franco via the Italian consul in Tangiers and his military attaché. On 28 July he sent a squadron of twelve *Savoia SA-81* bombers and two merchant ships with *Fiat C.R.32* fighters. The use of these planes enabled Franco to elude the republican navy's blockade, move troops from Africa to Andalusia and thus begin the advance on Madrid. By 7 August, Franco was installed in Seville. In just a few weeks, over 13,000 soldiers had crossed the Strait of Gibraltar. Thus, in the words of Paul Preston, 'Mussolini and Hitler turned a *coup d'état* going wrong into a bloody and prolonged civil war'.[4]

By the end of July, the success or failure of the military rebellion had split Spain into two. It had met with success in almost the whole of northern and north-west Spain: Galicia, León, Old Castilla, Oviedo, Álava, Navarre and the three capitals of Aragón; the Canary and Balearic Islands, except for Menorca; and large areas of Extremadura and Andalusia, including the cities of Cáceres, Cádiz, Seville, Córdoba, Granada and Huelva. The republican zone still controlled the main cities, the principal industrial and mining centres, Catalonia, the Basque Country and Asturias, and the headquarters of the leading companies and banks. The Republic's financial advantage was very

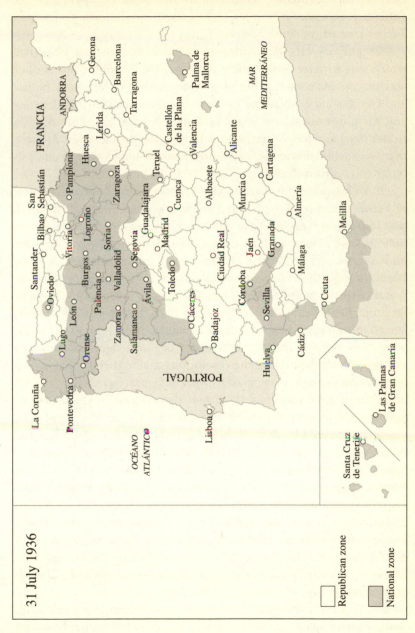

Spain: Republican and Nationalist territory, 31 July 1936.

clear at the beginning. It controlled the Bank of Spain and its gold reserves, some 700 tonnes, and its territory administered roughly 70 per cent of the State budget.[5]

The military rebellion failed to achieve its principal objective, which was to seize power and overthrow the Republic, but neither was the government capable of putting down the rebellion. Italian and German aid enabled the rebels to continue with their endeavour and the government also urgently sought foreign aid. The solution to this Nazi and Fascist harrassment lay in the democracies. At least, that was what the republican authorities believed was needed in order to confront the *coup d'état*.

On 19 July, according to the socialist Léon Blum, the prime minister of France, the recently appointed Spanish prime minister, José Giral, sent him a telegram: 'We have been caught unawares by a dangerous military coup. Please contact us immediately to supply us with arms and aircraft'.[6] The French government's initial reaction was, in Blum's words, 'to implement an aid plan, as far as we can, to provide materiel to the Spanish Republic'. But it was not possible. A military attaché in the Spanish embassy in Paris, an agent of the rebels, leaked information on the French government's decision to the right-wing daily *Echo de Paris*, and the paper began 'a vigorous campaign exposing in all their detail the resolutions taken, thereby stirring up considerable unrest, particularly in parliamentary circles'.

Public opinion was divided, as was also the case in Great Britain, between those who expressed their sympathy for the republican cause, represented by the left, and the political right, Catholics and broad sectors of the administration, who rejected this aid plan. The fear of revolution and that the conflict in Spain would spread to France, deep-rooted in the right-wing press and the armed forces, also convinced the two leading ministers in the Radical Party, Edouard Daladier, the minister of war, and Yvon Delbos, the Foreign Affairs minister, to hold back. 'French intervention in the Spanish Civil War would mean the beginning of the conflagration in Europe that Moscow so ardently hopes for', warned the weekly journal *Candide* at the end of July.[7]

Information transmitted to the British government by its diplomatic staff in Spain was of no help to the Republic either. From the outset, they described those defending the republican cause as being communists in the service of Bolshevism. On 24 July, British Foreign Secretary Anthony Eden urged Léon Blum to be 'cautious'. And two days later, Stanley Baldwin, the conservative prime minister, told Eden that 'on no account, regardless of what France or any other country does, should we join in the struggle alongside the Russians'. The British Conservatives, in power since 1931, were afraid that any intervention in Spain would hamper their policy of appeasement with Germany, and on 25 July, the French government followed the advice of its principal ally in Europe and announced its decision of 'complete non-intervention in Spain's internal conflict'.[8]

This saw the start of the non-intervention policy that would be implemented from the summer of 1936. The French authorities, with Blum at the head, believed that this was the best way of calming and controlling the internal division of the country, maintaining the vital alliance with Great Britain, and avoiding the internationalisation of the Spanish Civil War. Although this stance was immediately accepted by the British government, the extension of the Spanish conflict could not be avoided because Hitler and Mussolini had already begun to send military aid to Franco and furthermore, Nazi Germany and Fascist Italy never respected this non-intervention policy. Consequently, the Republic, a legitimate regime, was left initially without aid, until the Soviet Union began to intervene in the autumn of 1936, while the military rebels, lacking all legitimacy, received, almost from the opening shot, the aid that was vital to wage a war that they themselves had started.

Meanwhile, the republican State was reeling, public order had broken down and radical, destructive revolution was spreading like volcanic lava throughout the cities where the rebellion had failed. Wherever it had succeeded, the rebels implemented a system of terror that wiped out their political and ideological enemies.

NO RULES, NO GOVERNMENT

Suddenly, in this two-fold process of military rebellion and revolutionary response, blood began to flow extensively throughout Spain. The military rebels, with General Emilio Mola at their head, had given notice of this in the previous months when they were drawing up their plans for the coup. 'Bear in mind that the action will need to be uncommonly violent in order to bring down the enemy, who is strong and well organised, as soon as possible', said Mola in his Confidential Instruction number 1, signed by him as '*El Director*' on 25 May. 'Naturally, all leaders of political parties, companies or unions that are not sympathetic to the *Movimiento* will be imprisoned', he added, and that they would be dealt 'exemplary punishments (...) to stifle any rebellious or strike movements'. It was clear that if there was resistance, which was deemed likely, the rebellion would end up as a war of conquest to save Spain from anarchy.[9]

The combination of successes and failures in the rising soon showed the military rebels that the struggle was going to be hard, long and fought on various fronts. Hence the climate of premeditated, calculated terror that presided over their conquests from day one. In this regard, Franco had the military forces of the protectorate of Morocco, notorious for their brutality, at his disposal. Mola had the backing of several thousand Carlists from Navarre and Álava, with whom he quelled any resistance and terrorised thousands of republicans, socialists and anarchists along the banks of the River Ebro, in Navarre and Zaragoza.[10] In other cities such as Seville, Córdoba, Cáceres and León, the military and police forces were helped by the enthusiasm of hundreds of right-wingers and Falangists, who from then on devoted themselves to cleansing missions and building a new Spain on the ruins of the Republic.

Thus began an era of mass imprisonments, selective repression to crush resistance, systematic torture and terror. Mayors, civil governors, local councillors, trade union and *Frente Popular* leaders were the first to suffer all this. Compliance with the law was replaced by the language and dialectic of arms, by the rejection of human rights and the veneration of violence. Now that this new scenario of total war was under way, in which politics came to be assessed exclusively in military terms, one was either a friend or an enemy.

The killings were rife wherever there was the most resistance, wherever there had been social conflicts during the Republic and wherever a greater presence of leftist organisations triggered the settling of scores, swiftly and without quarter. The final days of July and the months of August and September 1936 saw the highest number of killings in regions that had been under the control of the rebels from the start: between 50 and 70 per cent of the total number of victims during the war was concentrated in this short period, which shows that it was not only a repression in time of war but an emergency 'surgical' extermination. Over 90 per cent of the close to 3,000 killings in Navarre and Zaragoza occurred in 1936. But the percentages were very similar in Córdoba, Granada, Seville, Badajoz and Huelva, the provinces which, together with Zaragoza, saw the most deaths in that wave of summer terror.

The victims would be arrested in the streets or in their homes for being 'well-known leftists', for opposing the 'glorious National Movement', sought because they appeared in the documents seized on the premises of political and trade union organisations, denounced by their neighbours or singled out for their irreligious behaviour. They would be shut up in gaols or in the large number of buildings equipped to be gaols in the early days, until they were removed to be killed during the night, just before dawn. Judges would sometimes appear on the scene to authorise the removal of the bodies, but more commonly in those early days, before the setting up of the military tribunals, the victims would be left, often without burial, where they had fallen, against cemetery walls, in roadside ditches, near rivers and in disused wells and mineshafts.

The flood of killings caused by that terror gave rise to all types of anomaly. Thousands of people were never registered, while many others appeared as merely 'male' or 'female', without being identified, and this is still hindering many of their family and descendants in their search for their remains, years after the death of Franco. Not all the dead were buried in the cemeteries; vast mass graves were dug, such as those in Lardero, near Logroño, the Pozos de Caudé, near Teruel, and in Viznar, just a few kilometres from Granada, where Federico García Lorca met his death.

In the cities where the uprising had failed, the officers who had rebelled against the Republic were treated without mercy. They were considered to be the main perpetrators of the violence and bloodshed that was spreading throughout the cities and countryside of Spain. Around 100 commanders and officers who had joined the uprising in the Barcelona garrison were executed between mid-August and February 1937. Examples of unpunished actions against officers in prison following their defeat reached levels of exceptional cruelty in Madrid, where in all the *sacas* ('removals'), particularly the mass *sacas* of November 1936, members of the army were picked out for execution. This scenario was repeated in Menorca, Almería, Málaga, Albacete, Guadalajara, Lérida, San Sebastián and other cities where the uprising had failed.

All these officers were assumed to be 'proven' Fascists, and 'proven' Fascists, as the anarcho-syndicalist newspaper, *Solidaridad Obrera*, declared on 1 August 1936, had to be killed. The military, and particularly the clergy, were the prime targets of the violent purges that predominated in the summer of 1936 wherever the defeat of the rising opened the gates to revolution. In addition, this persecution engulfed, during those first few weeks, conservative politicians, landowners, smallholders, farmers, the middle classes, shopkeepers, workers who were known in the factories for their moderate ideas, engineers and personnel managers in the various industries, and Catholics. Behind many of these killings were the armed militia, leftist party and trade union militants and the large number of works, district or village committees that had been set up in the heat of the revolution.

For what was left of republican Spain after the *coup d'état* of July 1936 was a melting pot of powers. A melting pot of armed powers, difficult to control, which tried to fill the power vacuum left by the defeat of the military rising in the principal cities of Spain and large tracts of the rural world, in large farming estates with absentee owners and in hundreds of small towns with no one in charge. The State no longer existed outside Madrid, if indeed it ever had done. It was time for the power of committees, of those who had never possessed it, the 'people in arms' as they were called by the anarchists, disconnected from José Giral's government in Madrid.

At first there were many people and circumstances that hampered control and favoured anarchy. From the collapse of the State, the disintegration of the administration and the distribution of arms among those who were willing to take them, emerged a wave of militant egalitarianism, millennialism, a 'spontaneous revolution' which,

CNT-FAI, 19 July 1936. The people in arms.

in the view of many witnesses, would collectivise factories and land, with wages suppressed and with the establishment of the earthly paradise that the people had been dreaming of for so long. This was the image that was, for example, handed down by George Orwell in his *Homage to Catalonia*, first published in English in 1938.

To George Orwell, who had recently arrived in Barcelona, this exterior aspect of the city seemed to him to be 'something startling and overwhelming: it was the first time that I had ever been in a town where the working class was in the saddle'. The buildings were adorned with red and black flags; the churches looted; the shops and cafés collectivised. Apparently, 'the wealthy classes had ceased to exist': there was no evidence of 'well-dressed' people, wearing ties or hats. Overalls, or 'rough working class clothes' had replaced middle class outfits.[11]

The changes in 'Barcelona's aspect' also made an impression on Francisco Lacruz who wrote about the revolution and terror from the winning side's viewpoint in 1943: 'Everything in this city, created by the effort of a hard-working bourgeoisie, a population exceptionally equipped for a comfortable, disciplined and pleasant life, had become sordid and grim. A proletarian multitude, stirred up by the most perfidious of vengeful feelings, imposed their plebeian outlook on life on the terror-stricken masses'. Anything beautiful, graceful or refined had been banned 'with implacable fury'. Wearing a suit, being clean-shaven or perfumed 'was tantamount to declaring oneself a "fascist", and thus openly condemning oneself to death'.

Women had to do without hats, fine dresses, jewellery, 'dainty footwear', and be dressed in 'the standard attire of certain women of lower social classes'. For their part, men 'made an effort to look like labourers who had just finished work'. People went around in shirtsleeves, 'with the oldest clothes they possessed or else in deliberately tattered garments'. Such was Barcelona at the time, where the 'sweaty, ragged, unwashed' rabble (. . .) 'looked like the population of Moscow'.[12]

While these exaggerations are typical of the images and propaganda heralded by the winning side in the civil war, the fact remains that, from the very beginning, the revolutionary tide of the summer of 1936 brought with it a wave of terror. For in order to destroy all these symbols of social distinction in clothing and manners, the corpses of thousands of people had to be trampled upon, political and class enemies, the military, the clergy, conservative Catholic owners and workers, estate owners and smallholders, *caciques* and the gentry. And in order to attain the collectivisation of lands and factories, it was necessary to confiscate the assets of these owners, who had either fled, been killed or were in prison: a process that was repeated, with varying degrees of violence, in the industries of Barcelona, Madrid and Valencia, and the farmlands of Aragón, Jaén and Ciudad Real.

But before any building, the 'social ill' and its main causes had to be weeded out. This was what revolution meant for most anarcho-syndicalist leaders and militants, but also for many other socialists and UGT members: the radical elimination of the symbols of power; the overthrow of the existing order; propagating an aggressive rhetoric that spoke of a society with no classes, no parties, no State. All this climate was a throwback to the Jacobins, the revolutionaries of the nineteenth century or those of the Russian revolution, reflected in the 'Public Health Committees' which, as in Lérida or Málaga for example, devoted themselves to the repression of counter-revolution in that summer of 1936.

The radical elimination of all these representatives of power was achieved by the *paseo*, the 'handing down of summary justice' to settle scores, feed class hatred or extract revenge. The description of these methods left to us by the anarchist Juan García Oliver, the republican government Minister of Justice between November 1936 and May 1937, makes the matter quite clear: 'Since the military rising meant the breaking of all social constraints, because it was carried out by the classes that traditionally maintained social order, the attempts to re-establish legal equilibrium saw the spirit of justice reverting to its oldest and purest origin: the people: *vox populi, suprema lex*. And while this abnormality lasted, the people created and applied its own law and procedure, the *paseo*'.[13]

Attacks on prisons, *paseos* and *sacas* were how the terror unleashed by the revolutionary storm in the name of the sovereign people manifested itself in the summer of 1936. All through that summer, as with the other 'hot-blooded' terror initiated and served up by the military, the gentry and landowners, judicial procedures were considered superfluous. The *paseo* was much quicker. And as with the zone controlled by the military rebels, the violence meted out in republican territory was concentrated within the months of August and September, except notably for Madrid, where several thousand people were killed in November 1936, during the first siege of the capital by the Nationalist troops.[14]

Not every one wanted to see blood spilt, and from the beginning there were some voices that were raised against the massacre from republican, socialist and anarchist leaders, something that was rarely seen among the authorities and the Catholic Church hierarchy on the other side. However, the defeat of the uprising released shackles, bringing about complete liberation from the yokes of the past, and saw the arrival of the long-awaited revolution and final judgement for the rich, exploitative bosses, a favourite theme in the most radical propaganda and rhetoric. With no rules or government, with no mechanisms for forcing people to comply with laws, the 'thirst for justice', revenge and class hatred spread with a devastating force to wipe out the old order.

The fury of the army rebels and Falangists was particularly aimed at the republican authorities and the *Frente Popular* coalition deputies elected in February 1936. A report drawn up by the secretariat of the *Congreso de los Diputados*, published on 22 August 1938, stated that 40 had been murdered and twelve were either prisoners or 'missing' in 'rebel territory'.

Of those killed, 21 were socialists, two communists and the rest republicans; 18 belonged to Andalusian provinces and five to Galicia, a region in which leftist and nationalist politicians were wiped from the map. One of them was Ángel Casal, an editor in the *Partido Galleguista*, Mayor of Santiago de Compostela and Vice-President of the La Coruña Provincial Government in 1936. He had been a member of the commission that presented the draft statute of autonomy in the *Congreso de los Diputados*. His body was found in a ditch on 19 August that year.

Although the exact date is not known for certain, reliable indications suggest that it was the day before when the poet Federico García Lorca, the fascist military terror's most memorable victim, must have been murdered. Following the success of the uprising in Granada, García Lorca took refuge in the house of the Falangist poet Luis Rosales, believing that there he would not be discovered. But on Sunday 16 August, he was taken from there by Ramón Ruiz Alonso, a right-wing ex-CEDA deputy who was well-known in Granada. That same morning his brother-in-law, Manuel Fernández-Montesinos, the republican ex-mayor of Granada who was married to the poet's sister Concha, had been murdered.

According to Ian Gibson's version of the events, Ruiz Alonso was accompanied by two CEDA colleagues when he called on the Rosales home in the Calle Angulo: 'Juan Luis Trescastro – a well-known landowner and typical male chauvinist loudmouth to be found among the young Andalusian upper classes – and Luis García Alix, the party secretary in Granada'. They took García Lorca to the Civil Government building, under the command of Major José Valdés Guzmán, who had been purging Granada of '*rojos*' since the beginning of the uprising.[15]

García Lorca was killed along with a schoolmaster and two anarchist *banderilleros* (bullfighter's assistants), and they were buried in the area around Viznar, a few kilometres from Granada, where mass graves had been dug by masons and 'reds' before being murdered by volunteers of the Fascist 'Black Squad'. One of his murderers was Juan Luis Trescastro, the 'male chauvinist' 'loud-mouth' who said that he was fed up with 'queers' and later swaggered through Granada saying that he had 'put two shots into García Lorca's arse'. His death certificate made use of one of the many euphemisms that were employed in the Nationalist zone to falsify the cause of death: 'from wounds produced by acts of war'.

In the republican zone, the biggest name to be killed was that of José Antonio Primo de Rivera, the martyr of the Crusade who, already during the war but more so in the post-war years, had new build-ings dedicated to him, as well as hundreds of streets, squares and schools; church walls bore the inscription 'José Antonio Primo de Rivera *¡Presente!*'

Born in 1903, five years after García Lorca, he was the son of the dictator Miguel Primo de Rivera. In 1933, following the rise to power of Adolf Hitler, he became interested in fascism, and after ensuring the political and financial backing of the traditional right, he founded *Falange Española*, the party that did most to incorpo-rate violence in its rhetoric and display it in the streets in the charged atmosphere of 1930s Spain.

He stood as a candidate for the province of Cádiz in the February 1936 elections, but was not elected. A month later, three Falangists tried to murder Luis Jiménez de Asúa, a law professor and socialist deputy. They failed, but they did kill his bodyguard. On 14 March, José Antonio Primo de Rivera and other leading Falangists were arrested, and the party went underground.

On 5 June he was transferred, along with his brother Miguel, to the prison at Alicante, possibly in order to prevent an escape attempt, and to distance him from the capital, then the main scene of Falangist street violence. The military rebellion failed in Alicante and on 18 November a Popular Tribunal sentenced him to death. He was shot in the prison at dawn on 20 November 1936.[16]

The Spanish Civil War has gone down in history, and in memory, for the way it dehumanised its adversaries and for the horrific violence that it generated. Painstaking research in recent years suggests that there were at least 150,000 deaths as a result of this violence during the war, almost 100,000 in the zone controlled by the rebels and somewhat fewer than 60,000 in the republican zone.[17]

Over the two summer months following the military uprising, this terror spread beyond the limits of political organisations, the apparatus of the State in the republican zone and the army in the rebel zone. New powers came to occupy the empty spaces left by the supplanting of order caused by the military coup. More or less autonomous powers, such the Falangist squadrons or revolutionary committees, operated within the realm of punishment and justice that had hitherto been administered by the State, while at the same time setting up mechanisms of terror that at that time were unchecked by any type of control or authorisation.

FROM 'HOT-BLOODED' TO 'LEGAL' TERROR

From November 1936, however, things began to change. Following the unsuccessful Nationalist offensive on Madrid, nobody really believed, despite the propaganda to the contrary, that the war would be a short-lived affair. The fronts stabilised and, except for Madrid where a decisive battle raged for weeks, any attacks were to result in small gains, strengthening of positions or events of little military signif-icance. Between the entry into Toledo at the end of September 1936 and the conquest of Málaga at the beginning of February 1937, Franco's troops failed to win a single victory, while the various forces still loyal to the Republic were still able to forestall them. During those four long months, the paramilitary and 'uncontrolled' groups practically disappeared from the scene and the militias definitively submitted themselves to the discipline of the army, a process which obviously took longer to materialise in the republican than the rebel zone.

The concentration of power was not easy, not even on the rebel side where everything pointed to the fact that the supreme command would be assumed by General Franco. But there was clear evidence that the terror was being controlled on both sides 'from above': the killings resulting from the *sacas* and *paseos* decreased considerably. The terror, like the atmosphere, cooled down, and a phase of 'legal' violence meted out by the tribunals began.

The enemy was still there, there were many still left to be killed, but the need to put the war first and the concentration of power and discipline on the home front began to put a brake on excesses. On the republican side, the government and the political and trade union organisations managed to halt the killing almost entirely; on the Nationalist side, the downward trend in violence developed more slowly and whenever they took a city, the 'hot-blooded' terror of wholesale killing would return.

Restoring control took some time in the republican zone. The first decrees of what was then called 'popular justice' were issued on 23 and 25 August 1936, immediately after the killing of leading right-wingers and politicians in the Modelo prison in Madrid.[18] They led to the setting up of special tribunals 'to try crimes of rebellion and sedition, and those committed against the security of the State'. They were to be made up of 'three judicial officials, who would act as *de jure* judges, and fourteen jurypersons who would rule on the facts of the case'. This 'emergency justice' of the Republic incorporated 'summary judgement' and several elements of military procedure without the need to resort to 'martial law', something the republican government did not declare throughout its territory until 9 January 1939.[19]

On 24 and 28 August the Generalitat (the Catalan regional government) issued very similar decrees setting up 'popular juries for the repression of fascism'. And it was not just a feature of Madrid or Barcelona: popular tribunals were soon to be set up in almost all the provinces of the republican zone. It marked the change, or so it seemed, from 'abnormality' in which the 'people', as García Oliver wrote, 'created and applied its law and procedure', in other words, the *paseo*, to 'normality', a stage in which 'suspicious elements were to be handed over to the popular tribunals and tried with impartiality, with punishment meted out for the guilty and immediate release for the innocent'.[20]

The 'hot-blooded' terror was finally superseded by 'legal' violence from the beginning of 1937 onward, although in most provinces the downward trend had begun at the end of the previous year. There were various reasons for this. Firstly, because the arrival of Largo Caballero in the government on 4 September 1936, accompanied by socialists, communists and, from 4 November on, anarchists, involved all these organisations in the defence of responsibility and discipline. Nothing illustrates this change better than the fact that it was an 'anarchist of action', García Oliver, who consolidated the popular tribunals and created work camps for the 'Fascist prisoners' instead of a shot in the back of the neck. Secondly, because most of the revolutionary and anti-Fascist committees set up in the wake of the defeat of the uprising were replaced by municipal councils formed by agreements between the various political organisations of the *Frente Popular*. And finally, because the armed groups and militias that were rife on the home front and front lines were by that time militarised and incorporated into the new army of the Republic. With stronger and more disciplined political and military powers, and with the war on centre stage, the revolutionary storm blew over, and the violence of the *sacas* and *paseos* was halted.

The main crime for which those who passed through the popular tribunals were charged was military rebellion. The accused were army personnel and members of the security forces, Civil Guards particularly; citizens who took up arms in support of the uprising; and rightwingers or members of Catholic and monarchist organisations. The profile of those sentenced to death by the popular tribunals in various provinces was very similar to that of the victims of the *paseos* and *sacas*, although there were hardly any clerics, many of whom having been murdered in the first few months. Several thousand people were tried in the various popular tribunals in the republican zone between September 1936 and May 1937, when most of those accused of these crimes were brought to judgement. Ninety-seven of the 427 tried in Barcelona were executed; and in Madrid, 45 of the 566. Much harsher was the tribunal in the province of Valencia, where 43.82 per cent of the 89 accused were sentenced to death, although finally only 23 were executed.

In the other zone, everything seemed to be under the control of the army, with Franco acting as the highest authority from October 1936 onwards. However, documentary evidence suggests that it was not military justice that held sway on the home front. Between late 1936 and early 1937 there were very few victims who had the opportunity to appear before courts-martial and military tribunals. A year into the war and still the *sacas* and *paseos* conducted by armed civilian groups were the norm. The phase of 'legal' terror took much longer to appear than in the republican zone and only from autumn 1937 did it manage to replace the 'hot-blooded' terror.

Of the 186 victims of violent death registered during 1937 in the city of Zaragoza, only 47 were executed after being sentenced by courts-martial. This was a notable 'improvement' as against the months of 1936 following the uprising, when only 32 of the 2,578 victims of repression appeared before military tribunals. In the province of Cáceres, fewer than 100 people were executed after appearing before courts-martial until the spring of 1937, while over 1,000 had been 'taken for a *paseo*' and even thrown into the Tagus from bridges.

There was, in fact, a long period, lasting between six and eight months, in which the army failed to implement the mechanism of summary justice. In order to 'regenerate' the Fatherland and rid it of republicans and reds, there was no need for judges or court proceedings.

And even if proceedings were initiated, there was no need for numerous testimonies or charges of some serious crime committed by the accused. For example, these were the crimes which, according to the proceedings of a court-martial held on 15 and 16 February 1937, had been committed by Emili Darder, the republican ex-mayor of Palma de Mallorca: 'He was a disruptive element who stirred up the workers against their bosses. He was a member of *Izquierda Republicana* (. . .) He is reported as having taken part in the Soviet movement that is being prepared in Mallorca'.[21]

Emili Darder was born in Palma in June 1895. He qualified in medicine and entered the Academy of Medicine and Surgery in Palma. In 1933 he became mayor of this city and at the time of the military uprising he was very ill, as the result of an angina that had been diagnosed a few days previously.

On 20 July he was arrested in his home. He was taken to the Provincial Hospital and thence to the Castillo de Bellver. He was held there, incommunicado, for six months. The night before his execution, his wife, Miquela Rovira, and their daughter Emilia were allowed to see him in the sick bay. According to Georges Bernanos, in *Los grandes cementerios bajo la luna*, that night the nurses kept his heart, 'which was rapidly weakening', beating with the help of injections: 'he was taken straight from hospital to the place of execution'.[22] He was executed on the morning of 24 February 1937 in the cemetery in Palma, together with the socialist ex-deputy Alexandre Jaume and the Mayor of Inca, Antoni Mateu. Darder, unlike Jaume, asked for and received 'the Holy Sacraments'. Father Anastasi, a Capuchin friar, had to give him communion with a spoonful of water.

'We are waging war because it is being waged on us', said Manuel Azaña in a speech in the City Hall in Valencia, then the capital of the Republic, on 21 January 1937.[23] A terrible war which in barely half a year saw the cruel terror of the rebel army and Falangists accompanied by a violent upheaval of social order. Tens of thousands of people had been killed on both sides. Many thousands of others were dismissed from their jobs, with 'purges' that were to spread through the administration and education. The military rebels and their allies, those who had lost their political posts in the February 1936 elections, put all their effort into this cleansing, destroying the social networks that republicans, intellectuals, socialists and libertarians had set up in towns and cities, the news and cultural media, community centres and athenaeums, and associations and trade unions.

It soon became clear that this transition from rebellion to war, from social tensions to the extermination of the adversary, was going to have long-term repercussions. In Tenerife, the vast warehouses of the English Fyffes Banana Company were used to house republican prisoners instead of fruit. From there, they were taken by the 'dawn patrols' and thrown into the sea. In León, the San Marcos building, a former inn and fine example of plateresque architecture, was used as a gaol by the military rebels.

Peaceful co-existence would have to return, declared Azaña in the University of Valencia a few months later, on 18 July 1937: 'both sides have to get used to the overwhelming yet unavoidable idea that there are twenty-four million Spaniards, and that however many of us are killed, there will always be enough of us left, and those of us that are left have the need and obligation to continue living together so that the nation does not perish'.[24]

There was still room for optimism and dreams, something somewhat hard to believe after all that had happened. Or perhaps they were things that Azaña, a master wordsmith, wanted to transmit as proof of his firm commitment to peace. And this in spite of the fact that certain battles were already lost, and would remain so for decades. For example, the battle for peaceful co-existence. What could those two words do amidst so much incitement to kill?

The call to violence and the extermination of the adversary were enduring values in the dictatorship that emerged from this war, a regime that was to last for almost four decades. During the war the Catholic Church, by turning a civil armed conflict into a religious crusade, by combining the sword and the cross, had already sanctioned the right of the military to rebel and justified the repression that they were to embark on. The entrance of the church onto the stage, far from reducing the violence, increased it, blessing it on the one hand and kindling even more the popular feeling against the clergy that had broken out at the same time as the defeat of the military uprising.

2

HOLY WAR AND ANTICLERICAL HATRED

Catholicism was the only religion in Spain, identified with political conservatism and social order. In spite of the liberal revolutions of the nineteenth century, the confessional State had remained intact. Since 1875, the Bourbon monarchy had opened new avenues of social power and influence to the Catholic Church and the land-owning aristocracy and good bourgeois families gave new impulses to the Catholic revival with numerous donations of buildings and money to religious congregations.

THE KEYS OF THE DISPUTE

For the Pope and his bishops the Catholic Church was the only source of absolute truth. Catholicism saw itself as the historical religion of the Spanish. As custodian of the highest virtues and a perfect society, in close harmony with the State, the Church was secure. This was because at the height of the twentieth century, Spain represented the epitome of a society with a 'single, dominant and coherent religion', a religion directed and followed by people, bishops, religious orders and laymen, who considered that the thorough preservation of social order was unrenounceable, in view of the close relationship between order and religion in Spain's history.

However, against this constant power and presence of the Church a counter-tradition of criticism, hostility and opposition had emerged.

Anticlericalism, already in evidence in the nineteenth century, with liberal intellectuals and a bourgeois left prepared to reduce the power of the clergy in the State and in society, entered the twentieth century in a new, more radical phase, to be joined by militant workers. And thus emerged, beginning with Barcelona and followed by other Spanish cities, a network of athenaeums, newspapers, lay schools and other manifestations of a popular culture, basically anti-oligarchical and anticlerical, in which republicanism and organised labourism – anarchist or socialist – joined forces. The objective, according to Joan Connelly Ullman, was no longer to just control or reduce the influence of the clergy, but to eliminate the Church as a public power, as a branch of the government and also a socio-cultural force in society.[1]

The Church resisted with vigour these impetuous onslaughts of modernisation and secularisation. And it built a solid rampart against individuals who disagreed with its opinions and life-style of the very order that it blessed and protected. Thus was forged a history of constant resentment between clericalism and anticlericalism, order and change, reaction and revolution which, heightened during the years of the Republic, was ended in 1939, following a bloody battle, with the violent and long-lasting victory of clericalism.

For the Church and most Spanish Catholics, the so-called 'social question' was of secondary consideration at the beginning of the twentieth century. They still clung to traditional concepts and charity mentality that was typical of the *Ancien Régime*. Hence the reception they gave to the *Rerum Novarum*, the encyclical published by Leon XIII in 1891, was unenthusiastic and slow in coming in Spain. And this was why, at the beginning of the twentieth century, the Catholic Workers' Circles overshadowed other types of association such as cooperatives, mutual aid societies, rural credit banks and, above all, trade unions.

The authorities, the most conservative political media and the Church put more faith in 'the good Spanish people, scarcely contaminated by socialist ideas'.[2] In a confessional State, in which Church and political power were so closely united, there was nothing to fear from mass apostasy. At least, that is what it thought. And it would go on thinking this as long as it held the monopoly on education, as long as its charitable works received the moral and financial blessing of respectable society; in short, as long as Catholics played a leading role in the early stages of social projects.

But industrialisation, urban growth and the escalation of class conflicts substantially changed this situation during the first three decades of the twentieth century. Some writers on Catholic affairs, concerned by the consequences of these changes, noted that the urban poor displayed a deep distrust of Catholicism, as it was always on the side of the rich and the employers, and the Church was considered to be a class enemy.

On the eve of the Republic, so these writers say, the urban proletariat in Madrid, Barcelona, Valencia, Seville, and from the mining areas of Asturias and Vizcaya, rarely entered a church, and were unaware of Catholic doctrines and ritual. Many priests in the large estate regions of Andalusia and Extremadura would often draw attention to the growing hostility shown to them and the Church by day-labourers 'polluted' by socialist and anarchist propaganda. As far as religious practice and the role of religion in daily life were concerned, there was a vast difference between these 'de-Catholicised' areas, with no Church influence, and the rural world in the north. In Castilla la Vieja, Aragón and the Basque provinces, going to church was part of the weekly and, for many women, daily routine. Nearly everyone in these regions had some member of the family in the Church, providing most of Spain's priests, monks and nuns, and it was in the well-to-do districts in these areas that nearly all resources were destined. For example, while in the diocese of Vitoria there were, at the time, over 2,000 priests to minister to the population, in the much larger diocese diocese of Seville, there were barely 700.

The gulf between these two conflicting cultural worlds, practising Catholics and hardened anticlericalists, opened up with the proclamation of the Second Republic, and a large number of Spaniards who had hitherto displayed indifference to this struggle were caught in the middle. All the alarm bells started ringing. Lluis Carreras and Antonio Ruiz Vilaplana, two priests who worked with Cardinal Vidal i Barraquer, put it plainly in the report that they sent on 1 November 1931 to the Vatican State Secretariat: under the 'evident grandeur' of the Church during the monarchy, 'Spain was becoming religiously impoverished', with the enlightened elite and the common people distancing themselves from religion, and the nation needing a 'restoration of Christian society'.[3]

The clauses of the republican Constitution, passed in Parliament during the last few months of 1931, that most upset the Chuch were the ones that declared the non-confessional nature of the State, removed the financing of the clergy, brought in civil marriage and divorce and, worst of all for the Church, displaced religious orders from the classroom.

As well as these important issues that were given priority by the republican legislation, there were also some apparently lesser matters that cannot be ignored if we wish to examine more closely the violent clerical and anticlerical reactions displayed on both sides in the civil war.

The arrival of the Republic also revealed an acrimonious, heartfelt struggle for religious symbols. The Royal March, the Spanish national anthem which, during the time of the monarchy, was always played at mass when the host was being consecrated, became one of the distinguishing marks of reaction, a provocation, as was the case with processions. The removal of crucifixes from schools met with vehement disapproval in many towns and villages in the north of Spain. Others protested over the banning of processions. All this shows the close links between order and religion, the monarchy and the authoritarian politics of the right.

The blame was placed on the Republic for its obsessive persecution of the Church and Catholics, while in fact the conflict was far-reaching, with its origin in previous decades. It was not that Spain was no longer Catholic, as Manuel Azaña put it so graphically, by which he meant that the Church no longer guided Spanish culture, having turned its back on the working classes a long time before.[4] It was that there was one Spain that was extremely Catholic, another not so much, and a third that was highly anti-Catholic. There was more Catholicism in the north than in the south, among landowners than among the dispossessed, among women than among men. The majority of Catholics were anti-socialist and people of order. The republican and working-class left was associated with anticlericalism. It is hardly surprising that the proclamation of the Republic meant rejoicing for some and mourning for others.

Following several months of disorientation and disorganisation, political Catholicism burst onto the republican scene. As Santos Juliá has pointed out, the founders of the Republic, with Manuel Azaña at the head, never took it seriously enough, rejecting it as a reaction from a Church which it saw as being decayed, with the air of a dethroned monarchy, a marginal force that was no match for a regime supported by its people. The reality, however, was different: in two years, Catholicism took root as a mass political movement that was to influence the future of the Republic. Firstly through free elections, and subsequently with the force of arms.[5]

However, the Catholic Church hierarchy was not content simply to support this movement or put pressure on the republican authorities. *La Ley de Confesiones y Congregaciones Religiosas* (Religious Confessions and Congregations Act), passed by the Cortes on 17 May 1933, which banned religious orders from any teaching activity, caused a huge commotion in its ranks. The bishops, who since April 1933 had been led by the fundamentalist, Isidro Gomá, reacted with a 'Bishops' Declaration' in which they regretted the 'harsh attack on the divine rights of the Church', and reaffirmed the superior, inalienable right of the Church to set up and run educational establishments, while rejecting 'non-Catholic, neutral or mixed schools.' On 3 June, the day after the Act had been endorsed by the President of the Republic, Alcalá Zamora, the Vatican issued an encyclical of Pius XI, *Dilectissima nobis*, devoted exclusively to this Act which attacked the 'inalienable rights of the Church.'

In the anticlerical camp, its most radical and destructive version also had its chance to show itself. In the revolutionary disturbances of October 1934 in Asturias, 34 seminarists and priests were killed, with the legislative persecution of the first biennium giving way to the physical destruction of members of the Church, something which had not occurred in the history of Spain since the massacres of 1834–35 in Madrid and Barcelona. Furthermore, the purifying fire appeared once more in Asturias: 58 churches, the Bishop's palace, the Seminary with its magnificent library and the *Cámara Santa* in the Cathedral were burnt or blown up.

The subsequent repression carried out by the Army and the Civil Guard was extremely harsh, an exemplary lesson, and thousands of socialists and anarcho-syndicalists filled gaols all over Spain. But the Church and the Catholic press devoted themselves to remembering the atrocities suffered by its martyrs, by calling for punishment and repression as the only remedy against the revolution. The Church's blinkered attitude with regard to social matters was what Canon Maximiliano Arboleya, familiar with the working class environment in Asturias, deplored in a letter to his friend in Zaragoza, Severino Aznar, following the storm of 'hatred and dynamite': 'Nobody, but nobody, has stopped to wonder whether this atrocious criminal revolutionary movement of nearly 50,000 men has any explanation other than the usual perverted socialist propaganda; nobody ever thinks that we too may be largely responsible'.[6]

Apart from the rural areas of the north of Spain, this social Catholicism which was championed by people such as Maximiliano Arboleya or Severino Aznar had not gained much ground. As far as the miners and inhabitants of the industrial suburbs of the major cities were concerned, the Catholic Church seemed to be sided with 'oppressive' capitalism, and the only aim of the Catholic syndicates was to defend the Church and capitalism: 'Whether we like it or not', reflected Arboleya, this was the view taken by 'nearly all our workers'.

Changing this image, attracting all these wayward lambs to the Church's fold was an 'arduous, costly, extremely difficult, long-term and maybe painful' task. This was something that now seemed unattainable and impossible at the beginning of that ill-fated year of 1936 when the election result ruined any hope of this. These catastrophist positions took hold of the few Arboleyas to be found in Spain, Basque Catholics such as Manuel Irujo and José Antonio Aguirre and the renovation sectors of Catalan Catholicism led by Cardinal Vidal i Barraquer. Not even Francesc Cambó's *Lliga Catalana* was exempt from this ultra-Catholic image, labelled by many, according to Borja de Riquer, as '*el partit dels rics i dels capellans*' (the party of the wealthy and the clergy).[7] With peaceful 're-Catholisation' through the Church's trade unions and social work no longer an option, it took just a few months to shift to violent 're-Catholisation' via a holy and patriotic war.

And this was the direction taken from the day after the *Frente Popular* coalition election victory. As early as 20 February *El Pensamiento Alavés* was saying that 'it will not be in Parliament that the final battle is fought, but on the terrain of armed struggle'. The Catholic and extreme right-wing press was calling for rebellion against so much disorder. Back in 1934 the canon preacher of Salamanca, Aniceto Castro Albarrán, had published *El derecho a la rebeldía* (*The Right to Rebellion*), presenting rebellion as a patriotic and religious crusade against the atheistic Republic.

In short, the confrontation between the Church and the Republic, between clericalism and anticlericalism, divided Spanish society in the 1930s as much as agricultural reform or the major social conflicts had done. Officially established as the state religion, the Catholic Church had, during the Restoration and Primo de Rivera's dictatorship, made full use of its monopoly in education, its control on people's lives, to whom it preached doctrines that were historically connected with the most conservative of values: obedience to authority, redemption through suffering and confidence in gaining reward in heaven.

With the proclamation of the Republic, the Church lost, or felt that it had lost, a large part of its traditional influence. Privilege gave way to what the ecclesiastical hierarchy, and many Catholics, considered to be open persecution. The Spanish Church found it harder to take root among the urban workers and rural proletariat. There was ever clearer evidence of the 'failure' of the Church and its 'ministers' to understand social problems, exclusively concerned as it was with the 'kingdom of the sacred' and the defence of the faith. This is what a reformist, liberty-driven regime such as the Republic revealed, as well as legislative persecution, popular anticlericalism and sporadic violence. The Church fought hard against losing all this influence, and prepared itself to combat the large numbers of Spaniards that it considered to be its enemy, a feeling that was reciprocated by the Spaniards. And Catholicism, used to being the religion of the status quo, moved onto the attack and became, in the words of Bruce Lincoln, 'a religion of counter-revolution'.[8]

When a large part of the army took up arms against the Republic in July 1936, the majority of the clergy and Catholics immediately supported it and gave its blessing to the defenders of Christian civilisation against Communism and atheism. As Manuel Irurita, the fundamentalist bishop of Barcelona, had previously said to his faithful in a pastoral letter on 16 April 1931: 'You are ministers of a King that cannot be dethroned, who came to the throne not through the votes of men, but by His own right, the right of inheritance and conquest'.[9]

Given the impossibility of an earthly king rescuing his people from 'the dishonourable situation' of sin, a 'Redeeming God' would have to come to bring the Fatherland 'days of glory and splendour'. This is what all Catholics were asking for, all immersed in the same idea in the spring of 1936: *Adveniat Regnum Tuum*.[10]

THE CIVIL WAR AS A RELIGIOUS CRUSADE

The uprising was not undertaken in the name of religion. The military rebels who planned and brought it to fruition were more concerned with other things, which they saw as saving order, the Fatherland, casting out liberalism, republicanism and the socialist and revolutionary ideologies that were serving to orientate large sectors of urban and rural workers. But from the outset, the Church and most Catholics lent their not inconsiderable resources to furthering this cause. They did this to defend religion, but also this order, this Fatherland that would liberate them from anticlericalism and restore all their privileges. The rebels did not even have to ask the Church for its support, which it gladly offered, and the Church did not waste any time in coming to its decision. While some said they wanted order and others said they were defending the faith, they all recognised the benefits of the arrival of the sacred onto the scene.

The anticlerical violence that was immediately unleashed wherever the coup failed matched the fervour and enthusiasm displayed by the clergy wherever it was successful. These were not rare or inexplicable outbursts of rage. It was the *coup d'état* that buried political solutions and gave way to armed procedures.

There are three things I hope to show in this section. Firstly, that the Church was delighted that it was to be arms that would ensure

51

'material order', eliminate the unfaithful and give it back its 'freedom'. Secondly, that in order to justify its involvement, the Church needed to employ a great deal of rhetoric, construct various myths and give constant reminders of the martyrdom suffered by the clergy. Finally, I shall trace the effective manner in which the Church idealised the figure of Franco, famously consolidated him as supreme leader of rebel Spain and forged his authority as dictator in the future.

The uprising was 'providential' wrote Cardinal Isidro Gomá, Primate of the Spanish bishops, in his 'Report of the military-civilian rising' which he sent to the Secretary of State of the Vatican, Cardinal Eugenio Pacelli, on 13 August 1936. 'Providential', because 'it has been proved, from documents now in the hands of the insurgents, that the communist revolution was due to break out on 20 July'.[11]

Gomá repeated this idea, with more sophisticated arguments in the Collective Bishops' Letter signed in July 1937, just one year after the beginning of the armed attack against the Republic. The war was by way of 'an armed plebiscite'. The Church, because of its well-known 'spirit of peace', had not wanted it to be so. But, faced with the serious threat of being suppressed, 'it could not remain indifferent in this struggle'.[12]

Another bishop, Enrique Pla y Deniel, bishop of the Castilian diocese of Salamanca, who was to become the ideologist of the crusade and apologist of a 'necessary' war, published his well-known pastoral letter '*Las dos ciudades*' (the two cities) on 30 September 1936, when General Franco was about to be invested with absolute powers by his rebel companions. Pla y Deniel defined the Spanish war as a struggle between 'two concepts of life, two sentiments, two forces that are preparing for a universal struggle among all the peoples of the world': on one side, the earthly city of the 'godless'; on the other, 'the heavenly city of the children of God'. It was not, therefore, a civil war, but a 'crusade for religion, the fatherland and civilisation'.[13]

'Armed plebiscite' and 'crusade'. Other terms were used to define it, but these two were the favourites of the Church. The first bishops to use them were those who felt safer alongside the military rebels, basically because the coup had been a resounding success in the zone that contained their dioceses. These were the dioceses of almost the whole of northern Spain, from Pamplona and Zaragoza to Galicia, with Burgos, Valladolid, Salamanca and Zamora in between. Thirty-two sees of the 61 dioceses that existed then in Spain were to be found in the rebel zone by the second half of August. According to data furnished by Alfonso Álvarez Bolado from Ecclesiastical Gazettes, 'in no fewer than eleven dioceses (...) through eighteen interventions, the bishops had made their position absolutely clear before the first official declaration by the Pope on 14 September 1936'. Furthermore, three of them, the bishop of Pamplona and the archbishops of Zaragoza and Santiago de Compostela, had already labelled the civil war as a 'religious crusade' before the end of August.

Almost all of these declarations followed a substantially identical line: they unblushingly sided with the military coup, which they celebrated with the Catholic masses as a liberation; they urged people to join the struggle against 'the lay-Jewish-Masonic-soviet elements', an expression coined by the bishop of León, José Alvarez Miranda; and they saw no outcome to the conflict other than the resounding victory of 'our glorious army' over 'the enemies of God and of Spain'.[14]

Intoxicated as they were by this brutal atmosphere caused by the military uprising, most of the Spanish Church authorities never wanted to hear anything about negotiation or pardon. At the merest whisper of this cursed word, negotiation, they would be on the alert. So said the provincial father of the Company of Jesus in León, Antonio Encinas, to Father General W. Ledóchowski, in a letter he wrote from Hendaye on 1 September 1936, in which he commented on the rumours in the French press of a possible intervention by the Pope to bring the war to an end. It would be a grave mistake because 'Catholics see this war as being an authentic religious crusade against atheism, and they see it as being entirely unavoidable: either the battle is won or Catholicism disappears from Spain'. 'Unhappiness' and 'disappointment' is what all these Catholics who 'unreservedly offer their resources and lives for the campaign' would feel. And the Pope would lose 'much of his authority'. Most people would be left with the impression 'that he spoke of events in Spain without knowing what is going on here'.[15]

Father Ledóchowski passed on a copy of this letter to Cardinal Pacelli, who was aware of what was happening in Spain from the long report sent to him by Cardinal Gomá two weeks earlier. Gomá was thinking of a certain, although not immediate, victory of the military movement, something he shared with almost everyone until the Battle of Madrid in November 1936 forced them to contemplate a longer war: 'if it is successful, as is expected (...) it is certain that within a relatively short time material order will be firmly assured, and we shall see the beginning of an era of clear liberty for the Church'.[16]

Even before the Spanish Church hierarchy had officially termed the war 'a crusade', a trend which was becoming obvious in the second half of August, large numbers of Catholics, lapsed Catholic conservatives and non-Catholic Fascists had classified the assault on power as a '*bellum sacrum et justum*', a 'necessary' war against the enemies of Spain, in favour of centralism and authoritarianism and the preservation of the socio-economic order, with no reforms, against the non-property-owning masses in the country and cities. As Gomá said to Pacelli, this was 'the true, traditional Spanish people': some were motivated by 'religious idealism, their Catholic conscience having been deeply wounded by the sectarian and anti-religious laws and by uncontrolled persecution'; others, because 'their material interests were under threat'; many were motivated by the desire to 're-establish the material order that had been profoundly disrupted'; and there were plenty, added Gomá, who were motivated by 'the feeling of national unity, under threat from separatist tendencies in certain regions'.

They called it a crusade, when in fact what was behind the 'National' side was a broad authoritarian 'reactionary coalition', whose components were determined to seize power through the army, destroy the internal and external 'enemies', defend the social order of the property-owners and create a society that they called 'new' to start with, although it was later shown to be otherwise.

With the Republic established in Spain, with its reformist programme in motion, with its social, cultural and political mobilisation that Spanish society had attained, what happened in July 1936 could not be a 'military intervention' or classic *pronunciamiento*. The authoritarian solution called for mass support. And who better than the Church and the Catholic movement it sponsored to provide it, to 'unify' all these different forces. Catholicism was the ideal hub for bringing them together, for furthering the process of melding all these reactionary groups and interests. It provided a veritable recruitment liturgy, particularly in Old Castille, Navarre and Álava, a baroque politico-religious liturgy replete with symbols, beliefs and zealousness.

The success of this religious mobilisation, this liturgy that attracted the masses in the dioceses of 'liberated' Spain, encouraged the army to adorn its speeches with references to God and religion, hitherto absent from the proclamations of the military coup and subsequent declarations. The rebels were convinced of the importance of the emotional link, as well as of the destruction and annihilation of the enemy, at a time when they knew what they did not want, but still lacked a clear political focus. The symbiosis between 'Religion and Patriotism', the 'virtues of *la Raza*' (pedigree) reinforced national unity and legitimised the violence that they had meted out in that summer of 1936.

Religious and military ceremony, Aragón (Coyne Collection, Archivo Histórico Provincial, Zaragoza)

This identification of the clergy and the Catholic masses with the military rebels could be seen from the early days of the war in processional prayers and in the 'replacing' and 'return' of crucifixes in schools, banned as religious symbols by the Republic. The focus now was on abolishing the republican legislation and restoring traditional Spain, something which was to win many adherents and was enthusiastically greeted.

Republican, anarchist, socialist and secular symbols all caved in under the joint pressure of the military and religion. In Pamplona, one of the first things the Carlists did after the uprising was to shatter the plaques containing the names of notable socialists and republicans in the streets and squares. Old habits of popular religious life were restored. Religious feast days returned to the official calendar, and others of a 'national' character began to be celebrated, which were maintained during Franco's dictatorship until his death.

In short, the interpretation of the war as a crusade reached the Church hierarchy from the fronts and from the popular demonstrations of religious fervour throughout rebel Spain. The Church authorities, safe in their episcopal palaces, understood this spirit of religious rebellion and imbued it with reason and legitimacy. They only spoke after others had acted, and this served to reinforce the justice of their cause even more, helping them to give the impression that they only made an appearance when the anticlerical and revolutionary violence left them no option. They had neither taken part in the rising nor encouraged anyone to go to war. But there they were, obliged to take a stand against the material and spiritual decadence that 'the reds' had left the Fatherland in. They knew that this was the best approach for a rapid legitimisation of the military rising, in other words, the right to rebellion, and the exterminating war that ensued.

The union between the sword and the cross, religion and the 'civilian-military movement', was a recurrent theme in all the pronouncements, circulars, letters and pastoral preaching issued by the bishops during August 1936. Before the end of that month, three bishops had already explicitly described the war as being a 'religious crusade'. The first to do so was Marcelino Olaechea, bishop of Pamplona, on 23 August. He was followed three days later by

Rigoberto Domenech, the archbishop of Zaragoza. And the arch-bishop of Santiago, Tomás Muniz Pablos, put it categorically on 31 August: the war against the enemies of Spain was 'certainly patri-otic, very patriotic, but fundamentally a religious Crusade, of the same type as the Crusades of the Middle Ages, because now, as then, the struggle is for the faith of Christ and the liberty of the people. It is God's will! *¡Santiago y cierra España!*' ('for Saint James, and close ranks, Spain', a traditional Spanish battle cry dating back to the ninth century).[17]

For the impulses that moved it and for its transcendence, the 1936–39 crusade, went on the archbishop of Santiago, was the same as the one that 'fused the Iberian races in the same moulds', from Covadonga and 'the feats of El Cid' to the 'epilogue' of the Battle of Lepanto, when 'Europe could finally feel free from Muhammedan and Asian barbarism'. The whole of Spain's history had been a crusade. So said the bishops, as did the ultra-Catholic monarchist José María Pemán in Seville on 15 August. 'The providential and historical mission of Spain has always been this: to redeem the civilised world from all its dangers, expel Moors, stop Turks, baptise Indians . . .'[18]

With this idea pervading Spanish ecclesiastical and traditionalist thought, and the fact that it had been revived in the battle against the French in the Peninsular War in the nineteenth century, it was inevitable that it would reappear in those 'ominous' moments of 1936. General Emilio Mola, hardly one for theological musings, was one of the first officers to understand the benefits of bringing the sacred into the picture, and the advantages of setting forward higher principles to steer a political and class conflict. The quote is meaningful and is taken from his broadcast on Radio Castilla on 15 August 1936: 'We are being asked (. . .) what direction we are taking. The answer is simple and one that we have repeated many times. We are going to impose order, to give bread and jobs to all Spaniards and give everyone a fair deal. And then, on the ruins left behind by the *Frente Popular* – blood, mire and tears – we shall build a great, strong, powerful State that is set to be crowned by a Cross (. . .), the symbol of our religion and our Faith, the only thing that has remained untouched among so much savagery'.[19]

On 1 October 1936, in Salamanca, General Francisco Franco was appointed to the highest military and political authority in the rebel zone, in a ceremony in which Miguel Cabanellas, in the presence of diplomats from Italy, Germany and Portugal, handed over power in the name of the *Junta de Defensa* which he had presided over since 24 July and which was dissolved that day. Franco adopted the title of '*Caudillo*', in an allusion to the medieval warrior lords. From that moment on, Franco was treated by the Catholic Church hierarchy as a saint, the saviour of Spain and Christianity. Cardinal Gomá sent Franco a telegram to congratulate him on his election as 'Head of the Government of the Spanish State' and Franco answered him by saying that on taking on this post 'with all its responsibilities, I could receive no better comfort than the blessing of Your Eminence'.[20]

A veritable baring of the soul. Franco was anxious to hawk his religious piety at this time, and he had understood, as had the majority of his brothers in arms, how important it was to introduce religion into his public statements and mingle with the 'people' in solemn religious acts. Once established as Head of State, says Paul Preston, his propagandists moulded an image of him as a 'great Catholic crusader' and his public religious piety notably intensified. From 4 October 1936 until his death on 20 November 1975, Franco had a personal chaplain, Father José María Bulart. He heard mass every day and, whenever he could, he joined his wife, Doña Carmen Polo y Martínez Valdés, for the evening rosary. In short, the man was an 'exemplary Christian', a 'fine Catholic', said Gomá, 'who cannot imagine the Spanish State outside its traditional bounds of Catholicism at all levels'.[21]

Bishops, priests and the rest of the Church began to look on Franco as someone sent by God to impose order in the 'earthly city' and Franco ended up believing that, indeed, he had a special relationship with divine providence. Gomá praised him to the skies every time his name was mentioned and Pla y Deniel lent him his palace in Salamanca for use as a centre of operations, 'headquarters' as it was known throughout Christian Spain. There, surrounded by the Moorish guard, he held court. He was like a king in the golden age of the Spanish monarchy, entering and leaving churches beneath a canopy. Franco needed the support and blessing of the Catholic

Church. He needed to be acknowledged by all the Catholics and people of order of the world, with the Pope at the head. He needed the Church in order to wage a war of extermination and be seen as a saint. *Caudillo* and saint. And he needed the Church to remain untroubled because he would know how to express his gratitude later. Gomá had already said as much to Cardinal Pacelli on 9 November 1936, after Franco had been supreme Head for barely a month: 'I have had a long talk with the Head of State (...) My impressions are frankly favourable (...) He intends to respect the freedom of the Church, promote the interests of the Catholic religion, to propose a Concordat with the Holy See, to see to the temporal needs of the Church and its ministers, to defend education and give it an openly Christian orientation at all levels'.[22]

Franco and Gomá, the bishops and Franco in close alliance, and yet in some sectors of the world's Catholic press and certain European Catholic circles the 'justice' of the cause that had united them was called into question. Particularly so after General Mola's offensive in the north left as its mark cruel, intensive bombing raids carried out in order to break the civilian population's morale and destroy land communications. It began with the Condor Legion in Durango on 31 March 1937. One hundred and twenty-seven civilians were killed during the raid and roughly the same number died as a result of their injuries. Among the victims were fourteen nuns and two priests, one of whom, Father Morilla, was celebrating mass.

Crueller still, creating real mass terror, was the bombing of Guernica on 26 April organised by the head of the Condor Legion, Colonel Wolfram von Richthofen after consultations with Colonel Juan Vigón, Mola's chief of general staff. Guernica was a symbol of Basque identity and both Vigón and Mola were well aware of this. That Monday 26 April was market day in Guernica. Among inhabitants, refugees and peasants who went to the market that day in the former Basque capital, there were some 10,000 people. The town had no anti-aircraft defences. It was attacked in the middle of the afternoon for three hours by the Condor Legion and the Italian *Aviazione Legionaria* under the command of Colonel von Richthofen. The Basque government estimated a death toll of over 1,500 and said that a further thousand had been wounded in the air raid, although the number of deaths, while not known for certain, was probably less than 500.

Franco's press and propaganda services denied at first that any bombing had taken place in Guernica. When this position became untenable, they blamed the destruction of Guernica on the Basques themselves, a lie maintained throughout the years of the dictatorship. But there were witnesses, including four journalists and a Basque priest, Alberto Onaindía. Two days after the attack, George Steer, the correspondent for *The Times*, published in that paper and in *The New York Times* an account of the massacre which would be read all over the world. Everyone now knew that Guernica had been destroyed by explosive and incendiary bombs. What certain historians, except the Francoist apologists, wrote later also made it quite clear: the idea originated in Mola's general staff and the Germans implemented it. And thanks to Pablo Picasso, Guernica became a symbol of the horrors of war.[23]

Explosive bombs raining down on a defenceless civilian population. The massacre seemed to confirm what a few Catholic intellectuals were already saying abroad: that Franco's Christian Spain was a hotbed of ruthless killing. Concerned about the repercussions that this news might have in certain European government circles, Franco personally summoned Cardinal Isidro Gomá to a meeting, which was held on 10 May 1937. According to Gomá's own account, Franco asked him to arrange for 'the Spanish bishops (. . .) to publish a letter addressed to all the world's bishops, along with a request that it be published in the Catholic press, that would set the record straight, and coincidentally would be performing a patriotic act and revision of history, which would be of enormous benefit to the Catholic cause the world over'.

Gomá wasted no time in meeting Franco's request. On 15 May he sent a 'confidential' letter to all the bishops setting out his request. All of them replied positively, except for Vidal i Barraquer who, in a letter sent on 30 May insisted that a 'collective Document' was not the most 'effective, opportune or discreet' way, although he did agree that there was a pressing need for 'vehement propaganda in favour of our unfortunate Spain, particularly with regard to religious persecution'. Vidal advocated writing 'personal letters' to foreign cardinals and bishops. He was not happy (and here he was clearly thinking of Franco) 'to accept suggestions from people outside the hierarchy over purely Church matters'; in other words, the Church, instead of remaining outside 'party politics', was tarnished by the cause of the military rebels.[24]

The 'Collective Letter from the Spanish Bishops to the Bishops of the World' was dated 1 July 1937, but it was sent to the bishops three weeks later, with the request that they did not publicise it until it had begun to be published abroad. It was signed by 43 bishops and five capitular vicars. Around this time Gomá sent two copies to Franco, and he pointed out to him, as if Franco did not know, that it had been written 'so that the truth of what has been happening in Spain in recent years be known and, especially, what the National Movement means for our beloved Fatherland and for western civilisation'.

From a doctrinal point of view, there was nothing new in this Letter that had not already been said by bishops, priests and others in holy orders in the twelve months since the military rising. But the international impact was so great – it had been published immediately in French, Italian and English – that many people accepted permanently the Manichaean and tendentious version transmitted by the Church of the 'armed plebiscite': that the National Movement personified the virtues of the best Christian tradition and the republican government all the vices inherent in Russian communism. As well as insisting on the lie that the 'military uprising' put a stop to a definite plan for a communist revolution and offering the typical excuse of order, peace and justice that reigned in the 'national' territory, the bishops included a matter of capital importance which is still the official position of the church hierarchy today: the Church was an 'innocent, peaceful, defenceless' victim of this war and 'before being totally exterminated at the hands of communism', it supported the cause that ensured the 'fundamental principles of society'. The Church was the 'benefactor of the people', not the 'aggressor'. The agressors were the other side, those who had caused this 'communist', 'anti-Spanish' and 'anti-Christian' revolution.[25]

The Collective Letter was viewed favourably by some nine hundred bishops in thirty-two countries. 'We should congratulate ourselves that with this Document we have helped to dispel any misunderstandings and put a good light on the events and ideas that are being aired with the current war in Spain', wrote Gomá to Pacelli on 12 October 1937. This unreserved support for the rebel side served as a decisive argument for Catholics and people of order the world over. This was fundamentally because it was accompanied by a shameless silence regarding the destructive violence that the army had been practising since the first moment of the uprising. The Letter demonised the enemy, who were only moved by the desire for religious persecution, and decisively codified support for the war as a holy, just crusade against communism's assault on the Fatherland and religion.

Franco and the Catholic Church emerged notably strengthened. The transformation of the war into a purely religious conflict, ignoring the political and social aspects, justified all the previous violence and gave Franco licence to carry on with the killing. The Church, the military rebels' travelling companion right from the start of the journey, now took its seat at the front of the train bound for victory. Javier Conde, then director of Propaganda, informed the Jesuit, Constantino Bayle, the editor of *Razón y Fe* and a confidant of Gomá's, of the satisfaction expressed by those in the Francoist political and military circles over this wonderful document: 'Please tell the Cardinal that I, an expert in these affairs, want to say the following: he has achieved more with the Collective Letter than all the rest of us with our efforts'.[26]

By the time this 'collective Letter' appeared, tens of thousands of 'reds' had been killed. Most of the clergy, led by the bishops, not only hushed up this wave of terror but condoned it and even collaborated 'body and soul' in the repression. It was God's implacable and necessary justice that spilled the blood of the 'Godless' in abundance, in order to ensure the survival of the Church, the institution representing God on the Earth, the maintaining of traditional order and the 'unity of the Fatherland'.

The bishops and most of the clergy were accomplices in this military and Falangist terror, which in most cases saw no need for any trials or legal safeguards. They hushed it up, they approved of it and they publicly applauded it. Prison and army chaplains; rural friars and priests. They were all so enthusiastic over the religious resurgence in Spain that they were deaf to the tortures, the dawn shootings, the wailing of the widows. The priests denounced the reds, refusing them good conduct certificates so that the army would punish them.

Administering the last rites to those who were about to be killed became one of the principal concerns of the Catholic clergy. The question lay not in saving their bodies because, the clergy argued, they deserved their end, but in saving at least their souls. The death ritual was described in detail by Gumersindo de Estella, the Capuchin father who looked after the spiritual needs of the inmates of the prison in Zaragoza during the civil war and in the immediate post-war years.[27]

The chapel of Torrero prison in Zaragoza was a space devoted to a 'courtroom' where, on the days when there were executions, an improvised altar was set up with all the necessary trappings for mass. A portrait of Franco presided over the ceremony until, in mid-1938, Gumersindo de Estella managed to have it removed, having repeatedly informed the authorities that 'Franco's presence in the Chapel and on its altar as a saint set the prisoners' nerves on edge and caused them outraged indignation because they knew that he was the one who signed the death sentences'.

The prisoners would go into the chapel around five in the morning. The priest had one hour 'for the spiritual preparation of the condemned', which Don Gumersindo felt was too short, particularly when there were several to be executed. He would speak to them, ask them about their families, what they had been condemned for and, above all, whether they were practising Christians. Some accepted confession and communion 'with enviable consent'. Others had to be convinced of the need to 'seek consolation in the supernatural'. Finally, there were those who refused any dialogue or spiritual aid. 'No sir, please don't ask me to practise religion' said a condemned man on 11 June 1938. 'The right is killing in the name of Religion and waging war in the name of Religion. And I want no part in a Religion that inspires such cruelty'.

At six in the morning, the Civil Guard would begin 'the task' of tying their hands. They were taken from the prison to the cemetery walls in a truck. During the short ride, the 'pitiful cries of woe' were unceasing, and the priest tried to calm them by giving them the crucifix to kiss. He would accompany them until they were placed in a line facing the wall. After they were brought down by the firing squad, he would give them absolution and extreme unction, before the duty lieutenant approached and fired 'two or three pistol shots into the head'.[28]

Particularly venomous was the clerical and Catholic offensive against schoolteachers. The clergy were convinced that all the ills of modern society could be attributed to the 'erosion process' performed by intellectuals and schoolteachers. They saw them as rivals, competing for their custom and trying to strip the church of its monopoly in, and administration of, ethical values. From the beginning of the twentieth century, the attacks of the hierarchy and the Jesuits had focused on the *Institución Libre de Enseñanza* (Free Institute of Education), which had claimed the educated elite and displayed considerable success in what the Jesuits felt was their own field, that of influencing the formation of national culture through teaching the elite. As far as the rural and working-class district priests were concerned, schoolteachers, when they were laymen and anticlerical, competed in offering the community services that were similar to theirs: legitimising civil instead of religious power; acting as guardians of ethical and civil values; and influencing the new generations. The Church hierarchy and Jesuits from above, and the priests and monks and nuns from below created a 'Catholic mentality' which felt intimidated by the alien and modern. They saw the Second Republic as being the last straw in this intimidation. In the 'Holy War' and post-war years, now unreservedly endorsed by the alien-exterminating dictatorship, they settled old scores.

Those intellectuals and schoolteachers who had identified most closely with liberal, republican, anarchistic or socialist ideas, who had struggled the hardest against religious education, and had advocated 'sovietising' schools, were going to pay dearly. During the war and post-war years, over fifty thousand schoolteachers underwent purging investigations.

Friends and defenders of killers on one side and martyrs on the other. Such was the two-faced attitude of the Spanish clergy during the civil war. The Church hierarchy, diocesan priests and monks and nuns of the various orders did not need to juggle any balls to legitimise from the outset the violence organised and perpetrated by the rebels. But the anticlerical reaction that was unleashed by the military coup wherever it was unsuccessful contributed even more to the Church providing its ideological and propaganda services to the rebel army, encouraging them to pursue the infidels to their graves and to lend even greater support to the uncivil peace that followed the war.

'THE SONS OF CAIN'[29]

For one thing seems to be beyond all doubt, confirmed by all researchers: the clergy and sacred objects were the prime target of popular rage, of those who took part in defeat of the military rebels and who lead the 'cleansing' undertaken in the summer of 1936. There was no need to wait for orders from anybody to spring into action. Some Carmelite friars were murdered on 20 July in Barcelona just as the rebel cavalry regiment, holed up in their convent, was overcome. Nearby, in Igualada, the first violent act to occur was the burning of the Capuchin friars' convent. The same scenes were repeated in many towns and cities in Spain, including places where the repression against the 'elements of order' became more intense in the second fortnight of August and first few days of September. In Murcia, where the targeting of the clergy was not particularly violent, most of the convents were attacked in the final twelve days of July. And 90 per cent of the thousand or so clergy killed in Madrid fell in the first few months, some time before the mass 'sacas' of November.

In regions where the defeat of the military coup unleashed a sudden, destructive revolutionary process, the punishment meted out was extensive and devastating. The figures speak for themselves: over 6,800 churchmen, both lay and regular, were killed; a large number of churches, hermitages and sanctuaries were burnt or suffered looting and desecration, with their works of art and items of worship totally or partially destroyed. Nor did cemeteries or graveyards fare any better, with a great number of priests' graves desecrated and the remains of monks and nuns exhumed.

Burning a church or killing a priest was the first thing that was done in many villages and towns where the military uprising was unsuccessful. Particularly in Catalonia, where a third of the clergy killed in republican Spain fell. They were killed without any previous legal procedure. If there was a terror that was 'hot-blooded', it was the terror that was visited on the clergy, who were rarely sent to prison. Only 240 clergy were sent to the Modelo prison in Barcelona during the whole war, 1.8 per cent of the total nomber of inmates, and up to the end of 1936 only 46 were sent there. Naturally, under the circumstances, prison was a 'privilege' for them and obviously somewhere safe. So it was no surprise that there was the occasional priest who did not want to leave prison, such as Josep Ribas, 71 years of age, who had been imprisoned on 19 August 1936 and who refused to leave when the general commissar of Public Order ordered his release in April 1937.[30]

'Direct action', nothing less. That was what the clergy deserved. Andreu Nin, one of the big names in the *Partido Obrero de Unificación Marxista* (POUM), publicly stated as much at the beginning of August 1936. Nin, who a few months later was to be kidnapped and murdered by the communist secret services, thought and said the same as many other revolutionaries, leftist republicans and union leaders: that the 'bourgeois' Republic's anticlerical legislation had done nothing to solve the 'problem' of the Church. It had had to be solved by the working class in the revolutionary flare-up initiated by the military coup. And it had been solved by the workers and revolutionaries in the way that they knew how, by 'attacking the roots', leaving no church standing, suppressing 'the priests, churches and worship'.[31]

Without a doubt, the treatment meted out to the clergy by the revolutionaries and their leaders in the summer of 1936 was merely the fulfilment of what many had been saying would happen since the beginning of the century, when leftist intellectuals, radical politicians such as Alejandro Lerroux and militant workers saw the Church and its representatives as the ultimate enemies of freedom, the people and progress, a designation that had, in the revolutionary discourse, hitherto been reserved for capitalism and the State. They all promised that one of the many contributions of the revolution would be 'the purifying firebrand' for church buildings and the cassock-wearing 'parasites'. And when the time came, they put it into practice.

It was not the revolutionaries who unleashed the revolution. Nor was this revolution the direct result of the intensification of the class war. It was caused, as we know, by a frustrated military coup, an event provoked from outside. Once unleashed, however, the clergy appeared as an easily identifiable target. Old scores resulting from class conflicts, social struggles and their bloody repressions, a normal aspect of monarchist or republican Spain, were settled, but particular attention was paid to the clergy. It is true that the revenge of these revolutionaries was exploited by a great many opportunists, delinquents and reprobates, who had never contributed to the revolution, all of them absorbed into this 'people-proletariat in arms'. However mollifying that may be, it does not change history.

The Church was persecuted for many reasons, and here one should remember the opinion of its detractors and persecutors, even though what they expressly stated might not always have matched their innermost motivations. José Álvarez Junco argues that this long-winded, repetitive criticism of the Church, full of nuances, 'was due more to fundamentally ethical recriminations, rather than to an analysis of the social power of the Church and its consequences'. Naturally, there was a harsh battle between the Church and anticlericalism over basic themes related to the organisation of society and the State. But the issues that gave rise to demonstrations and counter-demonstrations, the burning of convents and violence against the clergy were 'more symbolic and cultural', with strong popular support.[32]

The Catholic clergy was accused of 'betraying the Gospel', 'pharisaism', abandoning the original virtues of brotherhood and poverty, a recurring feature in the anarchist press which Gerald Brenan seized on as an explanation. In Brenan's view, anticlerical violence was the expression of a 'deep religious feeling' in an 'intensely religious people who feel they have been deserted and deceived'. This view was shared by Gumersindo de Estella, the chaplain of the prison in Zaragoza, and the few Catholics who felt that anticlericalism was not only an expression of 'popular rage' manipulated by demagogues and revolutionaries. 'I always maintained that deep down, the burning of churches was an act of faith', Ronald Fraser was told by one of these Catholics, Maurici Serrahima, a lawyer and leading member of *Unió Democràtica*, who gave shelter to eleven Capuchin friars from the convent at Sarriá, and helped Cardinal Francesc Vidal i Barraquer of Tarragona to flee the country. 'In other words, it was an act of protest because, in the eyes of the people, the Church was no longer what it should have been. It was the disenchantment of someone who believed, loved and was betrayed. It came from the idea that the Church should have been on the side of the poor, but it wasn't, and in fact it had not been for many years, except for some of its members. It was a protest against the Church's submission to the well-to-do'.[33]

From the young Lerroux to the anarchist worker, as well as the most corrosive anticlerical publications such as *El Motín* at the beginning of the century and *La Traca* in the republican period, all shared the idea that the clergy had an insatiable lust for power and money. This went for the clergy in general and the Jesuits in partic-ular, extremely rich and with no moral scruples. They possessed everything and they were constantly greedy for more. As Alejandro Lerroux wrote in 1907: 'They take possession of inheritances, they receive pious donations, they catechise the daughters of rich families and shut them up in their monasteries'.[34]

The clergy was always portrayed in illustrations in the anticlerical press as being corpulent and resplendent, surrounded by sacks of money which they concealed while asking for alms. And in the civil war, in the anticlerical assault of summer 1936, the same militias and armed groups that seized the bishops to kill them, attacked their palaces in the quest for the large fortunes they assumed were hidden therein. Several million pesetas would have been found, for example, in the assault on the bishop's palace in Jaén, according to the Madrid socialist press. The bishop, Manuel Basulto Jiménez, was murdered a few days later.[35]

But the favourite topic of the anticlerical press and magazines, as Álvarez Junco has also pointed out, was the sex life of the clergy, who were accused of 'anti-natural' conduct, sometimes through weakness, which led them into all sorts of 'aberration', mostly through excess. 'The republican or working-class press delights in reproducing stories, jokes and cartoons about priests who cohabit with their housekeepers and have children with them, confessors who lasciviously caress their female devotees and chaplains who enjoy an orgiastic life in convents'. And the introduction of this 'anti-natural' element meant that the clergy were seen as a 'cursed' social group, a sect that was fair game because it was something alien to the community, different to all other mortals, with their black cassocks, external symbols of their 'black behaviour'.[36]

Today, many people might be surprised at this, and it would be difficult to understand if anticlericalism were seen to be merely an attack on the political clout and social influence of the clergy. Yet history tells us that in the attacks on convents during the *Semana Trágica* and nearly 30 years later, during the civil war, the crowd displayed a morbid curiosity for the tombs of monks and nuns, where they were convinced that foetuses or sophisticated pornographic items were hidden. It was not natural for them to be shut up in a convent and anything could be expected of them.

Convent life, states the British historian Frances Lannon, 'was a scandal and provocation for a large number of people on the political left, who lived outside the bounds of the Catholic cultural universe'. Life-long celibacy, freely chosen, was a phenomenon peculiar to Catholicism, for women as well as men, although many more women than men chose this path. Despite the fact that figures from different sources do not agree, in Spain in 1931 there were some 115,000 ecclesiastics, out of a population of barely 23 million. Of these, nearly 60,000 were nuns, 35,000 diocesan priests and 15,000 monks. At any event, the number of nuns was three times higher than that of monks and also higher than the number of monks and priests combined.

Hostility towards nuns was embodied on the same basis as criticism of ecclesiastics in general, beginning with the control of education as a powerful tool for the cultural reproduction of Catholicism, but feeling against them was enhanced even further because of this 'antinatural' element of renouncing sex and maternity. But, unlike with men, who seemed to have the capacity to choose freely, with women, especially the youngest ones, Lannon states that there was the suspicion that they adopted this antinatural option under coercion, and this was expressed in literary as well as popular culture.

There had to be some kind of deception and coercion involved for young 14 or 15-year-old girls to enter as novices into convents. This was the message of *Electra*, the play written by Benito Pérez Galdós, the performance of which caused major uproar in certain cities in Spain in 1901. Furthermore, *Electra* was based on a contemporary legal action in which the parents of a young girl who had entered a convent claimed that it could not have been of her own free will. And this was perfectly in tune with the popular notion that celibacy was not normal. Hence also the success of the famous article by Lerroux written a few years later, in 1906 in which, according to the interpretation by Álvarez Junco, 'he brilliantly informed his followers of the highest objective of the immature Catholic male chauvinist: the raping of novices'. To repeat his famous phrase: 'pull up the veil of the novices and raise them to the category of motherhood'.[37]

The ritual of disinterring the bodies of nuns was a common occurrence during the days of anticlerical and revolutionary violence in the summer of 1936. But the number of nuns who were killed was infinitely lower than that of monks and priests. And despite all the clichés and conventional images regarding the matter, the incitement to rape nuns that Lerroux had made thirty years earlier had no followers in 1936.

Let us look at the numbers. According to the study published in 1961 by Bishop Antonio Montero Moreno, the principal yardstick as far as the figures are concerned, the total number of nuns murdered in Spain was 283. That may be a large number if it is to be argued that not one of them should have undergone this martyrdom. But it is a very small number if it is compared with the 4,184 diocesan priests and 2,365 monks who suffered the same fate. And as Montero, who estimated the total number of nuns for that year to be 'some 45,000', pointed out, more than half of them remained in the 'red zone'. So it was not as if there was any lack of potential victims.[38]

There are unusual and surprising data to be found in this matter. For example, in the zones controlled by the anarchists the nuns were almost always left alive, although they were forced to leave their convents and their habits, and were assigned to social work or servitude. The case of the diocese of Barbastro, a staging post for anarchist militias from Catalonia, speaks volumes. Of the 140 incardiated priests in this diocese, 123 (no less than 87.8 per cent) were murdered. The same fate befell 52 Claretians, 18 Benedictines and nine Piarists, figures that make Barbastro the most heavily castigated diocese in Spain with regard to the proportion of incardinated clergy to killing. No nun underwent the same punishment.

In Catalonia, where the mass killing of monks was rife, only 50 nuns were murdered. To find mass killings of nuns, we have to go to the Valencian Region and particularly Madrid. In both cases these mass killings occurred in November 1936, by which time the rest of republican Spain had called a halt to the 'hot-blooded' terror against the clergy. The biggest massacre, according to research by Antonio Montero, occurred at dawn on 10 November 1936, when 23 Sisters of Adoration were shot against the walls of the Este cemetery in Madrid.

Thus it seems that there were specific reasons for respecting the life of nuns more than that of monks or priests. Firstly, there was the suspicion that young women entered the convents under coercion, pressurised by confessors, men or, as Lerroux said, Jesuits, who were in fact the ones who had the ability to manipulate political power and connect with oligarchic groups with economic and social influence. In the anticlerical collective mindset, and in real life, nuns were less politicised than the male clergy. Nuns were not the 'guilty ones'; priests and monks were.

Spanish society in the first third of the twentieth century provided very few opportunities for women in professional and family life, and the religious orders ended up, despite their sexual and social restrictions, representing an alternative to exclusion in everyday life. Furthermore, as Frances Lannon points out, the greater growth in female as opposed to male congregations was concentrated in active rather than contemplative communities, so that the Church was able to call on thousands of nuns who were teachers, nurses and social workers to become part of their networks in Spanish society. It seems no coincidence that the Little Sisters of the Poor escaped this persecution and that what the nuns were criticised for in anticlerical publications was that they were taking this social and educational role away from 'normal' working-class women, the ones who did know what a mother's love was.[39]

Sparing nuns, killing priests and monks, and burning all religious buildings. That was the formula for the summer of 1936, when the outbreak of revolutionary fervour lifted the curtain for the last time on what waves of anticlerical feeling had been rehearsing previously.

Fire as a symbol of destruction of the old and purification, a necessary stage to new life. In Manzanares (Ciudad Real), while the images and altar pieces of the parish church were being destroyed, 'a large number of people' helped to transport inflammable liquids in buckets, cans and other receptacles. They sprinkled the walls of the building and the staircase in the tower, and then set fire to it, 'shooting out the upper windows to help the draught'.[40] In the village of Hijar, in Teruel province, as the correspondent for *Solidaridad Obrera* wrote on 6 August: 'The churches were burning. Then all the documents of the Municipal Archive were piled up, and they are still burning, and will do so for several days more. The Property Registry was also burnt to the ground. The red and black flag flies resplendently over these glorious deeds'. And the glorious deed was erasing the past, the symbols of order. This is why, as well as religious items, documents from the municipal archive, court records, public and property deeds were fed to the flames. And in the villages, as well as priests, bosses and local politicians were murdered, representatives of 'capitalism, the State and religion', the three powers that the anarchist press repeatedly denounced for suppressing the people.

The anticlerical offensive that spread through the villages of the eastern half of Aragon, where the militias passed through, was widely fêted and left numerous scars, still present today. The militias, together with the local inhabitants, would collect religious images and artefacts from the houses. They entered the church on horseback, threw the saints to the ground and dragged them to the village square. There they piled them up – 'the male saints on top of the female saints' – along with other religious items, municipal and ecclesiastical documents and property registers, religion and order inextricably united, and in the evening, according to the description of the ritual that the North American anthropologist, Susan Harding, has provided for the village of Ibieca, in Huesca province, 'they set fire to the lot'.

All the churches were closed for worship, converted into supply markets, stores, militia billets, gaols, dance halls, public canteens or garages. The parish houses were used as dwellings for politicians and officers, cultural centres or revolutionary committee offices. In Benabarre (Huesca), the convent church of the Dominican nuns was converted into stables.[41]

The 'martyrdom of objects', as Montero Moreno sees it, revealed 'a blind rage against the religious world that was much more significant than if the object of destruction were men of flesh and blood'. Objects were more 'innocent' than people. Hence the obsessive 'ferocity' with sacred objects.[42]

There are, however, other intepretations. The anthropologist, Bruce Lincoln, maintains that an iconoclastic act is never an attempt to destroy the sacred power of an icon, since iconoclasts are convinced that it does not have any. Rather, their intention is to demonstrate to all the observers, be they iconoclasts, icon worshippers or neutrals, the *impotence* of the icon, while trying to show an intellectual, political and/or material power that is superior to that of the icon worshippers. Those who worship these images feel shame, perceiving the shattering of their most precious beliefs and, in the process, impotence in the face of the attack of their enemies.[43]

Foreigners from more advanced protestant countries who witnessed this iconoclasm were struck by such an exotic and colourful spectacle, particularly if they were revolutionary tourists passing through the earthly paradise built up by Spanish workers and peasants. The Australian, Mary Low who, like George Orwell, Franz Borkenau, Agustín Souchy and many others, came to Barcelona and passed through Aragon, enrolled as a militiawoman in the POUM's 'Lenin Column', later called the 29th Division, led by José Rovira. In these regions of Upper Aragon, she found that there were many rural workers who knew nothing about politics, but were clear in their minds that the blame for all ills lay with the Church and the saints. And this is why they burned them: Mary Low goes on to say that they used the coloured wooden statues to fuel the fire they cooked with. These images had been dumped in the square when the church was burnt. There was a shortage of wood so they chopped Saint Eduvigis, the virgin and martyr on one day and Anthony of Padua the next . . .[44]

Spectacular too was the frenzied, carnival-style mocking of ecclesiastical paraphernalia. In Ciudad Real, according to the Causa General (the special investigation set up after the civil war to judge crimes in the red zone), there were 'mock weddings with all the prostitutes of this city (. . .) and mock processions with all their sacred trappings'. In Alcañiz, a town in the province of Teruel famous for its Holy Week processions, some individuals parodied the Lamentation of Christ procession: they put on all the ceremonial clothing, placed a man in the Holy Sepulchre and processed through the streets. In nearby Hijar, another town famous for its processions, an individual dressed in the cloak of Jesus the Nazarene was paraded through the streets accompanied by others wearing full-length gowns. In Calanda, the town in Teruel that was the birthplace of the film director, Luis Buñuel, 'distinguished' inhabitants were forced to carry the image of the Virgin of the Column through mocking crowds to the bull-ring and there destroy it. And in Ciempozuelos (Madrid), on 13 September 1936, the feast day of Our Lady of the Consolation, right-wing citizens were forced to carry the patron saint in procession, while the anticlericals accompanied them dressed in liturgical clothes, amid lewd and blasphemous chants.

Blasphemy, according to many witnesses, became a sort of safe-conduct in the republican zone. Anyone who did not blaspheme became a suspect and, as the testimonies given to Montero Moreno and other martyrology authors bear out, the clergy and Catholics were submitted to beatings and tortures for refusing to utter blasphemies. The fact is that in one zone, priests wanted to hear confession from the reds at all costs and make them shout 'Long live Christ the King!' before dying, while in the other zone, those who killed priests forced them to utter blasphemies and live their dying moments in apostasy. Such was the extent of the religious component, for good or ill, in this conflict.

For a few months, Spain lived the dream, or the nightmare, of a secular society, disassociated from the Catholic Church, with its own customs, calendars and rites, something which, according to Julio de la Cueva, 'had been the object of the efforts of radical republicans, socialists and anarchists for several decades'. 'We married and divorced without the need for any more papers than the absolutely essential' wrote Eduardo Barriobero, the anticlerical federal deputy in the Constituent Cortes of the Republic, who had been appointed Chief Advocate of the Justice Office set up by the Generalitat (the Catalan government) on 28 August 1936.[45]

Streets, towns, geographical locations and people's names that included any divine or sacred reference changed their names for others adapted to the new revolutionary times. Everything that the republicans and socialists who created the republican Constitution of 1931 had tried to promote in order, they said, to modernise the State and Spanish society, was now put into practice without obstacles or restraint.

The long-running conflict between the Church and the secularising projects was resolved by the force of arms after a military uprising that divided Spain into two camps, identified in this case by the defence of the Church and the Catholic religion or by hostility towards them. Three major aspects suddenly changed with this replacing of political measures with armed procedures, all three simultaneously, and no one aspect can be said to have caused the other. The first one was that the Church felt it had been rescued by the uprising and so offered its resources and blessing to the rebels as soon as the first shot was fired. The second aspect was that the anticlerical violence, of unprecedented dimensions, unmatched in the rest of southern Europe, hardened the posture of the Church hierarchy and Catholics, reaffirming its patriotic and warlike zeal and erasing any chance of mercy or pardon. Finally, this need for 'recatholisation' through the force of arms showed the historic failure of the Church to attract large sectors of the urban and rural poor, who identified it with the prevailing system of class and ownership.

The Church suffered brutal persecution as a result of all this, but at great cost to society. The overthrow of the State, administrative chaos and the issuing of arms to those willing to take them up saw the start of times of disorder, with no rules or government, a veritable millennarist and egalitarian upheaval. The proletarians imposed their 'plebeian meaning of life', the bourgeoisie had to wear workers' clothes, the peasants seized the lands and delinquents acted as policemen. And this 'popular rage' lay the blame for all its past suffering on the clergy. The Church, in the words of Frances Lannon, 'had to pay a cruel price for its identification with a system of class and ownership that was not of its creation'.[46]

Thirteen bishops lost their lives as victims of the anticlerical violence of the civil war. Nine of them were killed in August 1936, a fatal month for the clergy as well. Only the bishop of Barcelona and the apostolic administrator of Orihuela managed to survive the 'hot-blooded' terror of that fateful summer of 1936, and then only for a few months. The bishop of Teruel, Anselmo Polanco, was the last to fall, barely two months before the final victory of Franco's army.

All the martyrologies say the same thing, to clear any doubt and to ensure that they be considered genuine martyrs of religious persecution. They died acclaiming Spain and Christ the King. They could have escaped but refused. Their bodies were subjected to all types of humiliation and mutilation. When they fell with other clerics or Catholics, they took it upon themselves to give absolution to the rest.

Twenty-eight of the 60 dioceses in Spain remained in the republican zone after the summer of 1936. In ten of them, the revolutionaries very quickly found the bishop and killed him. Some bishops managed to save their lives because at the time of the uprising they were not in the city where the episcopal seat was. Such was the case with Leopoldo Eijo y Garay, bishop of Madrid-Alcalá, but particularly with Cardinal Primate Isidro Gomá y Tomás. It is almost certain that had he, Cardinal Gomá, been in Toledo in view of his importance and self-confessed anti-republican stance, would have been killed.

But there were other bishops who managed to save their lives through the intervention of the republican authorities. This occurred particularly in Catalonia. It happened with Félix Bilbao, bishop of Tortosa, and Francisc Vidal i Barraquer, archbishop of Tarragona, who were taken by representatives of the Generalitat to the port of Barcelona where they embarked for Italy on 30 July. José Cartañá, bishop of Gerona, came under the protection of the Catalan Minister of Culture, Ventura Gassol, thanks to whom he arrived in Pamplona via France. The bishop of Vic, the Mallorcan cleric Juan Perelló, manged to stow away on board a ship and flee to Genoa, from where he later reached Mallorca in March 1937. Justino Guitart, bishop of Urgell, easily managd to escape to Andorra, of which he was the Sovereign Prince. However, moves to save Manuel Borrás Farré, suffragan bishop of Tarragona, failed and he was killed near Montblanc on 12 August 1936.

In Menorca, according to Montero Moreno, 'the blindness and advanced age of the bishop, Doctor Torres i Ribas, contained the hordes and he was allowed to stay in the Bishop's Palace until well into October 1936. On October 21 he was moved to the Municipal Hospital as a patient and stayed there until his death on 1 January 1939'. He was ninety-two years old. Very near there, in Ibiza, Archbishop Antonio Cardona Riera was in hiding for the month in which Captain Bayo's militias were in control of the island. In an exploit reminiscent of an adventure film, the bishop of Cartagena, Miguel de los Santos Díaz de Gomara, escaped from Alicante disguised as a German sailor.

The Basque nationalists saved José Eguino y Trecu, bishop of Santander, from certain death; he had been detained in the prison ship, *Afonso Pérez*, attacked after the Nationalist bombing of the city on 27 December 1936 by an 'enraged mob' who released 156 inmates, 13 of them ecclesiastics. Another unusual case was that of Remigio Gandásegui, the archbishop of Valladolid, who managed to escape from Guipuzcoa through the intervention of the PNV (the Basque Nationalist Party) and end up in his own diocese, safe and sound, surrounded by officers and Falangists, whom he congratulated with an embrace for General Mola. He also expressed his gratitude with a donation for the cause.[47]

All this anticlerical violence represented an attack not so much against religion as against a specific religious institution, the Catholic Church, closely linked, it was thought, to the rich and powerful. Not that most of these thousands of murdered ecclesiastics, priests and monks were rich; they were not and that was not what mattered. It was that they preached poverty and aspired to wealth. They would speak of heaven when in fact they were only concerned with worldly values. It was a plague, said the republican and workers' press, the national disgrace that stopped the people from making progress. A criticism, as we have attempted to show, charged with symbolism, cultural ingredients and ethical reproach. Without them, it is very hard to explain the background to this killing.

There are some who are seduced by the well-worn argument that the anarchists were responsible, although this anticlerical violence was often taken to excess in many areas dominated by socialists, communists and republicans. The rage against the clergy was especially intense in the region of Valencia, particularly in the inland districts of Valencia and Castellón, but it did not lag far behind in the provinces of Toledo, Ciudad Real, Cuenca, Málaga and Jaén. In the last-named city, as early as 20 July 1936 some men from the recently created popular militias attacked the convent of La Merced, looted it and murdered four monks. In fact, with the exception of the Basque Country, where only 45 clergy were murdered, wearing a cassock became a symbol of relentless persecution in the whole of the republican zone, albeit to a lesser degree in Murcia, Albacete, Badajoz and Santander.[48]

Catholicism and anticlericalism were passionately involved in the battle over basic themes related to the organisation of society and the State that was being unleashed in Spanish territory. Religion was extremely useful from the outset because, as Bruce Lincoln maintains, it proved to be the only element that systematically generated a current of international sympathy for General Franco's nationalist cause. On the other hand, the violent anticlericalism that broke out with the military rising brought no benefit at all to the republican cause. Stories of the public burning of religious images and artefacts, the use of churches for stabling and storage, the melting down of church bells for ammunition, the suppression of religious acts, the exhumation of monks and nuns, and the killing of regular and lay clergy were recounted and spread in all their grisly detail, at times illustrated with macabre and shocking photographs, throughout Spain and beyond the Pyrenees, as the symbol of 'hot-blooded terror' *par excellence*.

Thus the civil war acquired a religious dimension that condemned anticlericalism to go down in history as a negative ideology and practice, not as an important phenomenon of cultural history, with its particular view of the truth, society and freedom. All the supporters of the defeated Republic were forced to go on the defensive as far as religion was concerned, although they knew how important the battle for education, the creation of a secular bureaucracy and submitting religious orders to the legislation of civic associations had been. All this was overshadowed by the death toll left behind by anticlericalism, the 6,832 murdered clergy. Thus since the war, as Lincoln goes on to say, even the most liberal of historians was forced to acknowledge the existence of these events and describe them as a deplorable outrage perpetrated by unrestrained fanatics caught up in the tension of the crisis.[49]

Anticlericalism was also used by the victors to settle the score with the vanquished, by reminding them for decades of the devastating effects of the killing of clergy and destruction of the sacred. After the war, churches and public spaces all over Spain were filled with commemorations of the victors, with memorial plaques for those who had 'fallen for God and for the Fatherland', while a veil was cast over the 'cleansing' in the name of God carried out by the pious and people of order. The upheaval caused by anticlericalism served to cover up the religious extermination and gave rise to the false idea that the Church only supported the military rebels when it felt harrassed by this violent persecution.

As Rigoberto Domenech, the archbishop of Zaragoza, said at the beginning of August 1936: 'This violence is not in the name of anarchy, but is being carried out licitly in favour of order, the Fatherland and Religion'.[50] The fact that this violence was meted out in the name of values as elevated as the Fatherland and Religion, with their capital F and capital R, made things much easier, in comparison with the other side's violence 'in the service of anarchy'. Furthermore, while what was being defended was so important and decisive as the survival of the Church, the perfect society, the institution representing God on the earth, the spilling of blood of the 'Godless', the 'sons of Cain', was just and legitimate, the consequence of a 'holy war of spiritual reconquest' that called for this bloodbath in order to extirpate this impurity.

These sacrilegious acts and clergy killings caused such devastation among the clergy that the memory of murdered martyrs took on fresh emotional impact for the Church and its followers. They enhanced its influence on the eventual victors, and by so doing, eliminated any last vestiges of sympathy for the vanquished that there might have been, heightening the clergy's thirst for revenge for many years to come.

Thus it is impossible, and hence the detailed examination we have devoted to it, to overlook the religious dimension of the Spanish Civil War, a 'just and holy' war in one camp, and ruthless fury unleashed on the clergy in the other, which has left major marks on the memory of the Spanish.

3

AN INTERNATIONAL WAR
ON SPANISH SOIL

The Spanish Civil War was first and foremost a brutal political combat between two sides with opposing views as to how society and the State should be organised. It has gone down in history for its horrifying violence, but for all its bloodshed and destruction, it should also be considered in its international dimension, for how it raised the collective consciousness in other countries. For the war in Spain contributed to the Manichaean beliefs of the time when people thought, as Piers Brendon notes, 'that the World was the scene of a cosmic duel between good and evil'.[1]

On the international scene that had been overturned by the crisis affecting democracies and the arrival of communism and fascism, Spain, until July 1936, had been a marginal, second-class country. However, everything changed as a result of that month's military uprising. In just a few weeks, the Spanish conflict occupied centre stage in the concerns of the main powers, deeply divided public opinion, generated passions, and the country became the symbol of the struggle between fascism, democracy and communism.

What had been in origin a conflict between citizens of a single country very soon evolved into a war with international players. The international scene was not very beneficial for the Republic or a negotiated peace at that time, and this heavily influenced the duration, course and outcome of the Spanish Civil War. The Depression had fuelled extremism and undermined people's faith in liberalism and democracy. Furthermore, the rise to power of Hitler and the Nazis in Germany and the rearmament policies undertaken by the principal countries of Europe since the beginning of that decade created a climate of uncertainty and crisis which undermined international security.

THE HOUNDING OF THE REPUBLIC

The legal government of the Republic had few defenders in western European diplomatic circles, least of all Whitehall. Alarmed by the social revolution breaking out in supposedly republican government-controlled cities, and by the risk of the advance of communism, the British conservatives, then in power under Stanley Baldwin, from the outset saw the Spanish Civil War as a question of 'Rebel versus Rabble'. This was the expression used by Sir Henry Chilton, the British ambassador in Madrid, who found himself in San Sebastián at the time of the military uprising, from where he went to Hendaya, on the French border, to remain there for the rest of the war. Chilton, like other colleagues of his, believed that the military rebels, with General Franco at their head, were defending their interests, those of 'our class', and feared that a republican victory would bring about a return to 'red' Spain.[2]

The basic components of this international dimension of the Spanish Civil War are well known thanks to the research of a distinguished group of historians. Ever since Hitler's rise to power at the beginning of 1933, the British and French governments embarked on an 'appeasement policy', which consisted of avoiding a new war in exchange for accepting the revisionist demands of the Fascist dictatorships, as long as they posed no risk for French or British interests. According to Enrique Moradiellos, the response of these two countries 'to the outbreak of the Spanish Civil War and its international implications was at all times subject to the basic objectives of this general appeasement policy'.[3] On the other hand, says Ángel Viñas, 'the Third Reich's support was a key element in transforming the 1936 military coup into a Civil War, and its development as such'.[4]

A victory for the military rebels re-establishing order and putting an end to the revolutionary experiments had many more advantages for Great Britain than a republican victory. Hence from the outset, the British, following the French proposal, defended the principle of refusing to support either side in the struggle and to abstain from intervention.

On 1 August 1936 the French government under Léon Blum had proposed to the British, Italians and Germans an agreement not to intervene in Spanish affairs. This position, transmitted by the French Foreign minister, the radical Yvon Delbos, was rigorously imposed from then on. The French High Command also wanted to avoid an intervention that would turn Italy against France and endanger peace in the Mediterranean. France's proposal also included a ban on the export and sale of arms to the republicans and rebels. On 13 August, the French government closed the Pyrenees border.

The Baldwin government's reaction was immediate, as it tallied perfectly with the policy then advocated by Great Britain's diplomatic circles. The British amabassador in Paris, Sir George Clerk, warned Delbos, in a meeting at the beginning of August, that hiding behind the 'Madrid government' were 'the most extreme anarchist elements' and asked that, until the non-intervention agreement was signed, there would be no supplies of arms or military materiel to Spain.[5]

The British amabassador made no secret of his sympathies for the military rebels, whom he considered to be 'the only ones capable of defeating anarchy and the soviet influence', nor did Anthony Eden, the British Foreign Secretary, nor, above all, did the ambassador in Spain, Sir Henry Chilton, who instead of returning to Madrid, remained in Hendaya, expecting a swift rebel victory. Luis Bolín, the London correspondent of the monarchist newspaper *ABC*, whom Franco appointed as his new press officer, and the Duke of Alba, who was also Duke of Berwick, lobbied the highest circles of British politics, informing them of the 'atrocities of the reds'. And the naval base at Gibraltar was 'flooded with pro-nationalist refugees'.[6]

The danger of communism seemed to be present in Spain and certain British authorities had no qualms in broadcasting it. The consul general in Barcelona, Norman King, cabled the Foreign Office at the end of July to say that British companies were being collectivised by the anarchists and that if the government of the Republic managed to crush the military rebellion, 'Spain will rush headlong into some form of Bolshevism'.[7]

In general, the aristocratic diplomatic circles, the middle class and the Anglican Church authorities, with the exception of the Bishop of Cork, supported the military rebels, while the Labour Party, the trade unions and many intellectuals were behind the republican cause. British society, as K. W. Watkins stated some time ago, experienced a 'deep' divide within over events in Spain, a division which was also influenced by 'a menacing European situation'.[8]

From the outset, Washington's position, in line with Britain's, was, as the Secretary of State, Cordell Hull, told the US ambassador in Spain, Claude Bowers, 'to abstain scrupulously from any interference into the unfortunate situation in Spain'.[9] This US and British policy, embodied in what Douglas Little calls 'benevolent neutrality', placed a legitimate government on the same footing as a group of military rebels.

By the end of August 1936, all the European governments, except Switzerland, whose constitution decreed its neutrality, had officially subscribed to the *Non-Intervention in Spain Agreement*. France and Great Britain signed it on 15 August; Italy, the 21st; the Soviet Union on the 23rd; and Germany, the 24th. In this agreement, after deploring 'the tragic events being enacted in Spain', they decided 'to strictly abstain from all interference, either direct or indirect, in the internal affairs of this country' and banned 'the exporting (. . .) re-exporting and delivery to Spain, Spanish possessions or the Spanish zone in Morocco, of all types of arms, munitions and war materiel'.[10] To monitor the application of this agreement, a Non-Intervention Committee was set up in London on 9 September, chaired by Lord Plymouth, parliamentary under-secretary for the Foreign Office, and a sub-committee made up of delegates from countries bordering Spain and the major arms producers, which included Germany, France, Great Britain, Italy and the Soviet Union.

Although Hitler, Mussolini and the Portuguese dictator, Oliveira Salazar, signed the Agreement, because they wanted to maintain good relations with Great Britain and France, they had no intention of complying with it; they systematically contravened it and continued sending arms, munitions and logistic support to Franco. By the end of August, Franco had received 48 fighter aircraft from Italy and 41 from Germany.[11] For Nazi Germany and Fascist Italy, intervention in the civil war marked the beginning and consolidation of a new diplomatic alliance which, via the 'Rome-Berlin Axis' formally set up in October 1936, was to have major repercussions on international politics in the future. It was made clear that Germany and Italy were not going to respect the agreement they had signed when, on 28 August 1936, Admiral Wilhelm Canaris and General Mario Roatta, the heads of their respective countries' military intelligence, met in Rome and decided to 'continue (in spite of the arms embargo) supplying war materiel and munitions deliveries, in response to the requests of General Franco'.[12]

Thus in practical terms, this Italo-German treachery and the feeble response to it offered by France and Great Britain determined the failure of the Non-Intervention policy and left the Republic at a clear disadvantage against the army that had risen against it. Even so, Léon Blum, the French prime minister, in the light of the continuing Nazi and Fascist intervention, at times turned a blind eye to the smuggling of arms purchased in various countries by the Republic across the Pyrenean border. In July 1938, France closed her frontier and left the Republic, in the last few months of its war just before its final defeat, to stand alone against the Fascist offensive.[13]

Although the Nazi and Fascist propaganda tried to show that their intervention was merely for ideological purposes, to halt the spread of communism, it was much more to do with military strategy and their alliance policy. Hitler considered, as research by Ángel Viñas some time ago has shown, that by helping Franco he would be able to further the interests of his foreign policy, so that a democratic and pro-French regime could be replaced by one similar to the Third Reich. Mussolini, meanwhile, had clearly calculated that a victory for Franco would weaken France's military position and make it easier for Italy to develop its expansionist plans in the Mediterranean.

Hitler believed that the defeat of France, his prime objective for realising his expansionist ambitions in central and eastern Europe, would be much easier with a Spain under the control of anti-Communist generals. A victory for the Republic, on the other hand, would

Image from *Mi Revista*, No. 51–52 (November 1938)

reinforce Spain's links with France and the Soviet Union, the two powers, one in the east and the other in the west, that opposed the Third Reich's imperialist aspirations. The Nazis' intervention also enabled them to use Spanish soil as a testing ground for new weaponry. As Hermann Goering, the Nazi aviation minister, declared before the International Military Tribunal in Nuremburg: 'I was able to test my young air force (...) fighters, bombers and anti-aircraft guns, giving me the chance to see whether the materiel was fit for purpose'.[14]

While international diplomacy was making moves to agree to non-intervention in the war in Spain, the Second Republic had been left with practically no diplomatic corps. As a result of the military uprising in July 1936, most of those working in Spanish embassies and consulates in Europe deserted, while others who officially had not left their posts were in fact in the service of the military rebels. The ambassadors in Rome, Berlin, Paris and Washington resigned in the first few weeks and out of the large representation that the Republic had in Great Britain, only the consul general in London, the commercial attaché and the consul in Southampton remained loyal to the Republic.[15]

The socialist Julio Álvarez del Vayo, the Foreign Minister in Francisco Largo Caballero's government formed on 4 September 1936, calculated that 90 per cent of Spain's diplomatic and consular corps had left their posts. Under these conditions, with an overwhelming need to rebuild its diplomatic corps, it was very difficult for the Republic to obtain foreign support. To replace the disaffected diplomats, it used distinguished intellectuals and university staff, almost all of them from the Socialist Party: the jurist Fernando de los Ríos, who had been a minister in the Republic between April 1931 and September 1933, was sent as ambassador to Washington; Doctor Marcelino Pascua to Moscow; the journalist Luis Araquistain to Paris; and Pablo de Azcárate, the only one who really had any experience in international diplomacy, was put in charge of the embassy in London.

The military rebels, on the other hand, boasted distinguished members of the aristocracy in diplomatic and financial circles with good connections with the elite groups of international diplomacy, such as the Duke of Alba and Juan de la Cierva in London, José María Quiñones de León in Paris, and the Marquis of Portago and the Baron of La Torre in Berlin. On 4 August 1936, José Yanguas Messía, who had been the foreign minister in Primo de Rivera's dictatorship, and recently appointed head of the Diplomatic Office of the *Junta de Defensa Nacional* in Burgos, reported to the military authorities that 'the general tone of the diplomatic situation is favourable to our movement (...) because all over the world the overwhelming influence of the totalitarian States are being felt', and he forecast that 'the capture of Madrid' would be 'be the determining factor for the official recognition of the absolute legitimacy of our movement'.[16]

The forecast by the military rebels regarding a swift 'capture of Madrid' did not come to fruition because, among other reasons, when what appeared to be the final battle occurred, in the autumn of 1936, the first shipments of Soviet military aid to the Republic reversed the trend of continuous rebel victories and republican defeats that had pertained from the beginning of the war. The first Soviet shipments of heavy weaponry arrived at the port of Cartagena on 4 and 15 October. The troops led by General Franco, now head of the rebels since 1 October, were advancing unfalteringly onto Madrid. The Italians and Germans had managed to strengthen the system of military aid to the rebels, while Great Britain and France were strictly observing the non-intervention agreement. In an international context, all this seemed to favour the military rebels. Things changed when Stalin decided to intervene in the conflict. Two months had gone by since it broke out.

ARMS FOR THE REPUBLIC

When the war broke out, in July 1936, the Soviet Union did not even have an ambassador in Spain, even though the Republic had established diplomatic relations with the Soviet regime for the first time three years earlier. For Stalin and Soviet foreign policy, the outbreak of an armed conflict in Spain created a serious dilemma. It was not in his interest to leave the Republic to its own fate, something which would strengthen Germany's position, but neither did he want to go against the policy mapped out by the democratic powers, whom he needed to put a brake on Hitler. Stalin believed at first that the war could be limited to a conflict among the Spanish and that if Fascist intervention could be avoided, the Republic could survive.

For this reason, since the Spanish Civil War afforded no advantage to the interests of the Soviet Union from the outset, Stalin's government, via the Foreign Affairs commissar, Maxim Litvinov, signed the Non-Intervention Agreement on 22 August. A few days later, the Soviet Union officially stated that it would not be supporting the Spanish Republic with arms, and it appointed Marcel Rosenberg as ambassador in Madrid. The instructions given to him by the Kremlin specified that 'it was not possible' to help the Republic with war materiel, and that 'our support would provide Germany and Italy with an excuse to organise an open intervention and a volume of supplies that we could never match'. However, the instructions went on, 'if there is evidence that in spite of the Non-Intervention declaration aid is still being given to the rebels, then we might change our decision'.[17]

The signs and evidence that Hitler and Mussolini were nevertheless aiding the rebels alarmed Stalin. If the Republic were defeated quickly, France's strategic position with regard to Germany would be radically weakened, and the increase of Nazi and Fascist power would also have negative repercussions for the Soviet Union. Stalin prepared the way. He notified the Non-Intervention Committee that he would be forced to breach the agreement if Germany and Italy continued doing so, and he calculated the potential costs of the aid so that the British government would not see it as support for a revolution that was spreading throughout the republican zone, and the Nazis would not take it as open intervention.

In October the first shipments of arms arrived in Spain. The Soviet Union began to do what Italy, Germany and Portugal were already doing: breaching the Non-Intervention accords without officially abandoning this policy. From that moment on, Soviet military aid to the Republic, paid for with the Bank of Spain's gold reserves, was continuous till the end of the war and was vital for sustaining the Republic's cause against Franco's army and the support of Hitler and Mussolini. As well as war materiel, a substantial quantity of aircraft and armoured vehicles, numbering some 700 and 400 units respectively, the USSR also sent food, fuel, clothes and a considerable number, around two thousand in total, of pilots, engineers, advisers and members of the secret police, the NKVD, under the command of Alexander Orlov. The Soviet people donated millions of roubles to buy clothes and food, thereby generating foreign humanitarian aid of unprecedented proportions.[18]

To buy arms and finance the war, the Republic had the gold and silver reserves of the Bank of Spain which, as the socialist leader Indalecio Prieto said shortly after the start of the conflict, belonged to the legitimate Spanish government, the only entity that could touch them. This money was vital for waging a war lasting nearly three years against the military rebels and the backing of their German and Italian allies. 'Without gold', wrote Pablo Martín Aceña, 'the regime would have collapsed in a matter of weeks'. And for this reason, as well as on the battlefields and in the chancelries, the Spanish Civil War was also fought 'in the sedate offices of Finance Ministers and governors of central banks'.[19]

The gold and silver reserves of the Bank of Spain were stored in the basement of its headquarters in the Plaza de la Cibeles. They amounted to 707 tonnes in ingots and coins, with a value at that time of 805 million dollars. It was one of the richest banks in the world, and a large proportion of these coins, mainly dollar deposits, had been there since the First World War, a time when the economic growth caused by Spain's neutrality enabled it to purchase vast amounts of gold on the international market.

At the end of August 1936, the Africa Army troops were closing in on Madrid and the government of the Republic had to make a decision as to what to do with the gold reserves.[20] On 12 September, following a proposal from the socialist Juan Negrín, the new finance minister in the government led by Francisco Largo Caballero, the government decided to remove the Bank of Spain gold reserves from the capital, so that they would not fall into the hands of the enemies of the Republic. Negrín relayed this decision to Luís Nicolau d'Olwer, the governor of the Bank of Spain, and told him that the gold was to be transferred to the Naval Base in Cartagena, on the south-east Mediterranean coast.

The Bank of Spain board was highly critical of this measure, and the few members that had supposedly remained loyal to the Republic deserted. The only member to stay in his post, Lorenzo Martínez Fresneda, who represented the private shareholders, 'did not waste any opportunity', says Martín Aceña, 'to leak secret deliberations' to his ex-colleagues who had gone over to the rebel side. This was because, just when the decision to transfer the gold to Cartagena was being taken, the *Consejo del Banco de España nacional* was holding a meeting in Burgos, and the entire board decided that forthwith the Republic should be stopped from using the gold to defend its cause.[21]

However, the gold did not stay long in Cartagena. The non-intervention policy had been applied to the Republic from the start, but the western democracies were not doing anything to stop the supply of aid to the rebel army. Because of this, in view of the Republic's desperate military situation, Arthur Stashevski, political commissar of the Soviet Union, suggested to Negrín that his government look after the gold in exchange for ensuring a permanent supply of arms. Francisco Largo Caballero, the Prime Minister, accepted this offer and notified the Soviet ambassador in Madrid, Marcel Rosenberg, that it had been decided to send the gold to the Soviet Union, to be deposited in that country's People's Finance Commissariat. Some days later, Spanish sailors and Russian tank crews loaded four merchant ships with 7,800 crates containing 510 tonnes of gold. The ships left Cartagena Naval Base on 25 October, bound for the port of Odessa. From there, the gold was transported by train to Moscow, where it arrived at the beginning of November.

The government of the Republic always maintained that, with the phony policy of non-intervention imposed by the democracies, they had no alternative but to confide in the Soviet Union. Historians have recently questioned the timing and wisdom of this decision. Paul Preston, following Ángel Viñas' line, believes that 'banking circles in England and France had already shown their hostility to the Republic by, in some cases, freezing Spanish assets, by virtually blocking credit and systematically hampering the Republic's financial transactions'. The Soviet Union was the only country that guaranteed the supply of arms and food in exchange for gold. On the other hand, Pablo Martín Aceña states that this decision was hastily adopted and the other alternatives, such as France or the United States 'were not seriously examined'.[22]

What lies beyond any doubt, following the exhaustive study made by Ángel Viñas several years ago, is the fact that the money raised by the sale of the gold was spent in its entirety on war materiel. As a result of the sale of these operations, the republican authorities obtained 714 million dollars, and this was the financial cost of the civil war for the Republic. However, the detailed study by Gerald Howson shows that many of the rifles they were sold were of pre-First World War design and others were in a poor state of repair. The Republic's go-betweens had to negotiate with arms dealers and acquire obsolete equipment for which they had to pay much more than the true cost. Franco, on the other hand, had a constant, direct supply of high technology arms from Germany and Italy at his disposal.[23]

The financial cost of the war on the Francoist side was very similar, between 694 and 716 million dollars, but Franco had to use credit to pay his costs, because he did not have any gold. And from what we learn from the most reliable studies on this matter, the head of the military rebels had no trouble in financing his war. It was

Hermann Goering, Hitler's right-hand man, who first designed the strategy for obtaining economic advantages, food, raw materials and minerals in exchange for supplying arms to the military rebels, through the setting up of bilateral Hispano-German trading companies.

However, the most useful aid that the Germans and Italians sent to Franco was in the form of loans: between 413 and 456 million dollars from Italy and close to 240 million dollars from Germany. The Francoist authorities became indebted to the Axis powers and they offset this by progressively increasing their exports to these two countries. Germany and Italy became Spain's largest customers, to the detriment of Great Britain and France. When the civil war was over, Germany was the Spanish market's largest customer and supplier.

Robert Whealey's research on how Franco financed his war has also provided conclusive data. The military rebels were not only helped by the Axis powers: some of the most important capitalists and businessmen in Great Britain, France and the United States supported their cause from the beginning, because they saw the Spanish republicans as socialists, anarchists and communists, even though they said that they were fighting for democracy. This was the case with the British Rio Tinto company, the biggest mining company in Spain, which cooperated with the military rebels from August 1936 until the end of the war, selling its minerals to the bilateral Hispano-German trading companies.

Then there were the Anglo-American oil companies, Texaco, Shell and others, who earned vast profits, some 20 million dollars, from their oil sales to Franco throughout the war. Without this oil, Franco's war machine would not have worked, since Italy and Germany, like Spain, depended on Anglo-American oil for their supplies. Franco received 3.5 million tonnes of oil on credit, more than twice the amount of oil imported by the Republic, and some of these oil magnates also hampered trade to the Republic and blocked credits in its banking system.[24]

Economic aid also reached Franco from the richest capitalists in Spain, who made their fortunes available to the military rebels to annihilate the 'reds'. Juan March, who had been at the forefront of the battle against the Republic since the day it was proclaimed in April 1931, contributed 15 million pounds sterling. Alfonso XIII, who in exile had also supported the rebel cause from the beginning – 'your first soldier is me', he said to Generals Mola and Franco – donated 10 million dollars, part of the funds that he had managed to transfer abroad after his fall.[25] In addition, a 'national subscription' provided the rebels with jewels and gold coins; the donations were made either voluntarily or under coercion. Lists of some of the principal benefactors were published in the press, and this encouraged others to donate so that they would not be tainted as being 'disloyal'.

In the closing years of Franco's dictatorship, certain pro-Franco military historians attempted to show that the republicans and the military rebels had received the same amount of materiel, that foreign participation was not the factor that tipped the balance in favour of Franco, and that the claim that non-intervention had harmed the republicans was made up by the Communists and the International Left who sympathised with the Republic. In the words of one of these historians: 'Foreign intervention, invoked and obtained at the same time by both sides, was relatively evenly balanced (...) To attribute the Republic's defeat to a lack of resources is to prolong historically the excuses for the Republic's ineptitude and squandering'.[26]

As against these arguments, which are not usually accompanied by documentary evidence, the foremost experts on the financing of the war and its international dimension, historians such as Ángel Viñas, Enrique Moradiellos, Gerald Howson and Pablo Martín Aceña, have pointed out the imbalance in favour of the Nationalist cause not only in terms of war materiel, but also of logistic, diplomatic and financial aid. Leaving aside the question as to whose interpretation is more faithful, these historians emphasise the importance of foreign intervention in the course and outcome of the war. The intervention of Nazi Germany and Fascist Italy and the rebuff, at best, from the western democracies played a major, if not decisive, role in the evolution and duration of the conflict and its final result.

'Italy and Germany did a great deal for Spain in 1936 ... Without the aid of both countries, there would be no Franco today', said Adolf Hitler to Galeazzo Ciano, the Italian Foreign Affairs minister and son-in-law of Benito Mussolini, in September 1940.[27] Hitler expressed a similar opinion in his 'after-dinner chats' during the Second World War and before that, in the final days of the civil war, the German ambassador in Spain had explained, in one of his reports to Berlin, that 'the decisive victory of Franco lies in the greater morale of the troops fighting for the Nationalist cause, as well as their superiority in the air and in their better artillery and other war materiel'.[28] And it seems no little coincidence that the British military attaché in Spain, not known for his sympathy for the Republic's cause, also insisted on 'the persistent material superiority of the traditionalist forces on land and sea (. . .) The material aid from Russia, Mexico and Chechoslovakia (to the Republic) was no match in quantity or quality to that of Italy and Germany (to Franco)'.[29]

But not only arms and war materiel came to Spain. Many foreign volunteers for the International Brigades also came, recruited and organised by the Communist International, which was well aware of the impact of the Spanish Civil War on the world, and of the desire of many anti-Fascists to take part in this struggle. To counter the Soviet intervention and the International Brigades, the Nazis and Fascists increased their material aid to Franco's army and also sent thousands of professional servicemen and volunteer fighters. The war was not just a Spanish domestic matter. It became internationalised, thereby increasing its brutality and destruction. Spanish territory became a testing ground for new weaponry that was being developed during those rearmament years prior to a major war that was on the horizon.

Jason Gurney, a Briton who left his country to fight alongside the Republic, wrote in his memoirs of the civil war, *Crusade in Spain*, that for him 'and a great number of people like me, it became the great symbol of the struggle between Democracy and fascism everywhere'.[30]

It was not just a battle between fascism and democracy. There was more to it, since within this war on Spanish soil there were various different conflicts. Firstly, a military conflict, initiated when the *coup d'état* buried political solutions to replace them with arms. It was also a class war, between differing conceptions of social order, a war of religion, between Catholicism and anticlericalism, a war revolving around the idea of *patria* and nation, and a war of ideas, beliefs that were at that time at loggerheads on the international stage. In short, the Spanish Civil War was a melting pot of universal battles between bosses and workers, Church and State, obscurantism and modernisation, settled in an international context that had been thrown out of balance by crises of democracies and the onslaught of communism and fascism.[31] This is why so many people from other countries, workers, intellectuals and writers, felt emotionally committed to the conflict.

SOLDIERS OF IDEOLOGICAL BATTLES

The decision to send volunteers to fight in the Spanish Civil War was adopted on 18 September 1936 by the Comintern Secretariat. The recruitment centre was Paris and the organisational aspects were put into the hands of French Communist Party leaders, with André Marty at the head, and other leading agents of the Comintern such as Luigi Longo ('Gallo') and Josep Broz ('Tito'). There were a good many in the Brigades who were Stalinists, especially at the organisational level, but there were thousands who were not.

They started arriving in Spain in October, from Poland, Italy, Germany and other countries under the control of dictatorships and fascism, although it was France that provided the largest number. Those from North America arrived later, at the end of the year, and the Lincoln Battalion, the subject of some of the legends most widely spread by writers and intellectuals, did not enter into action until the battle of Jarama, in February 1937. Before them, several hundred left-wing sympathisers, who at the time of the coup happened to be in Barcelona, attending the Popular (also known as Anti-Fascist) Olympics, organised as an alternative event to the Olympic Games being held in Berlin, had already joined the anarchist and socialist militias.

The number of brigadists varies according to sources, from the 100,000 quoted by the Nationalists to exaggerate their influence and the significance of international communism, to the 40,000 referred to by Hugh Thomas in his classic study on the civil war. One of the latest and most exhaustive studies on the International

Brigades, by Michel Lefebvre and Rémi Skoutelsky, provides a figure of nearly 35,000, accepted today by quite a few historians, although there were never more than 20,000 combatants at a time, and in 1938 the number had reduced considerably.[32] Some 10,000, from over 50 countries, died in combat: France provided almost 9,000 brigadists, and there were 2,000 Germans, around 1,000 Austrians, 2,000 Britons and almost 2,500 North Americans, while there were barely 150 Portuguese.

A large number of these volunteers who fought on the side of the Republic were unemployed, but there were many others who left their jobs. There were also mavericks, looking for adventure, intellectuals and middle class professionals, who were the ones that later wrote about their experiences. Most of them, however, were convinced that fascism was an international threat and that Spain was the right venue to combat it. So wrote an English worker, neither a poet nor an intellectual, in a letter to his daughter, reproduced by Watkins in his study on the division caused by the Spanish Civil War within British society: 'Now I want to explain to you why I

International brigades in the Defence of Madrid (Ministerio de Cultura)

left England. You will have heard about the War going on here. From every country in the world working people like myself have come to Spain to stop fascism here. So although I am miles away from you, I am fighting to protect you and all children in England as well as people all over the world'.[33]

These manual labourers, making up 80 per cent of the volunteers from Great Britain, had felt drawn by the Communist Party, which provided them with protection and a solid doctrine to adhere to. This was also the time that vast numbers of exiles from eastern and central Europe and the Balkan States converged on Paris, fleeing from Fascist and military repression. From there they went through Barcelona and Valencia, till they reached Albacete, the main base of the combatants, where they were galvanised into action by André Marty, the head of the International Brigades.

There were also many foreigners fighting with Franco's forces. They, like the brigadists, came from a wide range of countries. Not many of them were volunteers, because the majority of those who fought, particularly Germans and Italians, were regular soldiers, fully-trained, who were paid in their countries of origin. Chief among the genuine volunteers, between 1,000 and 1,500, were Irish Catholics, under the command of General Eoin O'Duffy, who subscribed to the idea of the crusade as held by the Spanish Catholic Church and Pope Pius XI in the Vatican. They bore various religious emblems, rosaries, images of the *agnus dei* and the Sacred Heart, like the Spanish Carlists, and they left Ireland, according to O'Duffy himself, 'to fight Christianity's battle against Communism'. They only fought in the Battle of Jarama, in February 1937, where, in view of their lack of military experience, they failed to acquit themselves well, and a few months later they returned home.[34]

As well as these Irish 'blueshirts', among Franco's troops were White Russians who had honed their skills in the struggle against the Bolsheviks, a mixed group of Fascists and anti-Semites from eastern Europe, and some 300 Frenchmen from the ultra-right *Croix de Feu* making up the Jeanne d'Arc Battalion. The almost 10,000 'Viriatos' (Portuguese volunteers) who had enlisted and were paid in Portugal were not volunteers, however, although Franco's camp always presented them as such. With all these new forces and the intensive recruitment of Rif tribesmen for the Africa Army, Franco's troops numbered some 200,000 men by the end of 1936.

And then there was the largest contingent of foreigners, the tens of thousands of troops that Germany and Italy sent to fight on the military rebels' side. At the same time as Franco's major offensive on Madrid, Hitler decided to set up an aviation unit as an autonomous combat force, with its own commanders and officers, which would be integrated into the Nationalist ranks. Called the Condor Legion, it arrived in Spain by sea in the middle of November under the command of General Hugo Sperrle and later of Colonel Baron Wolfram von Richthofen, both Luftwaffe officers. It consisted of some 140 aircraft divided into four fighter squadrons with Heinkel 51 biplanes plus another four squadrons of Junker Ju 52s, backed up by one battalion of 48 tanks and another of 60 anti-aircraft guns.

Research by Raymond L. Proctor reveals that the total number of Condor Legion combatants during the course of the war amounted to 19,000 men, including pilots, tank crews and artillerymen, although

Franco presides over a military parade of Spanish and Italian soldiers at Recajo (La Rioja), 2 October 1938 (Archivo Sandri, Bolzano-Alto Adige, Italia)

Farewell to the International Brigades, presided over by Juan Negrín, Prime Minister of the Republican Government, L'Espluga de Fancolí (Tarragona), 25 October 1938. The first person on the left is General Vicente Rojo (Archive: Spanish Ministerio de Cultura)

there were never more than 5,500 at a time, as they were frequently relieved so that as many soldiers as possible could gain experience. Thus the Spanish Civil War became the Luftwaffe's testing ground, a rehearsal for the fighters and bombers that would shortly afterwards be used in the Second World War. The Condor Legion took part in nearly all the military operations conducted during the civil war, and 371 of its members lost their lives in action.[35]

A much larger contribution was made by the Italians, who began to arrive in Spain in December 1936 and January 1937, after the secret pact of friendship signed by Franco and Mussolini on 28 November. Up to that time, the Italians piloting the Savoia 81s and Fiat fighters had been fighting in the Foreign Legion. After the signing of this pact, Mussolini organised the *Corpo di Truppe Volontarie* (CTV), commanded by General Mario Roatta until the disaster at Guadalajara in March 1937, and then by Generals Ettore Bastico,

99

Mario Berti and Gastone Gambara. The CTV had a permanent force of 40,000 soldiers and its total number, according to figures published by John Coverdale, rose to 72,775 men: 43,129 from the army and 29,646 from the Fascist militia. They were joined by 5,699 men from the 'Aviazione Legionaria', thus bringing the total number of Italian combatants to 78,474, much higher than the German or International Brigades figures.[36]

Furthermore, the Fascists went home later, with the end of the war and Franco's victory, while the members of the International Brigades had laid down their arms beforehand. On 21 September 1938, Juan Negrín, the Prime Minister of the Republic, announced in Geneva, before the League of Nations General Assembly, the immediate, unconditional withdrawal of all non-Spanish combatants in the republican army, in the hope that Franco's camp would do the same. At the time about one third of all those who had come to fight against fascism were still in Spain, and on 28 October, one month after their withdrawal from the front, the International Brigades paraded in Barcelona in front of over 250,000 people. Presiding over the farewell ceremony were Manuel Azaña, Juan Negrín, Lluís Companys and Generals Rojo and Riquelme. 'You can go proudly. You are history. You are a legend. You are the heroic example of democracy's solidarity and universality', they were told by the communist leader Dolores Ibárruri, 'La Pasionaria'. 'We shall not forget you, and when the olive tree of peace puts forth its leaves again, mingled with the laurels of the Spanish Republic's victory – come back!'[37].

They did not return because the war ended a few months later. Furthermore, many of them, close to 10,000, had died on Spanish soil, and another 7,000 were missing. Some were left with the bittersweet taste of anti-Fascist heroism mixed with disillusionment over what they had experienced: 'We deceived ourselves and were deceived by others', wrote Jason Gurney.[38]

But it was hard to forget the war and the ideological battles experienced in Spain, the striking contrast with what was happening in democracies such as Britain, where the people 'were in a deep sleep'. Or so it seemed to George Orwell, when he arrived there in late spring 1937, after spending six months of war and revolution in Catalonia and on the Aragón front. In marked contrast to 'bombs, machine-guns, food-queues, propaganda and intrigue', in London he found 'posters telling of cricket matches and Royal weddings, the men in bowler hats, the pigeons in Trafalgar Square, the red buses, the blue policemen (. . .) sleeping the deep, deep sleep of England, from which I sometimes fear that we shall never wake till we are jerked out of it by the roar of bombs'.[39]

At the same time as the International Brigades were leaving Spain, Mussolini withdrew 10,000 combatants 'as a goodwill gesture' towards the Non-Intervention Committee, just one quarter of those who were still fighting alongside Franco's army. They were seen off in Cádiz by Generals Queipo de Llano and Millán Astray and received in Naples by King Victor Emmanuel III. The last units of the Condor Legion were transported to Germany by sea on ocean liners after the victory parade of 19 May 1939 in Madrid. They were received in the port of Hamburg by Hermann Goering, Nazi Germany's Air Minister.

After the First World War and the triumph of the revolution in Russia, no civil war could be said to be solely 'internal' any more. When the Spanish Civil War began, the democratic powers were trying at all costs to 'appease' the Fascist powers, especially Nazi Germany, instead of opposing those who were really threatening the balance of power. The Republic found itself, therefore, at an enormous disadvantage in having to wage war on some military rebels who from the outset were the beneficiaries of this international situation that was so favourable to their interests.

4

THE REPUBLIC AT WAR

The military uprising of July 1936 forced the Republic, a democratic and constitutional regime, to take part in a war it had not begun. What followed this military coup was the outbreak of a social revolution that the republican state, in losing a large part of its strength and sovereignty, was also powerless to prevent. This revolutionary process began suddenly, violently, its objective being to destroy the positions of the privileged classes, the Church, the army, the rich, but also the republican authorities who were trying to maintain legitimacy.

Until it was defeated, on 1 April 1939, the Republic went through three different stages, with three prime ministers. The first government, led by the republican José Giral (1879–1962), was marked by its resistance to the military uprising and the revolution. Since Giral did not represent the new revolutionary and trade union powers that emerged in the summer of 1936, he was forced to resign and hand over to the workers' and socialist leader Francisco Largo Caballero (1869–1946), who began, with the collaboration of all the political and trade union forces, the reconstruction of the State, the creation of a regular army and control of the revolution. After the serious events of May 1937, he handed over to Juan Negrín (1892–1956), a socialist member of parliament and university professor, who resolved, as one of his main objectives, to change the democratic powers' non-intervention policy. The three prime

'Women are able to contribute to victory' (Republican propaganda)

ministers died in exile: Giral in Mexico and Largo Caballero and Negrín in Paris.

WAR AND REVOLUTION

A counter-revolutionary *coup d'état*, whose intention was to halt a revolution, ended up by unleashing one. It is very likely that but for the coup, and the collapse of the State's coercion mechanisms, this revolutionary process would never have got off the ground. Naturally, if support for the rising among the armed forces had been unanimous, any resistance would have easily been put down. The trade union militias, even with arms, would not have been able to do anything against a united army. The revolutionary organisations had the ability to undermine and destabilise the Republic, but not to overthrow and replace it. In the Spanish army in July 1936 there was hardly any sympathy for revolutionary ideas, while a large number of officers were clearly in favour of the authoritarian and counter-revolutionary cause.

Anarchist leader Buenaventura Durruti (Private collection, Zaragoza)

The streets in the towns and cities where the coup failed were taken over by new players, armed men and women, many of whom were well-known for their passionate opposition to the existence of this selfsame State which was now tottering. They were there not exactly to defend the Republic, which had had its chance, but to take part in a revolution. Wherever the Republic had not gone far enough with its reforms, they would with their revolution. Politics was giving way to arms.

For the anarchists, who so far had maintained strained relations with the republican regime, at times involving open conflict, their moment had come. We have a great deal of documentary evidence regarding this revolutionary celebration filmed by the anarchists themselves, showing how it all started in Barcelona, the revolutionary and libertarian city *par excellence*, spreading later to other places, to the Aragon countryside and the battlefronts. It was a revolution that extended to production resources and consumer goods, with historic images such as that of the Hotel Ritz in Barcelona, the archetypal example of bourgeois luxury, that was converted into a people's canteen.[1]

The first symbol of the new power of the anarchists was the militias, 'the people in arms', armed columns formed by workers, peasants and those of the army and forces of security that had not joined the rebellion. During the early months of the war, the militias, before converting themselves into regular units of the Republic's army, dominated large areas, created revolutionary committees to replace the old councils in any town they passed through, settled scores with people of order, right-wingers and the clergy, and preached a revolution of expropriation and collectivisation. The commanders of all these anarchist columns (Buenaventura Durruti, Ricardo Sanz, Antonio Ortiz, Gregorio Jover and Cipriano Mera) were 'men of action', members of the main anarchist groups of the FAI (Iberian Anarchist Federation), the organisation set up in 1927 to safeguard the purity of the anarchist ideas within the CNT (National Labour Confederation).

No one represented the strength and fame of the anarchists in those golden months of the revolution better than Buenaventura

Milicianos in Aragon Front (Private collection, Zaragoza)

Durruti. Born in 1896 in León, this labourer sought his fortune in France and Latin America, spent long periods in prison during the Second Republic and was in the line of fire on 19 and 20 July 1936, when the rebel troops were defeated in Barcelona.[2]

He led the militias that departed from Barcelona for Aragón to 'snatch it from fascism', and subsequently went with his column to a Madrid under siege by the Nationalists, where he died, in as yet unexplained circumstances, in the Ciudad Universitaria sector on 20 November 1936. Since he died in the city that the republican government, including the new anarchists ministers, had abandoned to move to Valencia, Durruti's legend grew: it was the final proof of his strength as against the weakness of those who, in spite of being anarchists, had become involved in the game of politics. Durruti died as a martyr, sacrificing himself in the fight against fascism, at the same time, so many anarchists were to say for a long time afterwards, as the best and purest manifestation of the Spanish revolution. In fact, Durruti had contributed little to the history, theory and practice of Spanish anarcho-syndicalism. But myth has always superseded reality.

His phrases and statements, some of them made to foreign press correspondents, seemed to incorporate the spontaneous spirit of the revolution started by the anarchists. A decree signed by Durruti himself in the Aragonese town of Bujaraloz on 11 August 1936, barely three weeks after the military uprising, abolished private ownership of 'large estates', declaring 'the people's ownership', under the control of the revolutionary committee, of 'all farming tools, tractors, machinery, threshing machines, etc., belonging to the Fascist owners', and called for the inhabitants of Bujaraloz to show their 'enthusiastic and unconditional support, both material and moral' because 'the armed struggle of the anti-Fascist militias is the safeguard of the interests of the working people'.[3]

The collectivisation of lands seized by the militias and the power exercised by anarchists and socialists in many towns in republican Spain in the first few months of the civil war were in fact a direct assault on the connection between ownership, authority and established power. Clichés apart, the abolition of paid labour, private ownership of production resources and money, and discussion in popular assemblies on the fuctioning of this new system of production and consumption are phenomena that show how social order in the early stages of this revolutionary process was being overturned.

This overturning of social order was also a genuine phenomenon of the revolution in Barcelona, with the collectivisation and workers' control of industry. Although the features and leading players were different to those that pertained in the countryside, their memory provokes the same ambivalence: destructive, radical transformation for some; for others, a demonstration of the creative capacity of the workers in factories without bosses. Worker self-management or the imposition of the stipulations of a ruling minority.[4]

The revolution and the war against fascism also brought about a new understanding and different image of women. The patriarchal culture had been strongly rooted in Spain prior to the proclamation of the Second Republic. According to the roles traditionally assigned, the man was a superior being, the family bread-winner, while the woman was predestined by nature and biology to motherhood and devotion to the family and home.

Barcelona, October 1936. Workers of a textile factory with donations for milicianos (Arxiu Fotogràfic de Barcelona)

Female Republican soldier, Barcelona. In the revolutionary fervour of the first few weeks, the figure of the militiawoman, the active and belligerent heroine, was portrayed graphically in numerous posters as an attractive woman in blue overalls, rifle on her shoulder, striding purposefully to the front to hunt the 'Fascist enemy'.

This image of the woman as the 'perfect wife' and 'angel of the household' gave way, in the revolutionary fervour of the first few weeks, to the figure of the militiawoman, the active and belligerent heroine, portrayed graphically in numerous posters as an attractive woman in blue overalls, rifle on her shoulder, striding purposefully to the front to hunt the 'Fascist enemy'. While the rejection of the 'middle class outfit' was for men a sign of political identification, as Orwell had observed, for women, according to Mary Nash, wearing trousers or overalls took on a deeper significance, since women had never before adopted this male costume, which challenged the traditional female appearance.

In fact, this aggressive image of the woman as part of the revolutionary spirit of adventure that was current in the summer of 1936 quickly disappeared to be replaced by the slogan 'men to the front, women on the home front', more in keeping with the roles assigned to both sexes in the war effort: the former, occupied with combat duties in the trenches and the latter giving aid and support on the home front. After the upheaval of revolution, the exaltation of motherhood and the right of mothers to defend their children against the brutality of fascism made for a much more powerful form of female mobilisation.

Starting in September 1936, with the socialist Largo Caballero as Prime Minister, a new policy began to be implemented which required women to return from the front. At the end of that year, the posters and propaganda with militiawomen had disappeared and these heroines in overalls were history. As far as we know, no women's organisation, not even the anarchist '*Mujeres Libres*', publicly protested against the decisions, taken by men, to force the women to give up armed combat. All these organisations saw the integration of the female work force into production on the home front as being 'an essential ingredient for winning the war'.[5]

This was because the revolution, for all its destruction and radicalism in the summer of 1936, occurred within the framework of a civil war, a struggle against a well-organised army which from the outset had been aided by the Fascist powers. The dilemma that some faced as to whether to wage a revolution as against war, or postpone

Seeing off the militia (Arxiu Fotogràfic de Barcelona)

it until the defeat of the military rebels, had little to do with reality since, as Helmut Rudiger, the delegate of the International Workers Association (IWA) in Spain warned, 'if the war is lost, everything is lost, and over the next half century or more there will be no further discussion on the problem of revolution'.[6]

Republican Spain, the Spain that emerged from resistance to the *coup d'état*, that welcomed the revolution and the war against the rebel army, was made up in those early months of a set of armed and fragmented powers that were hard to control. On 21 July the Central Committee of Anti-Fascist Militias was established in Catalonia, upon which, despite representation by all the political organisations of the left, the anarchists, led by Juan García Oliver and Diego Abad de Santillán, tried to impose their law. Very soon afterwards, at the beginning of August, the Popular Executive Committee made its appearance in Valencia. In Malaga and Lérida there was a Committee of Public Health. In Santander, Gijón and Jaén, provincial committees of the *Frente Popular*. In the capital of Vizcaya, Bilbao, a Defence Board. And in Madrid, as well as a National Committee of the *Frente Popular*, which organised militias and the life of the city, there was José Giral's government which, made up as it was of left wing republicans only, could not represent this jumble of committees, militias and control patrols in which socialists and anarchists, UGT and CNT trade unionists, were running the revolution, a revolution of destruction and murder, a revolution which was attempting to coax something new out of the wave of political violence.

Furthermore, with so may centres of power competing, it was very hard to tread the right path towards a unified economy and an efficient army, two basic elements with which to combat the military rebels.[7] It was also essential that this revolution and melting pot of powers would produce a public order that could direct the war and control the home front. As we have seen, things started to go badly for the Republic on the international stage, and it was constantly losing ground on the battlefields.

In fact, since the stabilisation of the fronts at the beginning of August 1936, there had been republican losses and rebel advances. The advance from the south of Andalusia of troops from Africa gave

War and Propaganda, Barcelona, December 1936
(Archivo Nacional de Cataluña, Barcelona)

the rebels control of Extremadura and certain areas of Castilla-La Mancha. In the first fortnight of August, *regulares* and legionaries brought war and political violence to cities and towns of the province of Badajoz, such as Almendralejo, Mérida and Zafra, where thousands of republicans and socialists were murdered.

On 14 August, Lieutenant-Colonel Juan Yagüe's troops took Badajoz, showing, for all the world to see, that success on the war front was only achieved by leaving no possible enemies in the rear. Hundreds of prisoners were taken to the bullring where, again in the words of the socialist leader Zugazagoitia, 'leashed like hunting dogs, they were pushed into the arena as a target for the machine guns which, well positioned, remorselessly mowed them down'.[8] Such a massacre earned the defiant response that Yagüe gave the *New York Herald* journalist, John T. Whitaker: 'Of course, we shot them. What do you expect? Was I supposed to take four thousand Reds with me as my column advanced racing against time? Was I expected to turn them loose in my rear and let them make Badajoz Red again?'[9]

Yagüe was right. Badajoz was never republican again. Antonio de Oliveira Salazar's dictatorship in Portugal also lent Yagüe a hand. As had happened previously in other towns in Extremadura, quite a few people fled to Portugal after the fall of the city. Salazar's police refused them entry or else handed them over to the rebels. A large number of them were executed on 20 August, one week after the slaughter in the bullring. Those who met their death included the mayors, Sinforiano Madroñero and Nicolás de Pablo, who had been elected to the Cortes for the PSOE in the February 1936 elections.

After the fall of Badajoz, Yagüe's column continued its rapid advance on Madrid. On 3 September it arrived at Talavera, a town in the province of Toledo, just over a hundred kilometres from the capital. That same day, in the north, where Emilio General Mola had launched an attack on Guipúzcoa, Irún, on the French border, fell. On 12 September it was San Sebastián's turn. The conquest of the province of Guipúzcoa was an important victory for the rebel army's plans; it had now joined one part of Spain from north to south, via Castilla, while leaving Vizcaya, Cantabria and Asturias cut off, unable to communicate with the rest of the republican zone except by air and sea.

By the time San Sebastián was conquered by the military rebels, José Giral was no longer prime minister of the Republic. He had achieved quite a great deal, bearing in mind that he was only in the post for a month and a half. He asked France and the USSR for aid to defeat the military rebellion, started using the Bank of Spain's gold reserves to finance the war, dismissed any public servant suspected of siding with the rebels, and pronounced the first measures to check indiscriminate violence on the home front.

But this was not enough, and the obstacles he faced seemed insurmountable. 'The government of the Republic is dead. It has no authority or competence, no plan for waging all-out war and finishing it with an absolute victory for the revolution', wrote Luis Araquistain, the left-wing socialist ideologist, to Francisco Largo Caballero on 24 August. Giral, with the military rebels by now at the gates of Madrid, really thought that he lacked authority and support and decided 'to present to H.E. the President of the Second Republic the powers received from him, as well as the resignation of all the ministers', so that he could replace them with a government that would 'represent each and every one of the political parties and trade unions or workers' organisations acknowledged as having influence among the Spanish people'.[10] It was time for the trade unions and Largo Caballero, the undisputed leader of the UGT, to take the stage.

Summer was drawing to a close. In barely two months, ever since the *coup d'état* that had preceded the civil war, the lust for revolutionary and counterrevolutionary cleansing had sent tens of thousands of citizens to their graves. In military terms, the revolutionary fervour of the trade union organisations provided the republican cause with few advantages and a great many setbacks. In the rebel camp, these military victories were achieved through the concentration of political and military power in the person of General Francisco Franco. A general in rebel Spain and a trade union leader in the Republic, two very different approaches to war.

A TRADE UNION LEADER IN THE GOVERNMENT

Indeed, Largo Caballero's government was the first and only government in Spain's history to be led by a workers' leader. On 4 September 1936, the by now veteran socialist, Largo Caballero, born in 1869, who had opposed the idea of his party colleague Indalecio Prieto forming a government of republicans and socialists in May of that year, and who had also refused to take on this responsibility after the *coup d'état* in July, finally agreed to lead 'a coalition government', in which he himself would also be the Minister for War.

It was a government with socialists and republicans, which already included two people who were to have the biggest influence on the Republic's policy during the war: Indalecio Prieto and, particularly, Juan Negrín. Furthermore, Largo Caballero accepted the post on condition that, for the first time in the history of a western European country, communists would form part of the government; and so it was, with Jesús Hernández in Education and Vicente Uribe in Agriculture. Finally, he came to an agreement with José Antonio Aguirre, the leader of the Basque Nationalist Party (PNV), over the participation of the Basque Nationalists in return for the speedy passing of a Statute of Autonomy for Euskadi, and a few days later Manuel de Irujo joined this coalition government as minister without portfolio.

Certain leading lights on the republican political scene were not very impressed with this solution of a government presided over by a trade union leader, with communist participation, but others felt that, given the exceptional circumstances, it was the only one that would be able to put a brake on the sinking of the republicans, win the war and at the same time consolidate the revolutionary ground that had been won.[11] The participation in this government of José Giral, the previous prime minister, and of other republicans who had been in his government, seemed to confirm the continuance of republican legitimacy. Naturally, it was not a revolutionary conquest of power but a transmission of powers from one, uniquely republican, which no one was capable of leading, to another made up of all the political forces, including Basque and Catalan nationalists, which made the government one of 'national unity', the best of the options available at the time.

Absent was the CNT, to whom Largo Caballero had at first offered a ministry without portfolio, which seemed to be scant recognition of what the anarcho-syndicalist organisation considered be their strength, on the front line with the militias and on the home front with the revolution. The anarchists had already entered the autonomous government of the Generalitat of Catalonia on 26 September, and its leaders spent October in trying to convince themselves and their militants that forming part of the government of the Republic was necessary and, as their then national secretary, Horacio Martínez Prieto said, the only option open to them. This 'haggling' between Largo Caballero and Martínez Prieto over the exact number of ministries occupied the closing days of the negotiation. In the end, it was four, although Largo Caballero maintained in his memoirs that they had asked for six.[12]

On 4 November 1936 four CNT leaders became part of the government of the Republic at war. It was a 'momentous event', declared *Solidaridad Obrera*, the principal mouthpiece of the CNT, on the same day, because anarchists had never trusted the authority of government action and because it was the first time that this had happened in world history. Anarchists in the government of a nation: an extraordinary and unrepeatable occurrence. Furthermore, one of the four anarchists was Federica Montseny, the first female minister in the history of Spain, occupying a new ministry, Health.

Very few noteworthy anarchists refused to support this new situation, and there was also very little resistance from the grassroot anarchists, those who had hitherto displayed revolutionary opposition to the reformist leaders. The summer, that bloody but mythical summer of 1936, was over. Radical anarchists and moderate trade unionists, who in the first few years of the Republic had fought and split from each other, were now together, striving to obtain the support required for realising their new political ambitions. It was all about not letting other political organisations get their hands on mechanisms of political and armed power, once it was clear that what was happening in Spain was a war and not a revolutionary celebration.

However, their entry into the government did not come at the best of times. Franco's troops were at the gates of Madrid, the scene of what was to be the most decisive battle of the first phase of the war. General Franco, sole commander of the military rebels since 1 October 1936, ordered the concentration of all his forces to take the capital, with the Africa Army in the vanguard, reinforced by squadrons of German and Italian aircraft.

The government of the Republic was incapable of organising the defence of the capital effectively. On 6 November, during the first cabinet meeting attended by the CNT ministers, it was decided unanimously to transfer the government from Madrid to Valencia. This was an impetuous move, stealthily carried out, and no public explanation whatsoever was given. To the public, it looked as if the government was fleeing and the people were being left to their fate.[13]

Just before the transfer, Largo Caballero ordered the setting up of a *Junta de Defensa* under General Miaja, which was to run things in a Madrid that was under siege from that day until the end of April 1937. The capture of the capital by Franco's army appeared to be a matter of days away but, despite the confusion and chaos that had taken hold of the city in those few days, with massacres of right wing, military and ecclesiastical prisoners included, Madrid failed to fall into the hands of the rebel forces.

General Miaja and the then Lieutenant Colonel Vicente Rojo, his Chief of Staff, who was set to become the most important officer in the republican army, organised the defence with all the forces available including, for the first time in the war, the International Brigades. Arriving just in time was the Soviet military aid, by then paid for by the shipment of the gold reserves. And the whole city, stirred up by the constant air raids and bombardments from the rebel army, helped to stem the advance of the attackers. Many saw it as a decisive battle between international fascism on one side, and communism and democracy on the other. It was also the first major battle of the Spanish Civil War to be captured on film, with images of the bombing of a defenceless population, women and children who were shown lying dead among the rubble, which were published around the world.

Meanwhile in Valencia, during the months he was in power, Largo Caballero, with the collaboration of all the political and trade union forces fighting on the republican side, oversaw the reconstruction of the State, the militarisation of the militias and the creation of the People's Republican Army, the contention of the revolution and the centralisation of power, all the while having to deal with challenges from the regions and nationalism, as his successor, Juan Negrín, would have to later.

The conversion of the militias into an army with a centralised military command that would be able to confront General Franco's army became one of Largo Caballero's primary objectives immediately on becoming prime minister and minister of War, a difficult task because 'the coup had shattered army unity and the republican command had to begin almost from scratch'.[14] Militarisation created a heated debate between the anarchists, with the leading figures trying to convince the majority of the militants that the militias, what they called 'the people in arms', were not an effective resource for a long-term war against a powerful enemy. Helmut Rudiger, the IWA delegate in Spain, summed it up succinctly when he said: 'Union life is based on agreements at general assemblies; war, on command and obedience'.[15]

In early 1937, most of the militias on the Aragon front, the scene of the latest acts of resistance, joined the new army. There were desertions in various columns, such as the Durruti Column, and some 400 men left the Iron Column, the most radically opposed to this measure, when it was militarised in March 1937 and transformed into the 83rd Brigade. Many of these deserters and dissidents brandished their arms in the streets of Barcelona in May 1937. They were defeated, although the serious problem of order and discipline that they caused the Republic left its mark and was further evidence of the contrast between disunity on the republican side and unity under a single commander in the Nationalist camp.

The reconstruction of central power was no easy task either. This was because although Largo Caballero's government limited the power of the revolutionary committees, it could not stop Catalonia and what was left of Euskadi from increasing their autonomy, or regional powers in other areas from become consolidated. In Catalonia, the government of the Generalitat created its own army, enjoyed full political and economic autonomy and, up to May 1937, had full power over the police and public order. Particularly worthy of note was the Council of Aragon, set up by anarchist columns on this front in October 1936, which had its own police organisation, controlled the collectivised economy and administered justice. It was a formidable challenge to the government of the Republic, until it was dissolved by decree, with the help of the military, in August 1937.

The Basque Country, by then reduced to the province of Vizcaya, had from 1 October 1936 a Statute of Autonomy granted by the Cortes of the Republic, and a government with almost full sovereignty. Presided over by the leader of the PNV, José Antonio Aguirre, this government set up the army of operations of Euskadi, a constant source of friction with the government of the Republic, a new police force, took control of the economy and justice, and decreed a wide range of social policies. It lasted only eight months, until the fall of Bilbao on 19 June 1937.

One of the great successes of Largo Caballero's government, particularly from the beginning of 1937, was that the hot-blooded, brutal, lawless terror of the early months of the war almost completely disappeared. Revolution gave way to war and the control of the home front, with stronger and more disciplined political powers, replaced the violence of the *sacas* and *paseos* with the justice of popular tribunals.

However, the setting up of a regular army, controlling the home front and the reconstruction of the State were tackled in the midst of bitter disputes and political tensions between the factions in the government coalition. The communists, who were unsuccessfully pressurising Largo Caballero to unite the PSOE and the PCE within a macro-Marxist party, as the youth wings of the two organisations had done just before the war in the shape of the *Juventudes Social-istas Unificadas* (Unified Socialist Youth – JSU), began to protest, both publicly and privately, against the government's ineffectiveness in controlling the regional powers and the way the war was being conducted. Criticism intensified after the conquest of Málaga on 8 February 1937 by Franco's troops, supported by 13 Italian battalions under the command of General Mario Roatta.

The Communist Party, a small organisation with very little in-fluence before the outbreak of the civil war, began to grow rapidly following the defence of Madrid in November 1936. Its growth and the prestige it acquired were closely linked to the presence of the International Brigades, the order and discipline that its leaders managed to impose on the running of the war, and particularly the aid it received from the Soviet Union. Its power was also closely linked to the new army of the Republic, in which its militants commanded most of the divisions that had been set up. It would be too much to say that the communists were preeminent in this army, as Nationalist sources claimed and certain historians have written, but it is true that, with their penetration in the important command posts, particularly on the Centre front, they had the upper hand in the new military structure. And from there, it was merely one step towards a greater presence and control in politics, in a parallel process to that of the decline of the revolution and the anarchists.

The communists, as well as Manuel Azaña, the president of the Republic, wanted the anarchists out of the government. They accused Largo Caballero of being ultimately responsible for the fall of Málaga, and the Comintern was arguing strongly for his removal from the

Ministry of War, although he would still hold the post of prime minister.[16] At the same time, the socialists sympathetic to Indalecio Prieto, who controlled the PSOE national committee and also wanted to oust the trade union organisations from the Executive, informed Manuel Azaña in the middle of March of the need to replace Largo Caballero as Minister of War. It was the struggle between parties and trade unions, which very quickly became resolved in favour of the former.

And this resolution began in Barcelona, a city away from the front, and a symbol of anarcho-syndicalist revolution. The capital of Catalonia was a melting pot of unique social and political characteristics which gave rise to tensions on various fronts: an autonomous government with notable left-wing republican nationalist influences, a powerful anarchist movement, a communist party, the PSUC, set up at the beginning of the war, that controlled the UGT and a tiny revolutionary party, the POUM, bitter enemies of the communists. The backbone of its economy was industrial production, most of it collectivised by the CNT, which brought it into dispute with the UGT and the Generalitat. And it also had a high population density, with tens of thousands of refugees who had fled the Nationalists from other regions in Spain, and this complicated the smooth running of basic product supply. And finally, there was no lack of arms, wielded by the police forces, militants from the various political organisations and the ex-militiamen who were against militarisation who had brought them back from the front.

In the first quarter of 1937 the political and trade union forces in Catalonia became embroiled in bitter disputes over the shortage of bread, the scope of the collectivisations and control of armaments, war industries and public order, a vital issue that in March led to the dissolution of the spot-check patrols, a fundamental component of the CNT's armed power. The image of worker self-management gave way to women's demonstrations demanding food and fuel, and to bloody disturbances on the home front that resulted in various deaths among the demonstrators, including women, and members of the security forces.[17]

This fight for survival, political and trade union unrest and the feeling of revolutionary failure set the stage for the notoriously

Barricades at Plaza Sant Jaume, Barcelona, May 1937
(Archivo Nacional de Cataluña)

tragic events of May 1937. The spark that set them off, on 3 May, was the decision of the Generalitat's councillor for Security, the nationalist Artemi Aiguader, to seize the *Telefónica* (State Telephone Company) building in the Plaza de Cataluña, which had been occupied by the CNT since the defeat of the military rebels in July 1936. The assault groups that went there to carry out the order were met with gunfire from some anarchists who were in the building at the time. Armed anarchists arrived to help those inside. The fighting spread. Many workers left their posts. Once more the barricades went up in Barcelona. Behind them, against the forces of order, socialists and communists, were former militiament who had refused to join the new army, young libertarians, FAI anarchists who were no longer recognised by this organisation, and POUM militants.

Manuel Azaña, who was in Barcelona at the time, helpless and caught between two fires, asked the government in Valencia for help in dealing with what he considered to be an anarchist insurrection with 'serious consequences and deplorable effects', which had deprived him, the Head of State, of the freedom 'not only to move about freely but also to exercise his duties'.[18]

Largo Caballero's government decided to send a delegation of anarchists, with the ministers Juan García Oliver and Federica Montseny, and members of the UGT, who as soon as they arrived in Barcelona broadcast a plea for a cease-fire and anti-fascist unity. Five thousand police also went to Barcelona, occupying the city and snuffing out the final vestiges of resistance. By the afternoon of 7 May, wrote Orwell, an eye-witness to these events, 'conditions were almost normal'.[19] The official casualty figures were 400 dead and 1,000 wounded.

Things could never be the same after these events, even though 'normality' had been restored. What had happened in Barcelona and on the Aragón front was much more than a confrontation between the various political and trade union sectors of republican Spain. The fissures were much deeper and shook the core of political and military power. Therein lay all the basic problems that had remained unresolved since the beginning of the conflict, made worse by the passage of time: military failure after military failure; the government's inability to organise supplies to the home front; and ongoing dissension in the economic, political, social and military spheres.

In the Cabinet meeting held on 13 May, the two communist ministers, Vicente Uribe and Jesús Hernández, called for Largo Caballero to resign as Minister of War, and for the POUM to be dissolved. The Prime Minister refused to accede to the first demand and tried to shelve any resolution on the second until the full facts were known about who was responsible for the disturbances in Barcelona. The communist ministers walked out of the meeting. The crisis continued. After an exchange of letters and proposals, in which Largo Caballero failed to convince President Manuel Azaña of his proposal to continue with a government made up of all the political and trade union forces, the latter dismissed the former UGT leader and, on 17 May, asked Juan Negrín to form a government. The two trade union organisations were cast aside. 'A counter-revolutionary government has been formed', said *Solidaridad Obrera* in its editorial of 18 May.[20]

From that moment on, the wartime Republic took on a completely new direction. The POUM was eliminated, Largo Caballero found himself alone and isolated and the anarcho-syndicalists realised that their political and armed power was rapidly fading.[21] The CNT's spell in government left very few traces. They entered in November 1936 and left in May 1937. There was very little they could do in six months. People remember the significance of the participation of four anarchists in a government more than their legislative activity. Since the revolution and the war had been lost, those ministers could never presume to have left their footprint on history. As far as the collective memory of the defeated, exiled libertarian movement was concerned, that break with its anti-political tradition, its betrayal and error, could only give rise to fatal consequences.

JUAN NEGRÍN: 'VICTORY THROUGH RESISTANCE'

With the dismissal of Largo Caballero, the socialist Juan Negrín became the third, most influential and last prime minister of the wartime Republic. The decision was taken by Manuel Azaña, who recovered the initiative, freed of the presence of the anarchists and socialist left. In this new government, Prime Minister Negrín kept the finance portfolio, Indalecio Prieto was to be the strong man, with a new ministry, Defence, which combined the previous ministries of War, the Navy and Air; and there were also socialists, communists, republicans, a Catalan nationalist and a Basque nationalist in the government. It was a *Frente Popular* government, which had been received, according to Azaña, 'with great satisfaction' and relief.[22]

Negrín was nominated not by the communists, as many have repeatedly claimed, in an attempt to show that he was being controlled by Moscow, having sold out to communism and the International. He was appointed by Manuel Azaña who, as president of the Republic, was the one who had this prerogative and who thought of him for 'his effectiveness as finance minister of a nation at war', and also particularly for international political reasons.[23] Azaña believed that, because of the non-intervention policy of the democratic powers, the Republic would never be able to win the war, and that the only possible solution was a negotiated peace with international mediation. Negrín, not Largo Caballero, was the ideal man to achieve this. He was a well-educated politician who spoke several languages, had no revolutionary tendencies, and whose career was free of any confrontations with trade union organisations.

Juan Negrín was born in Las Palmas de Gran Canaria in 1892, the same year as Francisco Franco. In 1912 he gained his doctorate at the Institute of Physiology at the University of Leipzig and began a brilliant career as a physiologist until, with the coming of the Republic, he began his political career as a socialist deputy, winning the three elections, in 1931, 1933 and 1936, that were held in this democratic regime up to the military rebellion. A few months before his appointment as prime minister, Negrín, as finance minister in Largo Caballero's government, had organised the shipment of three quarters of the Bank of Spain's gold reserves to the Soviet Union.[24]

Negrín began his mandate by attempting to re-establish the Republic's authority in Catalonia and on the Aragón front. His government took on the responsibility for public order which had

Juan Negrín, Prime Minister of the Republican Government from May 1937 (Private collection, Zaragoza)

hitherto been in the hands of the Generalitat and on 11 August he dissolved the Council of Aragón, the last remaining organ of authority controlled by the anarchists.

The other unfinished business on the Catalan home front, what to do with the POUM, the Marxist revolutionary party that was such a thorn in the flesh of the communists, was also resolved swiftly and violently. What the Spanish communists wanted, urged on by the Russian consul-general in Barcelona, Vladimir Antonov-Ovsenko, was the destruction of this party of 'Trotskyite agents' and 'Fascist spies' who were moreover openly criticising the execution of former Bolsheviks carried out by Stalin in the Moscow trials.[25]

The 29th Division, controlled by the POUM, was accused of deserting the front. Its leader was arrested and it was disbanded and reorganised. Many of its militants ended up being persecuted and tortured. A worse fate befell Andreu Nin, the party's political secretary and number one, an anti-Stalinist and former secretary of Leon Trotsky in Moscow. He had been the Justice minister in the Generalitat until the middle of December 1936, when the POUM, by now beleaguered by the growing power of the Catalan communists of the PSUC, was removed from the autonomous government and politically ostracised.

On 16 June 1937, at the same time as the POUM was being declared illegal, Andreu Nin was arrested in Barcelona by the police, who transferred him to Madrid and thence to the prison at Alcalá de Henares. In spite of being guarded by members of the Directorate General of Security, he was kidnapped on 21 June and murdered, no one knows when, by agents of the Soviet Secret Service in Spain, under the command of the general of the NKVD, Alexander Orlov. His body never appeared and Negrín was never able to offer a convincing explanation either to Manuel Azaña or some of his ministers. Nor did he wish to confront the communists who were becoming increasingly more influential and whom he needed to ensure the shipments of arms from the Soviet Union, the only power to supply effective military aid to the Republic.

Negrín wanted to win by fighting with discipline on the home front, by attracting the support of the people and organising a solid war industry, although the primary aim of his strategy was to bring about a radical change in the non-intervention policy, thereby obtaining the vital support of the western democratic powers. The war would be long and it could be won. So thought Negrín when he took office, and in the two years of his premiership he experienced moments of optimism, but others that were disastrous, moments that seemed to herald the final defeat.

It started badly because on 19 June, barely a month after he assumed office, the Italian forces and the Navarra Brigades took Bilbao. The Basque battalions disobeyed the order to withdraw to Santander and Asturias and on 26 August they surrendered in Santoña to the troops of General Mario Roatta, the same troops that had marched victoriously into Málaga at the beginning of February and suffered a resounding defeat in Guadalajara in March. The same day the Nationalists entered Santander and the offensive, involving 60,000 men, continued until the fall of the entire republican zone of Asturias at the end of October. In just a short time the Republic lost the entire northern zone, with its important coal mines and iron production industry.

The collapse of the northern front forced Negrín to accelerate his organisation of the war industry policy. On 31 October 1937 he decided to move the government and the capital of the Republic from Valencia to Barcelona. This move relegated the government of the Generalitat to a secondary role, furthered control over the collectives and restricted any autonomy the trade unions still had in the running of businesses. Over the following months, the government of the Republic came to control the entire war industry in Catalonia, but it had taken them too long, almost two years, to do so.

The Republic's production resources were not enough and Negrín said as much publicly in a speech to the Permanent Council of the Cortes in November: 'The territory we occupy does not produce enough to supply it, and therefore we need to import a considerable amount of foodstuffs (...). Furthermore, we need to acquire large quantities of raw materials, essential for the war industry. And we need to acquire war materiel, although unfortunately not in the proportion we would like'. Under such adverse conditions, concluded Negrín, 'we need to proceed in a spirit of great economy under the most rigid of administrative control'.[26]

The progress of the war, despite these measures, gave very little cause for joy and and even fewer strategic victories. Leaving aside the occupation of Teruel in the harsh winter of 1937, the only provincial capital to be captured by the republican army during the war, even though it was lost a few weeks later, it was General Franco's troops who had all the success. They conquered republican Aragón in March 1938, with the collapse of the front in three weeks, and by the beginning of April they had overrun certain areas of Catalonia, including Lérida, one of its provincial capitals. On 15 April they reached the Mediterranean coast in the province of Castellón, the setting for the famous photograph of Carlist soldiers splashing about in the water. The Republic had been split into two, and Catalonia isolated.

These defeats revealed the deep divide between those who believed the war could be continued, starting with Negrín, and those in favour of negotiating a surrender with Franco-British support, a notion which Manuel Azaña had supported all along. The problem at this stage of the war was that the Minister of Defence himself, the socialist Indalecio Prieto, up to that time a friend of Negrín, shared this view, and this gave rise to the second great internal crisis in the republican camp, one year after the first one in May 1937.

While Indalecio Prieto had shown early signs of his defeatist attitude after the fall of Bilbao, the city in which he had built his political career, it came fully into the open during the days following the defeat of the Aragón front. The new ambassador for France in Barcelona, Eirik Labonne, asked Negrín on 27 March 1938 whether he had heard what the socialist leader was saying. How were the French or British going to change their policy if even the Republic's Minister of Defence was not confident of winning the war? Two days later, Prieto presented the Cabinet with a devastating report on the situation. On the night of 29 March Negrín decided to dismiss his close friend and collaborator from his post.

Negrín dispensed with him because he felt he was demoralising the government and those who still confided in the Republic; however Prieto always believed that he was sacked because he was bowing to the pressure exerted by the Communist Party. In fact, whether this was true or not, the growing influence of the communists had become 'the main seed of discord' within the coalition government.[27] 'In "sacking" Prieto, Negrín exposed the growing divisions within the republican political class'.[28]

In the new government, formed on 6 April 1938, without Indalecio Prieto, Negrín also took on the Ministry of National Defence portfolio; it once more included the two trade union organisations, the UGT and CNT, albeit with a token representation, now that both organisations were a shadow of their former selves, with the socialists excluded and impotent and the anarcho-syndicalists in disarray.

This 'war government', or government of 'national unity', kicked off with a programme passed by the Cabinet on 30 April and made public on, significantly, 1 May, which everyone called Negrín's 'Thirteen Point Plan'. Among other things, it called for the independence and territorial integrity of Spain; it claimed respect for private property and freedom of conscience and religion; and it proposed a general political amnesty to enable, after the war was over, the rebuilding of Spain. They were sincere proposals which could almost certainly never be carried out, given that neither the international stage nor Franco's stance, backed as it was by the Catholic Church, would tolerate them.

For the survival of the Republic after May 1938 depended not only on a good army and the resistance of the civilian population, 'Victory through resistance' as the slogan had it, but also on the abandonment of the Non-Intervention policy, something that was not to be despite the diplomatic efforts that Negrín made during the middle months of that year. If France and the United Kingdom were not going to change their minds, it was suggested that at least they could put pressure on the Fascist powers to convince Franco to offer a negotiated settlement, an armistice that would prevent the reign of terror and bloody vengeance that Negrín knew Franco would impose. And if diplomacy and negotiations failed, it would be necessary to keep on resisting until the conflict that was looming in Europe between the Fascist powers and democracies broke out. And then everybody would be able to see whose side the Republic was on and who backed Franco.

There was still hope in the summer of 1938, with the beginning of the Battle of the Ebro and the granting of a loan of sixty million dollars from the Soviet Union, now that the gold reserves that had been transferred there were about to run out. But hopes were dashed firstly on the international front, with the Munich pact on 29 September 1938, when the prime ministers of Great Britain and France, Neville Chamberlain and Édouard Daladier, accepted Adolf Hitler's proposal, which Benito Mussolini claimed as his, to annex the Sudetenland. This sacrifice of Czechoslovakia signalled the death sentence for the only democracy still surviving in central and eastern Europe. With this decision, linked to the appeasement of the Fascist powers, the democracies imposed the death sentence on the Spanish Republic as well.[29]

The Republic was also being crippled by hunger. Particularly in the final months of the war, the two largest cities in Spain, Barcelona and Madrid, suffered supply problems as a result of price rises in consumer goods, the use of inferior products and the sudden appearance of the black market.

As the war went on, in Catalonia, especially Barcelona, there were more and more people denouncing the inefficiency of the supply system and protesting against the appearance of the black market. Many of these complaints and accusations were lodged by women who raided food shops and town halls to ask for bread and provisions for their families. It is obvious that these protests should never be divorced from the exceptional conditions dictated by the war and the massive influx of refugees that Catalonia experienced. But they also highlight the contrast between the lives of luxury and plenty of certain sectors of the population linked to the new power base and the shortage of staple products suffered by most of the civilian population.

Following the loss of Aragón, in March 1938, agricultural production fell and hunger and pessimism increased among a rapidly rising population that saw the prosperity promised by the revolution receding at the same rate as it was experiencing a deterioration in its welfare. Every day there was less and less territory to defend. Some of the anarchist newspapers, for example, found it hard to survive those difficult months and disappeared. This hardship also affected *Solidaridad Obrera*, which had lived its golden age in the early months of the revolution. Newsprint was becoming scarce, and the censors showed no mercy on the newspaper that had epitomised the power of the CNT.

And if people were being ground down by the war in Barcelona, things were not much better in Madrid where conditions had already been extremely harsh in the autumn and winter of 1936. There also, the women demonstrated publicly in protest against the shortage of food supplies. The workers 'were going hungry' and 'mothers demanded milk for their children', wrote Palmiro Togliatti, the delegate of the Communist International in Spain. The bread ration fell sharply at the front and behind the lines. In Madrid, bread rationing went down from the 230 grams per day per inhabitant before the war to 100 grams at the end of 1938. As a result of all this, said a report from the Central-South Army Group on 19 November 1938, the troops' attitude was that *the war is drawing to a close* (. . .) That is what is being talked about at the front and behind the lines, in soldiers' letters from the front, in gatherings, in the streets, and places of entertainment'. Support for Negrín and his resistance strategy was fading fast.[30]

A confidential report at this time from Great Britain's diplomatic representative in the republican zone emphasised the internal ravage caused by military defeats and problems supplying both war materiel and staple products: 'The fact is that the vast majority of the population in Spain is suffering a serious food shortage, including in the rural areas. Rationing for workers in essential industries and troops behind the lines has recently been drastically increased'. The republican army, he added, would be able to resist 'as long as the food shortage does not cause a breakdown of morale'.[31]

However, it was not the 'food situation', serious as it was, as these sources of information show, that would hasten the end of the Republic. The loss of Catalonia, totally under Franco's control by the beginning of February 1939, saw the reappearance of internal disunity, one of the blights that had plagued the Republic throughout the war. Republican, socialist and anarchist leaders openly began to criticise Negrín's resistance strategy and his dependence on the Communist Party and the Soviet Union. On 5 March 1939, Colonel Segismundo Casado, commander of the Army of the Centre, initiated an uprising whose principal mission was to overthrow Negrín's government and negotiate a surrender with Franco. He managed to obtain some military and political support, including that of Cipriano Mera, the anarchist commander of the Fourth Army Corps, and the socialist Julián Besteiro, the first Speaker of the Cortes of the Second Republic, who had already held talks with the underground Falange in Madrid and with Franco's agents, who acted in collusion with international espionage, infiltrated in networks connected with embassies and the diplomatic corps.

This was a military rebellion against the legitimate government, still in power, although Great Britain and France had recognised Franco, and as Manuel Azaña, surprised that Julián Besteiro was involved, said, 'it was a repetition of Franco's *coup d'état* and, what was worse, motivated by the same reason: the excessive preponderance or intolerable dominance of the communists'.[32]

For a few days, what was left of the republican zone experienced a mini-civil war within the other one that was still being fought against the Nationalists. Fighting was intense in Madrid for a few days, until 10 March, leaving around 2,000 dead. Exhaustion and general malaise meant that Casado's supporters had little problem in quashing the communist resistance, and what was really caused by this rebellion was the definitive breakdown of the republican institutions. A few days later, Franco's troops entered Madrid. This saw the beginning of an uncivil, merciless peace, not a 'peace without bloodshed', which the supporters of Casado claimed as justification for their coup.

5

THE NEW ORDER

By the time a section of the Spanish army rose up against the Republic in July 1936, right-wing authoritarian regimes had already prepared the way in a large part of Europe. After the First World War and the coming to power of the Bolsheviks in Russia, the counter-revolutionary, anti-liberal and anti-socialist movement was quick to show itself in Italy, during the deep post-war crisis that shook this country between 1919 and 1922, became consolidated through right-wing and military dictatorships in several European countries and culminated with the rise to power of Adolf Hitler in Germany in 1933.

A great deal of this reaction revolved around Catholicism and the defence of national order and ownership. The Russian revolution, the rise of socialism and the secularisation processes that accompanied political modernisation intensified the struggle between the Catholic Church and its anticlerical opponents of the political left.

The dictatorship option in much of Europe after the beginning of the 1920s, with Miklós Horthy opening the way in Hungary, restored some of the traditional structures of authority that had been present before 1914, but it also had to look for new ways of organising society, industry and politics. This is what lay behind the fascism led by Benito Mussolini in Italy and it was the solution that was constantly being mooted by the right-wing parties and forces in Spain in the 1930s to overthrow the Second Republic.

The military rebels in Spain, under the supreme command of Franco after 1 October 1936, began to build the new State in wartime. The construction of this new State was accompanied by the physical elimination of the opposition, the destruction of all the symbols and policies of the Republic and the quest for an emphatic, unconditional victory with no possibility of any mediation.

MILITARISM

The military rebels were quite clear about what they wanted to destroy, less clear about what they wanted to construct instead. It was a Spanish nationalist movement, opposed to separatist decentralisation, and it rejected, with its attack on the Republic, left-wing ideologies, socialism, anarchism or, generically speaking, communism. The prevailing process in the territories occupied by the military rebels during the first few months was the imposition of military order as against the forces that had mobilised the masses in favour of socialism and revolution; the forging of an authoritiarian mentality as against liberalism, the parliamentary system of parties and free elections.

The 'exalted Spanish nationalism' which characterised the most senior coup leaders, all of them '*Africanistas*', so called for having served in the Army of Africa, laid the blame for the prolonged decadence suffered by Spain since the Peninsular War in 1808 on liberalism and parliamentary democracy, and was expressed in 'a militarist idea of political life and public order that made the Army a Praetorian institution that was virtually independent of civil power'.[1] This view was shared by many officers who had been born in the last two decades of the nineteenth century and had served in Morocco during the final years of the Restoration (1917–23) and the dictatorship of Primo de Rivera, such as Manuel Goded, Emilio Mola, José Enrique Varela, Juan Vigón, Juan Yagüe and Francisco Franco. The transformation of the *coup d'état* into a civil war helped them implement a regime of terror, with mass executions, imprisonment and torture for thousands of men and women.

The death in a plane crash, on 20 July, of General José Sanjurjo, who had been appointed leader of the uprising by his colleagues, forced the military rebels to take a swift decision to fill this power vacuum. On 24 July, on a recommendation by General Emilio Mola, who had acted as '*El Director*' of the plot in Pamplona, the *Junta de Defensa Nacional* (National Defence Council) was set up in Burgos, presided over by General Miguel Cabanellas, who had led the rebellion in Zaragoza, which included Mola himself and Generals Dávila and Andrés Saliquet. In theory, it was the first military coordination and administration body to be set up in the rebel zone, although the strategic direccion of operations was still being shared throughout the summer of 1936 between General Gonzalo Queipo de Llano in the south, with his headquarters in Andalusia, Mola in the north and Franco at the head of the Africa Army which had been transferred to the Peninsula and was beginning its advance on Madrid, the taking of which became the first and main objective of the rebels.

Four days after it had been set up, the Council extended the state of war to the whole of Spanish territory, an edict that was to remain in force until 1948. Its most significant measures began with the outlawing of left-wing parties and trade unions, with the confiscation of their assets and properties (16 September), to be followed shortly afterwards by the banning of all political activities, including those of right-wing groups who supported the military cause and had shown an outright rejection of the Republic. The CEDA, the grass-roots Catholic party, disappeared, its founder, José María Gil Robles, 'condemned to unpopularity' due to the failure of his *posibilista* policy with the Republic. The party's leading figures collaborated in the implantation of the new dictatorial order and thousands of its followers found a niche for themselves in the Falangist or traditionalist militias.[2] Nor did the Alfonsine monarchists, leaderless since the assassination of José Calvo Sotelo shortly before the military uprising, and without an organised social base, oppose the militarisation of the policy set in motion by the rebel command.

At the same time as the right-wing political parties that had been represented in the republican parliament were disappearing, the civil war was, from the outset, being accompanied by a mobilisation and massive growth of Falangist and traditionalist (Carlist) militias, who incorporated tens of thousands of civilians subjected at all times to military command. They were the hubs of civil mobilisation that helped the military rebels from the beginning, and together they did the dirty work of repression, the elimination of the reds, during the first few months until the military tribunals bestowed 'legal' status on justice in the Nationalist camp.

At the end of summer 1936, after two months of war, Franco's troops were at the gates of Madrid and some of the generals raised the question of the need for a single military command and a centralised political apparatus. The Nazi authorities who were negotiating the loan of war materiel with Franco had been urging him since the end of August to take sole command. Meanwhile, certain generals who were fiercely loyal to Franco, including Kindelán, Orgaz and Millán Astray, as well as his brother Nicolás, formed, in the words of Paul Preston, 'a kind of political campaign staff committed to ensuring that Franco became first Commander-in-Chief and then Chief of State'.[3] So Alfredo Kindelán, the former head of Aviation during the monarchy, who had asked to be released from the army when the Republic was proclaimed, moved that a meeting of the *Junta de Defensa Nacional* and other generals be held to choose a supreme chief.

There were two meetings, one on 21 and the other on 28 September. The first one, which took place in the barracks of an aerodrome near Salamanca, was chaired by General Miguel Cabanellas and present, among others, were Generals Franco, Mola, Queipo de Llano, Dávila and Saliquet. At lunch later on the estate of Antonio Pérez Tabernero, a bull-breeder, all were in favour of naming a single commander, except for Cabanellas, who advocated the continuation of a Council such as the one already set up, and which he chaired. And they all proposed naming Franco *Generalísimo*, except Cabanellas, who abstained, and later commented: 'You don't know what you've done, because you don't know him the way I do – he served under me in the Army of Africa as head of one of the columns under my command; and if you want to give him Spain now, he is going to believe it is his alone and will not allow anyone to replace him either during or after the war, until he is dead'.[4]

On 1 October Francisco Franco was named 'Head of the Government of the Spanish State', in the words of the decree drawn up by

General Francisco Franco (© Bettmann/CORBIS)

the monarchist, José Yanguas Messía, a professor of international law. The Defence Council was dissolved to be replaced by a State Technical Council headed by General Fidel Dávila. Franco adopted the title of *Caudillo*, which linked him to the mediaeval warriors, and the slogan that was most repeated from that moment on, and which was required to be used in any reference in the press, was: 'One Fatherland, one State, one *Caudillo*'. Thus began a personal, in principle temporary, dictatorship which replaced an improvised military council after the *coup d'état*.[5]

Francisco Franco was born in El Ferrol on 4 December 1892, and was forty-three years old at the time of the rising against the Republic. Almost all his military service had been in Africa, where he swiftly rose through the officer grades for his exploits in battle, and was awarded a large number of decorations and distinctions. He entered the Military Academy in Toledo in 1907, from where he only passed out 251st of the 312 officers in his year, but despite that he was a captain by 1915, and in February 1926, at the age of thirty-three, he had risen to brigadier. Between 1920 and 1925 he served in the *Tercio de Extranjeros* (the Spanish Foreign Legion), created in 1920 by José Millán Astray, with Franco as second-in-command. He was appointed Director of the Zaragoza Military Academy in January 1928, where he served until it was closed down by the Second Republic, and then during the years of the Republic he was military commander of La Coruña in 1932, general commander of the Balearic Isles in 1933 and 1934, supreme commander of the Spanish forces in Morocco at the beginning of 1935, Chief of General Staff from May 1935 until February 1936 and general commander of the Canary Islands from March until 18 July that year. He was promoted to major-general at the end of March 1934, on the recommendation of the then Minister of War, the radical Diego Hidalgo.

His brother officers saw him as a well-prepared and competent commander, but his path to the highest command was smoothed by the disappearance from the scene of some of his more qualified rivals for the position. General José Sanjurjo, who was due to fly from Portugal to Spain to head the rising, died on 20 July when his small aircraft, piloted by the Falangist Juan Antonio Ansaldo, crashed near Lisbon. Generals Joaquín Fanjul and Manuel Goded had failed to take Madrid and Barcelona, and they were arrested and shot a few days later. José Calvo Sotelo, the far-right monarchist leader, who had remained in close contact with the plotters, had been murdered on 13 July, and José Antonio Primo de Rivera, the head of the Fascist *Falange Española y de las JONS* party, was in prison at the time of the military uprising in Alicante, another city where it was unsuccessful.

Meanwhile, Gonzalo Queipo de Llano, who led the rising in Seville, was, like Franco, a major-general, although he had held this rank longer. The problem was that he had been a republican and plotted against monarchist governments, and thus would not have been accepted by all the rebel officers. That left Emilio Mola, who had prepared the plot and the rebellion as its Director, although he was a lieutenant-general, a lower rank than Franco. Potentially, however, he was a rival. It was his idea to set up the *Junta de Defensa Nacional de Burgos*, the first body to coordinate the military tactics of the rebels, and he had, with considerable help from the *requeté*, had gained control of a large part of the northern zone of Spain, including almost the entire province of Guipúzcoa, since the beginning of September.

Franco played his cards with astuteness and zeal. He presented himself to the media and diplomats as the principal general of the rebels, and this is what he also told the Germans and Italians, so that a few days after the *coup d'état*, certain European Foreign Ministries were already referring to the rebels as 'Francoists'. He also commanded the best-trained troops of the Spanish army, the 47,000 soldiers of the Foreign Legion and the *Regulares Indígenas* (Moorish troops), which he was able to transfer to the Peninsula thanks to the transport planes and bombers sent by Hitler and Mussolini. This, say the experts, was the decisive factor in giving Franco the advantage in the struggle for power: the control of the Army of Africa and the fact that he quickly transferred these troops to the Peninsula, thereby ensuring that any aid from the Fascist powers would be given to him alone.[6]

Once he was installed in power, the legend of General Franco, 'a life-long practising Catholic', grew apace, thanks to the veneration he was held in by the Church hierarchy. All the members of the *Junta Técnica del Estado* were noted for their 'religious beliefs', and were 'pious', but 'the one who stands out in this aspect is the *Generalísimo*'. Such was the view of Cardinal Isidro Gomá, the Primate of the Catholic Church in Spain, the first time he spoke about Franco to the Secretary of State for the Vatican, Cardinal Pacelli, later Pius XII, on 24 October 1936. And that was before Gomá had met Franco personally, but he already believed that 'he will be an exceptional collaborator in favour of the work of the Church from the high position he occupies'.[7]

From 1 October 1936 onwards, Franco began to enjoy absolute power, and in a speech broadcast after his appointment he gave a few clues as how he was going to organise the new State: 'within a broad totalitarian concept', with the most 'rigorous principles of authority', at the service of 'total national unity'. And to construct this, first it was necessary to destroy democracy, the Republic and the socialist and anarchist trade unions, something that was already being done in a radical and violent manner.[8]

During the first few months of the war, Franco was helped in this task of constructing something from the destruction of the adversary by his brother Nicolás, a conventional, lacklustre character who had participated in the supplying of arms to the rebels from Lisbon. Germany and Italy officially recognised Franco on 18 November 1936, and this, politically, sanctioned the support that the Fascist powers were giving Franco with the supply of war materiel, in spite of the non-Intervention treaty.

Despite this concentration of political and military power in the person of Franco, there were, for a time, still some centres of autonomous power, at least until April 1937. In Seville, where he initiated a brutal repression that was firmly backed by people of order, General Queipo de Llano issued a large number of edicts and orders without consulting the *Junta de Defensa*, and he gained considerable popularity with his radio talks and his effective and, for the republicans, threatening propaganda-mongery. However, beyond his lust for power or eccentricities, Queipo shared the basic ideas of the military dictatorship that was being exercised in the territory controlled by the rebels: 'Spain cannot be reconstructed until the entire political rabble is swept away', he declared in November 1926, when the cleansing was already well under way.[9]

In rebel Spain the military authorities were in control, but behind them there were the civilian masses to be subdued. Any conflicts that arose were always put down by Franco and the army. The recruitment of thousands of Carlists in Navarre and Álava gave them greater political influence in the early months of the war.[10] They set up a *Junta Central de Guerra*, presided over by the leader of the Communion, Fal Conde, divided into two sections, military and political, which exercised full power in Navarre. Anxious to have military control of this mobilisation, the Carlist leaders set up in December 1936 a Royal Military Academy for *Requetés*, in a bid to have military control of this mobilisation, a measure which was wholly incompatible with Franco's decision to incorporate the Carlist and Falangist militias into the regular army. Franco expressed to the Count of Rodezno, Fal Conde's rival for the leadership of the Communion, his 'displeasure' because, besides the 'Head of State', there was another power 'that was creating and regulating armies, and granting promotions'. He classed this as a 'crime of treason' and told him that Fal Conde would have to give up this initiative. General Dávila, acting on Franco's orders, gave Fal Conde forty-eight hours to leave Spain or face a court martial. Fal went to Portugal and Franco thus eliminated a potential competitor and put a brake on the activities of a group that was enjoying great success at mobilising followers at that time.

Also spectacular was the growth of the *FE de las JONS* in the early months of the civil war, when a good many of its leaders, some of them released from gaol by the military rising, concentrated all their efforts into recruiting new members who were flooding into the Fascist camp. It had been a small organisation before the elections of February 1936, although the defeat of the CEDA and the fascistisation of the right in subsequent months had swelled its membership by the eve of the *coup d'état*. Its radical thinking and paramilitary structure, added to the lack of credibility of organisations such as the CEDA that had decided to accept the legitimacy of the Republic, saw its membership swell when arms replaced politics. By October 1936 there were over thirty-six thousand Falangists on the fronts, together with over twenty-two thousand Carlists and more than six thousand members of other tendencies, such as the Alfonsines or the CEDA.

Although it had thousands of members, it still lacked solid direction with undisputed or charismatic leaders. José Antonio Primo de Rivera, the national leader, was in prison in Alicante with his brother Miguel. Onésimo Redondo was killed on 24 July in Labajos, Segovia, in a skirmish with republican militias. Julio Ruiz de Alda and Fernando Primo de Rivera, José Antonio's younger brother, were murdered in August in the Modelo prison in Madrid. Two months later, after a *saca* from the Las Ventas prison, the same fate befell Ramiro Ledesma Ramos. Also in prison were Raimundo Fernández Cuesta, who was exchanged in October 1937, and Rafael Sánchez Mazas, who managed to escape a mass firing squad a little before the end of the war. As one of the backroom Falangist leaders, José Luna, the provincial head in Cáceres and an infantry captain, said the *Falange* had gone from having 'a tiny body with a big head to a monstrous body with no head at all'.[11]

Falangist heads from the various parts of rebel Spain met in Valladolid on 2 September 1936 and set up a provisional command junta, presided over by Manuel Hedilla, a man loyal to José Antonio, who was then busy training Falangist militias. The junta moved to Salamanca at the beginning of October, to be near Franco's headquarters. From there various operations to rescue José Antonio were planned, directed by Agustín Aznar, head of the Falangist militias, but they all failed and in any case, the initiative was not on Franco's list of priorities. Before he was shot in the prison yard in Alicante on 20 November, José Antonio wrote his will, naming as executors his friends Raimundo Fernández Cuesta and Ramón Serrano Suñer, and after managing to cross over into the Nationalist zone these two were to play a major role in the unified *Falange*.

News of the death of José Antonio, published in the republican and foreign press, was suppressed in rebel Spain. Franco exploited the cult of '*el Ausente*' (the absent one) in order to create a vacuum in the party's leadership and manipulate the *Falange* as a tool for the political mobilisation of the civilian population. One month later, on 20 December, Franco issued a decree placing the Falangist militias and those of the other organisations under the orders of the military authorities. All combat personnel, militarised and regular, was now under the authority of the *Generalísimo*. The distinct centres of power began to disappear. All that remained was to create a single political force, a mass movement that would be able to identify with its Fascist and Nazi allies.

By the end of 1936, all the political forces that backed the military uprising, once they had accepted the supreme command of Franco, were in favour of some kind of unification, although the problem lay in figuring out which force would predominate. Franco was thinking of a party which would help him to gain even more power for himself. He was also being pressured in this direction by the Italian Fascists. In February 1937, an envoy sent by Mussolini,

Roberto Farincacci, who used the highly radical and violent influence of the *Squadristi* to get himself appointed secretary of the Italian Fascist party, urged Franco to create, 'with the political forces that have contributed combatants', a Spanish National Party with a genuine Fascist and corporatist programme.[12]

FASCISM AND CATHOLICISM

A key figure in introducing this Italian Fascist model into the ideology was Ramón Serrano Suñer, Franco's brother-in-law. Serrano Suñer, born in 1901, had been a CEDA deputy after the 1933 and 1936 elections for Zaragoza, the city where he practised law. He was married to Ramona Polo, the younger sister of Franco's wife, Carmen Polo, and had been a close friend of José Antonio since his time as a student at the Universidad Central in Madrid.

After the failure of the military uprising in Madrid, Serrano Suñer was arrested, although he managed to escape in January 1937. Soon afterwards he arrived with his wife and children in Salamanca, where Franco had installed his headquarters, traumatised by his captivity and by having seen his brothers José and Fernando killed for organising his escape. Serrano Suñer, an expert in administrative law, seemed to be the ideal person 'to establish the legal bases of the New State', a task for which neither Nicolás Franco nor the authoritarian monarchist José Antonio Sangróniz, the *Caudillo*'s two main collaborators up to that time, was suited. 'It was Serrano Suñer who was finally to give specific shape to Franco's ideas for setting up a single-party regime'.[13]

Serrano Suñer explained to Franco that what he was running was a 'camp State', with a barrack-room mentality, which should be replaced by a permanent political mechanism, a new State similar to those run by Fascist regimes. Serrano Suñer's plan consisted of creating a mass political movement based on the union of the *Falange* and the Traditionalist Carlist Communion, an initiative in which Franco's brother, Nicolás, his right-hand man until Serrano Suñer's arrival, had had no success.

Franco first called Rodezno and other Navarran traditionalist leaders to tell them his decision: there would be no negotiations

between the two groups, which could produce the party confrontations to be found in a democratic system, and that he would be the
one to decree unification. He was more worried about the *Falange*,
because it was a bigger party, with totalitarian aims, but since the
death of José Antonio, its leaders had been locked in a power struggle.

This power struggle developed into a bloody brawl between the
two rival groups on 16 April 1937, in which two died, until it was
put down by the army, a situation that was exploited by Serrano
Suñer to silence any focus of resistance to unification. Three days
later, the decree of unification, which he himself had drawn up, was
published. *Falange Española* and the Carlists would combine under
the leadership of Franco in a 'single national political unit', *Falange
Española Tradicionalista y de las JONS*, 'a link between the State
and society', in which the 'Catholic spirituality' of the Requetés, 'the
traditional force', would be integrated into 'the new force', fascism,
as had happened 'in other countries with a totalitarian regime'. All
the other groups that had also supported the rebel war effort, including
the Alfonsines and the CEDA, were excluded.[14]

In practice, this meant that the hierarchical structures of the
Falangists and *Requetés* would disappear because, from that moment
on, the supreme chief was Franco. Manuel Hedilla who, in the absence
of José Antonio Primo de Rivera, presided over the *Falange*, was
unwilling to take a back seat, and he told the provincial chiefs to
follow his orders alone. On 25 April, Hedilla was arrested along
with other dissident Falangists. Two months later, he appeared before
a summary court martial which sentenced him to death for 'endorse-
ment of rebellion' and resistance to compliance with the unification
decree. In the end, Franco pardoned him, but he spent four months
in gaol and never went back into politics.[15]

In view of the hold that Franco had on the situation, there was
little chance of resistance, however angry the Carlists or the hardline
sector of the *Falange* grouped around the founder's sister were about
the way unification had come about. From the beginning it was a
party dominated by Franco, and this left him without any political
rival. Antonio Goicochea dissolved *Renovación Española*, and Gil
Robles, who enthusiastically accepted unification and gave instructions for *Acción Popular* to comply with the decree, saw no

improvement in his situation. The Falangists never forgot his time in the government of the Republic and Franco had no intention of incorporating a representative of the old regime, especially as he had been his superior as Minister of War.

And if anyone still had any doubts as to Franco's position, barely a month and a half after unification his only remaining rival was also eliminated. On 3 June 1937, the aircraft taking General Emilio Mola to inspect the front, at the height of the campaign to control the north, crashed near Alcocero, a small village in the province of Burgos. According to the official version, the plane crashed into a hill because of the fog, although there were rumours of sabotage and also that the aircraft, an Airspeed A.S. 6 Envoy manufactured in Britain, was shot down by friendly aircraft by mistake. Franco felt 'relieved at the death of General Mola', wrote the German ambassador von Faupel, but from that moment he stopped travelling by plane and began to visit the front by car.[16]

The winds of fascism were blowing through Europe, Franco was supported in his war against the Republic by Italy and Germany, but this fascistisation process in rebel Spain could never call into question the power of the army, and it had to exist side by side with the presence of the Catholic Church as a highly influential social and cultural force. Thus, less than a year after the military uprising, Franco's personal dictatorship was established on the three pillars that were to accompany it until his death four decades later: the army, the Catholic Church and the single party.

Militarism, fascism and Catholicism were the essential components of the New State that emerged as the war progressed. On the one hand, the Caudillo was exalted like the Führer or il Duce, with the straight-arm salute and blue shirts; on the other, rituals and religious displays made their appearance with processions, open-air masses and political-religious ceremonies in the medieval style. Rebel Spain became a territory particularly suitable for the 'harmonisation' of fascism, of the 'modern authoritarian current', with 'glorious tradition'. There was therefore to be a two-fold process, running in parallel and simultaneously, 'of the gradual fascistisation of the State apparatus (and Spain's national political style) and of the restoration of religious life'.[17]

The call for a 'religious and military meaning to life', for author-itarianism and contempt for democratic systems was now to be part and parcel of the crusade discourse at all times. Priests and others in holy orders, particularly Jesuits and Dominicans, unblushingly sailed with the authoritarian and Fascist winds that were then blowing in many parts of Europe and provided definitions of fascism adapted to the circumstances in Spain: 'If we take Fascists to mean those who advocate a government that gets rid of the farce of the parlia-mentary system and universal suffrage; that chokes the trade unions and parties of the revolution, those dens of iniquity; that abomi-nates everyday democracy, that disguise of parasites and hair shirt for the uneducated public; that weeds out the venomous Judaeo-Masonic seed'; if all that was fascism, then 'the National Uprising, Franco's government and the whole of Christian Spain are Fascist'.[18]

For a time, throughout the civil war and during the early post-war years, fascism and Catholicism were compatible, in declarations and daily life, in the projects that emerged within the rebel camp and in the form of government imposed by Franco. Fascism was 'a forceful protest against an absurd democracy and a rotten liber-alism' and it was useless to oppose this 'torrent': 'we Catholics could not oppose the movement known as *Fascism*, which was eminently national in nature; we had to accept it with love and follow it along traditional, Christian paths: the modern authoritarian current had to be harmonised with our glorious tradition, and thus a new State would emerge, free of outdated democratic and liberal traces, impreg-nated in our historic institutions'.[19]

The Spain that was being built by the army, Fascists and Catholics was a territory particularly suitable for the 'harmonisation' of the 'modern authoritarian current', with 'glorious tradition'. The feeling of uncertainty and fear caused by the reform policies of the Republic, anticlericalism and the expropriatory and destructive revolution that followed the military coup were used by the army, the Catholic Church and the Falange to mobilise and establish a social base that would be ready to respond to what were seen as being clear symptoms of de-Christianisation and 'national disintegration'. The army, the Church and the Fascist party represented this base and, following victory in the civil war and the long dictatorship that ensued, they

Fascist salute (Archivo Sandri, Bolzano-Alto Adige, Italia)

supplied the ruling class, the system of local power and the faithful servants of the administration.[20]

The radicalisation that fascism brought to counter-revolutionary initiatives and practices, its totalitarian potential, its ideological purity and exclusivity and the experience of the war of attrition that had been waged by the military rebels since July 1936, was melded with the restoration of this historical unity between Catholicism and the Spanish national identity. Catholicism was the perfect remedy to the lay Republic, separatism and revolutionary ideologies. It became the perfect link for all those who joined the rebel camp, from the most hard-line Fascists to those who had proclaimed themselves to be rightist republicans.

Because of the influence of the army and the Church, the right-wing assault on parliamentary democracy in Spain never became a 'revolutionary' action for remodelling society from top to bottom; but then this was really only achieved in Germany with National

Socialism. In Fascist Italy, the model closest to that of Spain, the monarchy and the Catholic Church coexisted with the regime until the removal of Mussolini in July 1943.

The creation of this new State began with the unification of all the political forces into a single party. It took somewhat longer for this pet project of Serrano Suñer's to take shape, although major progress was already being made during the war. The 'camp State' gradually gave way to a more organised bureaucracy. In the summer of 1937, the monarchist general, Francisco Gómez Jordana, took over the presidency of the *Junta Técnica del Estado*, replacing another general, Fidel Dávila, who had been somewhat ineffective during the months he had presided over this body. Gómez Jordana, Count of Jordana, deplored the chaos and 'shambles' that had been left and, together with Serrano Suñer, he tried to restore order to the administrative apparatus. They both believed that what rebel Spain needed was a proper government, not a *Junta Técnica*. And they told Franco as much.

On 30 November 1938 Franco named his first government, based on suggestions from Serrano Suñer, if we are to believe what he himself claimed in his memoirs. As with all subsequent Francoist governments, the posts were carefully shared out between officers, Carlists, Falangists and monarchists; in short, between all the sectors that joined forces to rise against the Republic in July 1936. Each sector controlled the area that it felt affinity towards: the military and public order ministries for the officers; the syndical and 'social' ministries for the Falangists; the financial ministries for technocrats, lawyers and engineers; and education and justice for Catholics, traditionalists or ex-members of *Acción Española*. In thirty-seven years of Francoist governments no woman ever occupied a ministry. And what the *Caudillo* always required, above anything else, was loyalty to the 'command'.

This first government represented a victory for Serrano Suñer, the new Interior Minister, over Nicolás Franco, the representative of the poorly-structured administration that had prevailed during the first year of the war. As Franco said, the government would oversee the 'national-syndicalist organisation of the State', although rather than construction, what it oversaw was the destruction of republican legislation, particularly with regard to anything that had to do with the 'revision of lay legislation'. But above all, it was a government 'born for war and at war', and therefore, to win it outright, it took on Fascist overtones to keep to its commitment with the Axis powers.[21]

The principal political outcome of this new phase was the passing on 9 March 1938 of the *Fuero del Trabajo* (Labour Rights), a kind of mock Constitution based on the *Carta del lavoro* of 1927 in Fascist Italy. The text represented a compromise between Falangism, represented by Ridruejo, and Catholic traditionalism (the drafting of this part clearly being the work of Eduardo Aunós, of *Acción Española*); it struck a middle line between 'liberal capitalism and Marxist materialism', with the job of 'channelling (...) the Revolution that is still pending in Spain, and which will return the Fatherland, Bread and Justice to Spaniards once and for all'.[22]

A few weeks later, on 22 April, Serrano Suñer went a stage further in the process of Fascistisation with the passing of the *Ley de prensa* (the Press Act, which was to remain in force until 1966) and which imposed absolute government control on the media through censorship. January 1937 saw the setting up of *Radio Nacional* and January 1939 the birth of the State news agency EFE. By the time the war was over, Franco's government had established the bases of an information policy that defended the dictatorship and was directed towards the repression of dissidents.

THE ROOTS OF FRANCO'S DICTATORSHIP

The common link between Catholic tradition and Fascist ideology was the destruction of the Republic's social and cultural policies and bases. On 4 September 1936, before Francisco Franco came onto the scene as *Generalísimo* and *Caudillo* of the military rebels, the *Junta de Defensa Nacional* in Burgos ordered 'the destruction of all works with socialist or communist undertones that may be found in travelling libraries and schools' and the suppression of 'co-education', one of the *bêtes noires* of the Church hierarchy and Catholics opposing republican educational policy.

The revitalisation of religion reached the farthest corners of the territory under the power of the military rebels, with street names being changed, the restoration of public worship, the re-establishment of religious education in the schools and the 'return' of the crucifix in schools. The 'return' of crucifixes to schools, which had been removed during the republican years, acquired a special symbolic significance, with the children as witnesses. In most cases, mayors and priests ran the ceremonies, while bishops usually delivered the speeches.

At the first meeting of Franco's first government, held on on Thursday 3 February 1938, it was decided to 'revise' all the Second Republic's lay legislation, and thus one law after another was repealed by decree, from the Civil Marriages Act (March 1938) and the Divorce Act (August 1938) to the Religious Confessions and Congregations Act (February 1939), the Act passed in June 1933 that marked the climax of the alienation between the Catholic Church and the Republic.

This 'renovation of legislation' was so swift that only a few months later, on the last day of June 1938, José María Yanguas Messía gave an assessment of his government's 'Catholicity' in his speech while presenting his credentials as ambassador to the Holy See: 'the government has already returned the crucifix and religious teaching to the schools, it has repealed the Civil Marriages Act, it has suspended divorce, it has restored the Company of Jesus into civil law, it has officially recognised the identity of the Catholic Church as a perfect association (...) restored the sanctity of religious festivals, and has brought an authentically Catholic and Spanish conception to Labour Rights'.[23]

The Catholic Church was grateful and pleased with all these reformation measures by the government. Firstly, with the 'most glorious *Caudillo*', whom it considered as being undoubtedly the 'providential man chosen by God to lift Spain', in the words of the *Catecismo patriótico español* which the Dominican, Ignacio G. Menéndez Reigada published in Salamanca in 1937, a forerunner of the countless catechisms that would be published in the first few post-war years.

Spain was once more Catholic, One Nation, Great and Free, but to consolidate this state of affairs 'God and His works' needed to be involved in everything, in laws, the home and the institutions.

And it was necessary to cast out the 'false intellectual idols' and expurgate libraries, said Enrique Pla y Deniel, the bishop of Salamanca, in his pastoral letter of May 1938, 'particularly public and even school and educational libraries, into which so many adulterated and poisonous elements have been introduced in recent years'.[24]

The Church asked the regime for all this and much more, in return for the support it had given the uprising, the blessing it had bestowed on the violence against republicans and revolutionaries. This 'spiritual reconstruction' was to be seen particularly in schools. 'No more contempt for our history' said the monarchist-turned-Fascist Pedro Sainz Rodríguez, Minister of Education in Franco's first government, in a circular sent to the Inspectorate of Primary Schools at the beginning of March 1938. And a few months later the same ministry laid down the guidelines for the reorganisation of public education in Barcelona for when the city fell to Franco's troops: 'Schools will have to be equipped with Crucifixes, portraits of the Head of State, national flags and posters with a collection of emblems and captions, which will give children the idea that a new Spanish State is being formed and reinforce the concept of a Fatherland that they have hitherto been unaware of'.[25]

It was not all religion, however, on the Nationalist home front. And to escape the old concept of charity and assistance and to give expression to the Falangist dreams of 'social justice', the struggle against 'hunger, cold and misery' in the middle of a war, October 1936 saw the setting up of *Auxilio de Invierno* (Winter Assistance), later to become the *Delegación Nacional de Auxilio Social* (National Social Assistance Delegation) in May 1937. It was the brainchild of Mercedes Sanz Bachiller, the widow of Onésimo Redondo, and Javier Martínez de Bedoya, a former fellow-student of Onésimo's, who after spending some time in Nazi Germany, returned to Spain in June 1936 and in the autumn of that year he suggested to Sanz Bachiller, at that time provincial head of the *Sección Femenina* in Valladolid, that they set up something similar to the Nazi *Winterhilfe* to collect donations and distribute food and warm clothing to the most needy. In less than a year, they turned it into an institution at the service of the demographic policy of the Nationalist 'New State', defending motherhood, with the setting up of a charity to protect mothers and their children: 'We need strong, fecund mothers to give us plenty of healthy children to fulfil the desire for supremacy of the youth that has died in war'.[26]

The formation of this new State and the new concept of the Fatherland destroyed the political victories and dreams of intellectuals, professionals and administrative sectors who had developed a common political culture marked by republicanism, democratic radicalism, anticlericalism, and, in some cases, Messianism for the working classes. Teachers, doctors, civil servants and university professors were persecuted for having followed a 'disruptive' profession. Punishment, in the form of murder, was meted out to the rectors of some universities. Famous cases included that of Leopoldo García-Alas, the son of the writer Leopoldo Alas 'Clarín', a lawyer and republican politician, professor and rector of the University of Oviedo, shot in February 1937. And Salvador Vila Hernández, rector of the University of Granada, a distinguished Arabist and disciple of Miguel de Unamuno, who was shot in October 1936 in Víznar, the same spot that had seen the murder of the poet Federico García Lorca two months previously.[27]

And with the disappearance or silencing of these republican intellectuals, the way was opened for the Fascist project 'of the recomposition of the unity of the Fatherland', which until 1936 had barely managed to take root. The military uprising changed this trend and the 'political programme, rhetoric and symbols' of the Falange, a party, let us not forget, that was founded in October 1933, 'immediately attracted young intellectuals' from whom 'the only coherent project for building a Fascist State in Spain' emerged'.[28]

They obtained good posts in the government and administration, dominated the press and propaganda apparatus, and until the defeat of the Axis powers in 1945, they believed in the project and displayed great enthusiasm when carrying it out, while they replaced the purged civil servants and intellectuals who were undergoing reprisals from the politicians of the new State under construction. Among the most significant and enthusiastic of these figures were Dionisio Ridruejo, Pedro Lain Entralgo, Gonzalo Torrente Ballester, Luis Rosales and Antonio Tovar. Catholics and Fascists worked together

Nazi symbols in Franco's Spain (Ministerio de Cultura)

on the same task and strove to increase their power bases in education and the press and propaganda respectively. There was friction between these two projects 'with their liberalising pretensions', with some aspiring to restore a traditional Catholic monarchy and others to establish a Fascist State. It was Franco, the supreme leader, *Caudillo* and *Generalísimo*, who established order and balance, until they were disgraced and abandoned the Fascist ship to rebuild their Fascist past and present themselves as liberals after 1945.[29]

Yet apart from these differences, they were united in the memory of their murdered martyrs, because they were also united in the 'blood pact' sealed by the political violence that they applied and condoned on the home front during the war and the subsequent victorious years. The highly emotionally-charged ritual and myths surrounding the victims on the republican home front reinforced the power and presence of Catholics and Falangists in the coalition of forces commanded by Franco, fomented the thirst for revenge and

Ceremony of homage to Italian soldiers fallen in combat against the Republic. Cemetery in Santander, 1937 (Archivo Sandri, Bolzano-Alto Adige, Italia)

removed any trace of sympathy for the vanquished once the war was over.

A decree by the Head of State dated 16 November 1938 proclaimed that henceforth 20 November would be a national 'day of mourning', in memory of the shooting of José Antonio Primo de Rivera on that date in 1936, and established, 'with the prior agreement of the Church authorities' that 'on the walls of every parish church there was to be an inscription with the names of their fallen, either in the present Crusade, or as victims of the Marxist revolution'.[30]

This was the origin of the placing of commemorative plaques to 'the fallen' in churches. And although the decree did not stipulate as such, all these inscriptions were headed by the name of José Antonio, a sacred fusion of those who had died for political and religious causes, all of them 'martyrs of the Crusade'. Because, as Aniceto de Castro Albarrán, the senior canon of Salamanca, wrote in his *Guerra Santa*, all the victims of the 'Russian savagery' were religious victims, and not just the clergy: 'the most prominent Catholics, the most pious figures, the most evangelistic "right-wingers", in short, all those whose martyrdom exclusively involved religious hatred and persecution of the Church'.[31]

The quality of life seemed to be better in Franco's Spain, politically and ideologically more united than the republican zone, although this union had a lot to do with the way the war was progressing, with victory after victory and hardly any setbacks, thanks mainly to the effects of the non-Intervention pact which was observed by the democracies, and to the German and Italian intervention.[32]

In such a situation, the war fatigue which during the last few months was in evidence mainly in cities such as Madrid or Barcelona, with protests and unrest over food shortages on the home front, was not affecting Nationalist Spain, where supplies were plentiful. From the beginning, the rebels controlled the major agricultural production areas. The precedence of military over civilian rule was made clear from the beginning, with a united military leadership which 'ordered that all economic activities be steered towards the war effort. In contrast to the indiscipline caused by the revolution, in the Nationalist zone production was subject to an unwavering discipline'. And unlike the monetary chaos in the republican zone, with a great many coins and promissory notes in circulation, the 'Nationalist' peseta suffered a limited depreciation and there were no serious interruptions in supplies. The aid from Italy and Germany and the major international companies' acceptance of Franco's cause were also a basic factor in maintaining unity, morale and faith in victory.[33]

While the anarchists and Socialists were seizing and collectivising land, one of the first measures taken by the *Junta de Defensa Nacional*, set up in Burgos on 24 July 1936, and its successor, the *Junta Técnica del Estado*, was to dismantle the Republic's legislation and the activities of the *Instituto de Reforma Agraria* (IRA). Wherever possible, beginning with Andalusia, lands were returned to their former owners. In 1938, the Minister of Agriculture in Franco's first government, the Falangist Raimundo Fernández Cuesta, established the *Servicio Nacional de Reforma Económica y Social de la Tierra* (National

Land Economic and Social Reform Service), but the owners had not expected to recover their lands 'legitimately' and the violent counter-revolution of officers, landowners, *señoritos* and Falangists had already taken reprisals against thousands of peasants in Extremadura and Andalusia.

In the sphere of land ownership and labour relations, in agriculture and in industry, the military rebels mounted a swift counter-revolution with the aim of re-establishing the order that had been in place prior to the proclamation of the Republic. The defence of private ownership and capitalist social order were the main pillars of the reactionary coalition that supported the *coup d'état* of July 1936 and the violent destruction of the Republic through the civil war.

First in Málaga in February 1937, then in all the other republican cities, ending with Madrid at the end of March 1939, the entry of the Nationalist troops was celebrated with the Te Deum and other Catholic rituals which gave unity to all the reactionary forces. The bishops gave the Fascist salute at all the civilian-military ceremonies, they blessed arms, they rallied the troops and encouraged the persecution of the vanquished: re-Catholicisation by the force of arms never envisaged reconciliation, or mercy for the vanquished. The unconditional surrender of the enemy, the 'triumph of the city of God', would come with a rhetoric and a rule steeped in militarism, nationalism and Catholic triumphalism. Total conclusive victory.

Franco and his brothers in arms had been making it quite clear since the beginning of 1937 that they would not accept any mediation to end the war, 'just unconditional surrender'. Franco said as much to Gomá in June 1937, so that the Primate, by now a good friend of the *Generalísimo*'s, would inform the Holy See. He would not accept a settlement nor did he have to apologise for the alleged harshness shown by the army to the enemy 'because nobody has been condemned without going through the proper procedure as laid down in the military code'.

And Gomá believed this. 'General Franco is magnanimous', he would say to anyone who was in any doubt about it. He was close to him, he had appealed to him to ensure that, following the fall of Bilbao, 'the repression would be as subdued as possible', particu-

Republican prisoners in Franco's Army (Archivo General de la
Administración, Alcalá de Henares, Madrid)

larly with priests, to avoid a fresh occurrence of those 'appalling'
scenes of the murder of priests by Catholic troops after the fall of
Guipuzcoa.[34]

One year later, Franco's attitude to a possible mediation was
monotonously repeated: 'All those who want mediation, either
consciously or unconsciously, are helping the reds and the covert
enemies of Spain (...) Our justice could not be more dispassionate
or noble; its generosity is merely aimed at the defence of the highest
interests of the fatherland; no type of mediation could make it more
benign'. On 18 October and at the beginning of November 1938,
towards the end of the long drawn-out Battle of the Ebro, he offered
more of the same to the Reuters correspondent: 'The outright decisive victory of our army is the only solution for Spain to survive
(...) and there can only be one outcome: the unconditional surrender
of the enemy'.[35]

No mediation, no pardon. The only thing the officers talked about
was a process of 'cleansing', as if Spain needed to be 'purged' of her
'sick bodies'. And a good many church authorities, bishops, priests
and others in holy orders, went even further in their defence of this

killing hysteria. 'We are on the point of winning the war. Later we will need to win over the vanquished and help the victors to forge a great Spain for an almighty God', Martín Sánchez-Juliá, the leader of the *Acción Católica Nacional de Propagandistas* had said way back on 1 April 1937. Mediation was 'inadmissible', wrote Leopoldo Eijo y Garay, bishop of the diocese of Madrid-Alcalá, because 'to tolerate democratic liberalism, entirely Marxist in its nature, would be a betrayal of the martyrs'. Pacification through arms, at sword-point. That was the peace that was due to come.[36]

Voices calling for the extermination of the adversary thundered from the pulpits. We know this thanks to the reliable testimonies of certain priests, from the French author Georges Bernanos, or from Antonio Ruiz Vilaplana, the clerk of the court in Burgos, who 'bore witness' and related his experiences from Paris after fleeing from 'Nationalist Spain'. Burgos, with its overwhelming scent of incense and violent atmosphere since July 1936, was where the priest of the Merced Church called for a merciless punishment for the enemies of God: 'With these people, all of us need to be like fire and water ... there can be no pacts of any type with them ... there can be no forgiveness for the criminals who have destroyed churches and killed the sacred clergy. Their seed, the seed of evil, the seed of the devil, must be eliminated. Because the sons of Beelzebub are truly the enemies of God'.[37]

All attempts to end the war via a negotiated peace, as advocated by the President of the Republic, Manuel Azaña, and which was also welcomed by the Vatican in Spring 1937, at the same time as Franco was asking Gomá to publish a collective letter from the Spanish bishops abroad, failed. No one in Franco's Spain wanted to talk of 'coexistence', of 'continuing to live together so that the nation would not die', as Azaña asked for in Valencia on 18 July 1937, a year after the beginning of that 'terrible war, the war on the body of our own fatherland'.[38]

On this matter, Cardinal Gomá was just another military man, who rejected any type of peace that was not by force of arms and who, as primate of the Church of Spain and unofficial representative of the Holy See until October 1937, advised the Vatican not to collaborate in attempts to obtain an armistice, advice that was backed up in Rome by the Superior-General of the Jesuits, Wlodimir Ledóchowski. Few clergy, so few that their voice was not even heard, disagreed with this position.

The discordant voices came from outside Spain, from French Catholic intellectuals such as François Mauriac or Jacques Maritain who, shocked at so much condoned violence, set up the French Civil and Religious Peace in Spain Committee. But the Spanish Catholic Church dreaded a possible change of direction, a return to the Republic and its anticlericalism, particularly now that the sword and the cross were resurrecting an Imperial Spain, One Nation, Great and Free.[39]

There were some who managed to flee from this Great and Free Spain and took refuge in the mountains of Andalusia, Asturias, León and Galicia. They were the *huidos* ('fugitives') who remained hidden because they knew they could not go back home and that if they were captured, extremely harsh repression awaited them. In a good many cases, they were the seed of the post-war guerrilla activity which was maintained until the beginning of the 1950s. And although several hundred of them had died in confrontations with the armed forces during the war, they were never organised nor did they represent an alternative to open warfare on the battlefields. The Spanish Civil War never combined conventional war with guerrilla warfare, the strategy that had been used in the Peninsula War against Napoleon's troops and successive Carlist civil wars in the nineteenth century.

6

A LONG WAR

When the civil war broke out in 1936, the Spanish army had no modern weaponry, was top-heavy with officers and, with the exception of the troops stationed in Africa, the degree of organisation and preparation of the various units was somewhat deficient. It was a 'poor and antiquated' institution, 'with practically no tanks or anti-aircraft guns, whose air force flew in out-of-date machines that were frequently in bad condition'. All its high command were veterans of the conflict in Morocco where they had gained experience of colonial struggles against a 'primitive enemy' but none of them had taken part in modern warfare.[1]

As a consequence of the success or failure of the military uprising of July 1936, with two opposing groups of combatants, the government of the Republic, which in principle had more territory, more economic resources and held the most important and populous cities in its power, was left without military forces and unable to impose discipline on the revolutionary militias that arose in place of the army. The military rebels, on the other hand, had the Africa Army, which they were able to transfer swiftly to the Peninsula thanks to the aid from Nazi Germany and Fascist Italy, and they were professional soldiers who knew the ground rules of military technique.

The war lasted a long time, almost three years, and before its defeat the Republic was subjected to slow punishment, abandoned to its fate by the democratic powers, with battles that left its troops decimated against an army, under Franco, that was always able to count on the advantage of outside aid. There were no great battles as there were in the two world wars, and there are experts who believe that, militarily speaking, it was 'a vast botched operation on both sides'.[2] But it was the first war in the twentieth century in which aviation was used for premeditated bombing of the home front, and there is no doubt that the air attacks by the Italian air force on Madrid, Barcelona and Valencia, the three largest cities in Spain, also helped Franco's army to win the war.

ARMIES AGAINST MILITIAS

In the areas where the military uprising was defeated, the most active left-wing groups, basically socialists and anarchists, were armed and the tide of popular and revolutionary power eliminated or, in some cases, incorporated the army units loyal to the Republic. In the three months following the uprising, the war was a struggle between armed militias, who lacked the basic elements of a conventional army, and a military power that concentrated all its resources in authority and discipline.

The militias, which emerged in the cities, attempted to extend their armed power to other locations. Thus, as early as 21 July, one of the first decisions taken by the anarchists in Catalonia, once the military rebels had been defeated, was to set up the Central Committee of Antifascist Militias and to send armed columns to take Zaragoza, the main city of Aragón, three hundred kilometres from Barcelona, which had fallen into the hands of the rebels.

However, it is hard to accept the conventional image of thousands and thousands of militiamen prepared to set off for Aragón to fight fascism. The photographs and documents of the time show us crowds of people applauding their departure in the streets of Barcelona, but it seems that the number of those who were seduced by the rallying cries of certain anarchist leaders, climbing onto the trucks with their rifles, clenched fists raised, was lower than we have been led to believe. The figures given by the anarchists range between 20,000 and 30,000 men to cover the whole of the Aragón front. According to Nationalist sources, 15,000 'invaded' this region.[3]

Each political or trade union organisation had its militia and each militia its leadership committee. For the anarchists and socialists, the militias were a version of the 'people in arms' who were entrusted to create a revolution and destroy the traces of order that the army and social groups supporting them represented. Brought up in the anti-militarist tradition, in the mistrust of professional soldiers, many of these militiamen, starting with their leaders, were not about to give up their positions easily. This is why the organisation of armed columns, expropriations and the murder of political and ideological enemies went hand in hand from the outset.

In other words, the officers who remained loyal to the Republic and had to confront other officers in what was now open war found that they no longer had any subordinate officers and that, instead of troops, they now had thousands of highly enthusiastic and revolutionary workers and farm labourers, imbued with antifascist zeal, but with no training and no organisation or discipline to fight effectively in open warfare.

During the summer of 1936 the militias were an emergency resource to respond to the military rebellion and the scarcity of regular army units loyal to the Republic. Their uniform was blue overalls, with red (socialist) or red and black (anarchist) neckerchiefs and berets or caps with the badge of their organisation. They were armed with rifles and machine guns seized in attacks on barracks, but also with shotguns and a good many unserviceable weapons. They would discuss any decisions to be taken in assemblies, choose the leaders to command them and their newspapers and pamphlets, of which there were plenty during the early stages, emphasised their bravery and heroism against the 'Fascist beast'.

It was soon clear that these badly organised, ill-equipped militias, with very little discipline, were ineffective in waging war against an army that was advancing on Madrid with the troops transferred from Africa. On 7 August, José Giral, the prime minister of the Republic, appointed Lieutenant Colonel Juan Hernández Saravia, Manuel Azaña's former military cabinet head, minister of war, and he tried to recoup any available professional officers. Although the militias were to continue exhibiting their military power for a time, the new minister ordered the first calling to the ranks since the breakdown of the system of mobilisation caused by the military coup.

The rebels also had a great many volunteers, but from the outset their army had tens of thousands of soldiers, Civil Guards and uniformed police. The command network was re-established by the Africa Army officers and the rebel generals imposed military discipline from the very start. And thus, with these two different styles of warfare, the summer of 1936 ended with substantial rebel advances and republican losses, including two provincial capitals, Badajoz and San Sebastián. When the latter fell, on 13 September, the columns of Moors and Legionaries from Africa were close to Madrid. In four weeks they had advanced almost five hundred kilometres, killing poorly-armed militiamen and sowing terror wherever they went.

However, the Africa Army did not press on towards Madrid, the capital of the Republic, a city with weak defences at the time, and Franco ordered General José Enrique Varela to change course and make for Toledo to relieve the rebels who had been under siege in the Alcázar since 22 July. As a result of this decision the military rebels lost a perfect opportunity to sweep onto Madrid, before the republicans could reorganise their defences and the first major contingent of foreign aid arrived. But Franco was more interested in the 'political benefits of relieving the Alcázar', which would smooth the path for his appointment as supreme head of the rebel troops. The attack on Madrid was delayed for two weeks.[4]

Meanwhile, Franco had firmly consolidated his leadership and the relief of the Alcázar had boosted his legendary status. For Franco had promised one month previously that the thousand or so civil guards and Falangists, under the command of Colonel José Moscardó, who had holed up there in the first few days of the uprising, with the wives and children of a fair number of well-known left-wing militants as hostages, would soon be liberated. Moscardó's famous utterance 'all quiet in the Alcázar', repeated to Franco and numerous journalists in a staged event two days after its liberation, was suitably propagated. Franco was the saviour of the besieged heroes, the symbol of an army prepared to win the war at any cost.

MADRID

By the middle of October 1936, the rebel troops, now well equipped with Italian artillery pieces and armoured vehicles, had occupied most of the towns and villages around Madrid. The militiamen, rattled by the advance of the Africa Army, withdrew to the capital, where they were joined by hundreds of refugees fleeing from the occupied localities. Franco announced that he would take Madrid on 20 October and General Mola is reputed to have arranged to meet the *Daily Express* correspondent in the Puerta del Sol for coffee. On 29 October the first Soviet tanks and aircraft, sent by the Kremlin to counteract Italian and German aid, arrived in Madrid. The first shipment of arms from the Soviet Union had arrived at the port of Cartagena three weeks earlier.

Around this time, Largo Caballero's government decreed the setting up of the Popular Army, formed by Mixed Brigades which, through militarisation, was to convert the militiamen into soldiers. The indoctrination required for combat was provided by political comissars, a figure that appeared at this time and which had already been introduced by the communists in the 5th Regiment, the model for the professional army that they aimed to control, advised at all times by foreign communists.

On 19 October Franco signed the plan of attack on three fronts, with some 30,000 men divided into nine columns. General José Enrique Varela, an *Africanista* and Carlist sympathiser, commanded the colonial troops and attacked via the *Casa de Campo* park and the University campus. No one in the government, least of all the prime minister, Francisco Largo Caballero, was confident that Madrid would be able to withstand the onslaught of the military rebels, with their mercenaries from Africa, reinforced by the Luftwaffe and the Italian *Aviazione Legionaria*. And the foreign diplomats and press did not expect any other outcome either.

On 6 November, when the Nationalist columns were in reach of their objective, the republican government decided to leave Madrid and move the capital of the Republic to Valencia, far from the front.[5] General José Miaja, whom the Prime Minister, Largo Caballero, had left in charge of the *Junta de Defensa* of Madrid, and Lieutenant-Colonel Vicente Rojo, Chief of General Staff, had 20,000 men at

Women collaborating in the defence of Madrid against Fascism
(Private collection, Zaragoza)

their disposal. Two days later, the militiamen and the Moors were engaged in hand-to-hand combat in the University campus.

The attackers' principal force was the colonial infantry, 'used to a fluid war, with little artillery and against an enemy that was quick to abandon its positions and which never endeavoured to defend them until the last bullet was fired'.[6] Franco and Varela, after a triumphant advance from the south during the summer, expected to enter Madrid with infantry attacks. They proposed 'an unreasonable objective with scant resources. Thirty thousand men could not conquer a city with over a million inhabitants determined to defend themselves'.[7] Furthermore, delaying the attack in order to relieve the Alcázar beforehand provided the republicans more time to organise their defence, take delivery of the first shipment of Soviet aid and welcome the International Brigades. Vicente Rojo, however, in his book *Así fue la defensa de Madrid*, downplayed the role of these volunteer forces who had come from all over the world, and instead stressed the courage and bravery of thousands of anonymous citizens angered by the destruction wrought by the rebel air raids and who felt that their freedom

163

was under threat. It was a battle of resistance in which, in the republican camp, 'compliance with military duty, which began to prevail over any other type of duty', was seen for the first time in the war.[8]

Some organisations linked to the communists, such as the International Red Aid and the *Alianza de Intelectuales Antifascistas*, urged the inhabitants of Madrid to emulate the glorious exploits of 1808, the resistance of the people against the Napoleonic troops, immortalised in the paintings of Goya, and the poet Rafael Alberti dedicated his poem '*Madrid, corazón de España*' (Madrid, heart of Spain) to this heroic defence.[9] In demonstrations and on the most important buildings of Madrid could be seen banners bearing the legends '*No pasarán*' (they shall not pass) and '*Más vale morir de pie que vivir de rodillas*' (better to die on your feet than live on your knees), phrases that were forever linked to the communist leader Dolores Ibarruri, '*La Pasionaria*'.

Although the hero of the defence of Madrid might have been perceived as being General José Miaja, who was in evidence all over the city attempting to raise the people's morale, the technical and military aspects were in the hands of Vicente Rojo, an officer who remained loyal to the Republic because he believed that it was his duty to do so, and a few months later he became head of its army. He had always defined himself as a 'Catholic, officer and patriot', and according to his grandson, José Andrés Rojo, he felt caught between the world of the *Africanista* officers who took part in the coup, with whom he felt no affinity, and that of the armed militiamen who defended the revolution and burnt churches. Between these two worlds, he resolved to design a new strategy to organise an efficient force to confront the military rebels, in an attempt to establish the authority of professional officers like himself and the chain of command of this army.[10]

Vicente Rojo was born on 8 October 1894 in Fuente de la Higuera, a small town in the region of Valencia. He was two years younger than Franco and was not yet forty-two when the war began. His father, an officer who had served six years in Cuba, died three months before he was born, and when he was thirteen he lost his mother too. In order to continue with his studies, he was sent to a boarding school for orphans of Infantry officers and he entered the Toledo

Republican soldier, Madrid Front (Ministerio de Cultura)

Infantry Academy in June 1916. He left as a second lieutenant of the Infantry, having passed out second in a class of 390 cadets.

In 1915 he served as a volunteer in Africa, was promoted to Captain in 1918, and between 1922 and 1932 he taught at the Academy in Toledo. He then went to the War College to obtain the Staff Diploma and in June 1936, shortly after his promotion to Major, he joined the Central Staff. Following the chaos caused by the military uprising, Largo Caballero's first government reorganised the Central Staff and Rojo became second-in-command there under the immediate orders of Lieutenant-Colonel Manuel Estrada. On 25 October 1936, he was promoted to lieutenant-colonel 'for his loyalty', a few days before Miaja received the order to appoint him Chief of General Staff for the defence of Madrid. He was promoted to colonel 'for his war service' on 24 March 1937, and in May Juan Negrín appointed him Chief of Central Staff of the Republic, a post he held until the end of the war. On 24 September that same year, he was promoted to general.

One of the biggest drawbacks in the army that Largo Caballero's government began to set up was the shortage of professional officers. Of the 16,000 officers in the army that were in service before the military uprising, only about 20 per cent stayed in the republican zone, and this 'was totally inadequate for an army whose troop numbers increased five-fold in less than a year'. Very few of its officers had held high command before the war, and this shortcoming 'brought about the rapid promotion of officers who knew nothing about commanding large units'.[11]

Thus, this improvisation of commands posed a serious problem, even more so as one moved down the ranks, because most of the more junior officers were on the rebel side. The appointment of battalion and company commanders was necessarily improvised, and the army had to take in and commission the political heads of the militias and columns that were created in the days following the military uprising. In the opinion of Gabriel Cardona, one of the best specialists in military history, 'while the republicans were on the defensive, these shortcomings were not so dramatic as when the major offensives started, in which a clear chain of command was required'.[12]

But it is worth mentioning that, alongside Rojo, there was a group of professional officers, including Juan Hernández Saravia, Antonio Escobar, Francisco Llano de la Encomienda, José Fontán and Manuel Matallana, who remained loyal to the institutions of the Republic and yet they are now forgotten. Although many of them were the last to flee Spain, ultra-radical writers in exile, both anarchist and Socialist, branded them as traitors, Francoists or Stalinist puppets. With the bitter taste of defeat in their mouths, the communists also joined in the chorus of invective, and they never warranted respect from the victors. On the one hand, there were officers, those who won the war, who are still remembered in the street names of many towns and cities in Spain, and there were others, those on the losing side, who today are complete unknowns.

Then there were the republican army commanders who came from the militias. They had had no military aptitudes, although Enrique Lister had received some training in the USSR and Manuel Tagüeña had risen through the ranks. The most rapid promotion was that of Juan Modesto, who had been a corporal in the Legion, and in the summer of 1937 was appointed the first commander of the 5th Army Corps, a shock unit in which the communists played a major role. In addition, some of the anarchists who had been commanding columns since July 1936 joined the chain of command of the Republic's army, laying aside their anti-military prejudices. Prime examples included Cipriano Mera, Gregorio Jover and Miguel García Vivancos.

Franco's first major assault on Madrid failed, despite the relentless bombing carried out by the Junkers Ju 52. On 23 November Franco ordered the suspension of the attacks because his columns were fatigued, and because the republicans had managed to arm themselves, with the incorporation of Soviet fighter planes, and to become better organised. It was not yet a real army, but the republicans had overcome the state of initial disorder and the feeling of defencelessness. In spite of this early defeat, Franco had at that time obtained German and Italian recognition of the *Junta Técnica del Estado* as Spain's legitimate government. On the international stage, the military rebels continued to consolidate their positions. Mussolini and Hitler made it quite clear as to what side they were on in the battle being fought on Spanish soil.

Madrid under siege in November 1936, whose image was engraved on the collective memory of the republicans and members of the International Brigades for the heroic resistance of its population, was also the setting for the terrible slaughter of prisoners, particularly politicians, officers, right-wingers and clergy. Assaults on prisons, '*paseos*', '*sacas*' and murders had been occurring in Madrid since the defeat of the rebels in July that year, but all this faded into insignificance compared to the massacre of Paracuellos del Jarama, an unrepeatable event in the civil war, as was the situation that gave rise to it, the transfer of the government of the Republic to Valencia, and the setting up of a *Junta de Defensa*, which took on the coordination and control of the forces of order and security.

At that time there were over 5,000 inmates in Madrid's gaols. Around 2,000 were removed on 7 and 8 November and taken in buses operated by the Madrid Tram Company to locations near Paracuellos del Jarama and Torrejón de Ardoz. Most of them were shot and buried in mass graves. The *sacas* and killings went on for several days and escalated towards the end of the month. On 4 December, the new inspector general of Prisons, the anarchist Melchor Rodríguez, halted the *sacas*. In one month, this process had accounted for some 2,700 prisoners who were positively identified after the war, although in the veneration of the martyrs promoted by the eventual victors, this number was inflated to nearly nine thousand.

It was a bad time for the republican cause, with a Madrid under siege, no government, and armed groups systematically murdering prisoners. Not surprisingly, the affair gave rise to a string of justifications, accusations and controversial statements, which are still to be found in writings even now. It would be no exaggeration to place the blame on the police, under communist control with Soviet advisers, militants of the *Juventudes Socialistas Unificadas* (Unified Socialist Youth) and the top leadership of this police system: Manuel Muñoz, director general of Security; Santiago Carrillo, councillor in charge of Public Order; and Segundo Serrano Poncela, 'delegate for the Directorate-General of Security'. And although it is highly likely that the typical 'disorderly mobs', those who were always at home in chaotic situations, were acting of their own accord, the November *sacas* in Madrid suggested a full-scale cleansing of the home front dictated by the war, but one that was also coveted, a unique chance to eliminate the political, ideological and class enemy.[13]

The war went on and Madrid continued to be the prime objective of a Nationalist army that by the end of 1936 had been joined by tens of thousands of Italian troops, forming the *Corpo di Truppe Volontarie* (CTV), with generals who had gained experience in the First World War, and several thousand Germans who served in the Condor Legion and anti-tank and artillery sections of the *Wehrmacht*. At the start of 1937, the Nationalists had almost 350,000 men, a very similar figure to that of the republican army.

With his army bogged down on the outskirts of Madrid, Franco decided to attack Málaga in order to continue the conquest of the large expanse of Andalusia. The battle, which saw the debut of Italian participation, began on 5 February and on 7 February the motorised columns of the CTV entered the city, with air cover from a large number of bombers and fighters, and with cover also from inshore by cruisers and launches. It was also the first rehearsal of the *guerra celere* (the Italian version of *Blitzkrieg*), which was successful in Málaga because the republicans had no defences there and offered hardly any resistance.

Two days before the entry of the Italians, tens of thousands of people, men, women, the elderly and children, had begun to swarm out of the city towards Almería, to escape the reprisals and pillaging of their subjugators. A force was organised to pursue them, while they were being machine-gunned by planes and warships. The road was covered with dead and wounded and many families lost their children in the flight. Those who stayed in Málaga fared no better. At least 1,500 people were murdered over the following months, in gaols, cemeteries or 'taken for a walk' at night. Between 8 February and April 1939, the official end of the war, 818 women and 4,168 men were imprisoned in the city, figures that do not include those held in other gaols in the province and concentration camps. It marked the return of the 'hot-blooded terror' of the summer of 1936, with bodies that disappeared without being registered and murders with no trials or legal safeguards.

At the same time as the conquest of Málaga, the Nationalist army prepared a new attack on Madrid. This involved cutting off the road to Valencia, through the River Jarama valley, the route by which supplies and military materiel arrived in the capital. This operation was designed to be completed with an attack by the Italian CTV troops from Sigüenza towards Guadalajara to catch Madrid in a pincer movement. Over three weeks in February, from 6 February to the end of the month, both sides lost thousands of men, and while the Nationalists managed to advance their front a few kilometres, in the end the battle of the Jarama was somewhat unproductive.

A few days later, on 8 March, General Amerigo Coppi's motorised division began its attack, but it was held up in a heavy snow storm and within a few days it suffered a crushing defeat, among other reasons because Franco failed to carry out his diversionary operation from the Jarama and the republican troops, with the aid of the Garibaldi Battalion of the International Brigades and Soviet tanks, were able to concentrate all their efforts on halting the Italian advance.

General Roatta ordered the retreat. So ended the rebels' five-month battle to take Madrid, without success despite their military superiority. The republicans had managed to save the capital and offer the world an image of heroism and resistance against international fascism. Republican documentaries filmed with Italian prisoners tried to show the world that they were not Fascist volunteers but regular soldiers.[14] However none of this evidence, which ultimately may be considered as propaganda, was to change the posture of the non-Intervention Committee.

WAR OF ATTRITION

The succession of failures to capture Madrid brought about a change in Franco's strategy, and from that moment on he opted for a long, drawn-out war of attrition to grind the enemy down. And it did not matter that the Italian and German officers and strategists questioned his military competence, because his aim was to eliminate the enemy, the anti-Spain element, and at the same time 'tame' his brother-generals and consolidate his position as sole dictator.[15]

He intimated as much to Colonel Emilio Faldella, General Roatta's Chief of Staff, in February 1937: 'In a civil war, a systematic occupation of territory, accompanied by the necessary purge, is preferable to a rapid defeat of the enemy armies which leaves the country still infested with adversaries'. And he said it again, in more detail, to Mussolini's ambassador, Roberto Cantalupo, on 4 April 1937: 'We must carry out the necessarily slow task of redemption and pacification, without which the military occupation will be largely useless (...) Nothing will make me abandon this gradual programme. It will bring me less glory, but greater internal peace (...) I will take the capital not an hour before it is necessary: first I must have the certainty of being able to found a regime'.[16]

Franco held all the trumps with which to apply this military strategy. He had plenty of men, made possible by the continuance of the traditional system of recruitment and by the large number of Moroccan volunteers swelling the ranks of the Africa Army. Since September 1936 he had been able to use two Military Academies, in Burgos and Seville, to rapidly train university graduates as second

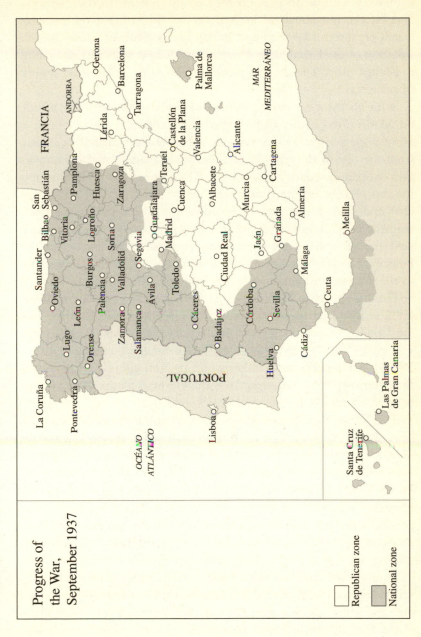

Progress of the War, September 1937

Republican zone

National zone

FRANCIA

ANDORRA

OCÉANO ATLÁNTICO

PORTUGAL

MAR MEDITERRÁNEO

La Coruña
Pontevedra
Lugo
Orense
Oviedo
Santander
Bilbao
San Sebastián
Pamplona
Huesca
Vitoria
Logroño
León
Burgos
Soria
Zaragoza
Palencia
Valladolid
Zamora
Salamanca
Segovia
Ávila
Guadalajara
Madrid
Toledo
Cáceres
Badajoz
Ciudad Real
Cuenca
Albacete
Teruel
Castellón de la Plana
Valencia
Alicante
Murcia
Cartagena
Almería
Granada
Jaén
Córdoba
Sevilla
Huelva
Cádiz
Málaga
Ceuta
Melilla
Lérida
Tarragona
Barcelona
Gerona
Palma de Mallorca

Lisboa

Santa Cruz de Tenerife
Las Palmas de Gran Canaria

Spain: Republican and Nationalist territory, September 1937

lieutenants and he also set up four establishments to train officers and NCOs. But above all he had the confidence that the international prospect of German and Italian backing for his cause and the isolation of the Republic by the western democracies was not going to change either. Thus he had plenty of men and a guaranteed supply of resources.

With all these resources, instead of pressing on with the attack on Madrid, the Nationalists turned their attention to the north, a weak region as far as defences were concerned, isolated as it was from the rest of the republican zone, with a substantial concentration of Spanish industry and mining. The Germans too were pushing for this change of direction in the war, because they felt that the coal and steel in this region would help Hitler's accelerated rearmament programme. And General Mola, whose troops were very near the objective, wanted to conquer these areas and teach the Basques a lesson: 'If submission is not immediate, I will raze Vizcaya to the ground, beginning with the industries of war'.[17]

For this operation Mola deployed the Navarre Division, the Italian CTV, reorganised under the orders of General Ettore Bastico, and the Condor Legion, under von Richthofen, who was to utilise this war in the north of Spain as a test bench for the bombing of cities. The Basque republican battalions had no anti-aircraft artillery and their territory 'was so narrow that the German planes were able to reach their targets before the sirens sounded'.[18]

The Nationalists began their campaign at the end of March with heavy bombing by the Condor Legion designed to shatter the morale of the civilian population and destroy ground communication networks. First it was Durango, on 31 March; then, Guernica on 26 April. On 19 June, the city of Bilbao, which was protected by an eighty-kilometre defensive perimeter developed by the Basque government, 'the iron belt', useless against the aircraft that flew above it, surrendered, 'reintegrated into civilisation and order' as was reported in the occupants' official dispatch.

A few days later, in his inaugural speech as mayor of Bilbao, the Falangist José María de Areilza warmly embraced the patriotic and anti-Basque atmosphere of the moment: 'Let us be clear about this: Bilbao has been conquered by force of arms (. . .) The winner has been a united, great and free Spain. We have seen the last of this fearsome sinister nightmare called Euskadi (. . .) Vizcaya is once again part of Spain *through military conquest, pure and simple*'.[19] A decree on 23 June repealed the Statute of Autonomy which had been passed by the Cortes of the Republic in October the previous year, and by virtue of Vizcaya and Guipuzcoa being considered 'treacherous provinces' they were stripped of the special economic and fiscal prerogatives that they had enjoyed since the end of the nineteenth century.

The 'united, great and free' Spain was then extended to Santander and in October to the republican zone of Asturias, with Gijón and Avilés as the last strongholds. With the fall of the industrial north and the control of iron production, the balance of power began to shift clearly towards the Nationalists, who had more men and better armaments at their disposal, as well as lines of communication to move their troops from one front to another. Franco was able to concentrate all his forces in the centre of Spain to attack Madrid again and the Mediterranean. The constant Nationalist victories began to spread a feeling of defeatism throughout the republican zone. International opinion believed that once the north was lost, the Nationalist victory was 'just a question of time'.[20]

From the summer of 1937 to the end of the year, Colonel Vicente Rojo, recently appointed by Juan Negrín as Chief of General Staff of the Republic, organised a defensive strategy aimed at limiting the Nationalist advance as far as possible, given the material superiority of the enemy and the difficulties involved in consolidating a true republican army. This was the objective of the surprise offensives in Brunete, near Madrid, in July 1937, to halt the Nationalist advance on Santander; in Belchite, near Zaragoza, in August and September, to delay the conquest of Asturias; and in Teruel, in December 1937, to pre-empt Franco's expected offensive on Madrid.[21]

This was because once the north had been occupied, Franco once again tried to attack the capital, via the Guadalajara sector, something which the Italians had attempted unsuccessfully a few months previously. Vicente Rojo, who had been promoted to general at the end of September, decided on a pre-emptive attack to conquer Teruel, the smallest of Aragón's three provincial capitals, with barely fifteen thousand inhabitants, of no military interest, although with a small garrison, and this enabled the taking of the first provincial capital by the republicans in the entire war.

Rojo, who personally directed the operation, moved some 40,000 men there, together with two of the divisions fighting on the Aragon front, the 11th, under Lister and the 25th under García Vivancos, as well as the Levante army, commanded by Colonel Juan Hernández Saravia. The attack, launched by Lister on 15 December 1937, caught the limited Nationalist forces that were defending the city, under the command of Colonel Domingo Rey d'Harcòurt, unawares, and counterattacks by Generals Varela and Aranda were encumbered by the extremely harsh weather conditions prevailing during that period.

On 22 December the republican tanks entered Teruel, an event captured in images spread throughout the world, although the defenders withdrew to the centre and took up positions in various buildings, in the midst of storms more typical of the Siberian climate, until on 7 January 1938 Rey d'Harcourt negotiated a surrender in which he asked 'for the lives of civilian personnel to be respected'.[22]

Teruel was retaken on 22 February by troops under the direction of General Juan Vigón, who deployed 100,000 men, including the Italian CTV. Once more Franco wanted to show that he would not cede an inch of territory to the republicans, let alone a provincial capital. Thus ended one of the cruellest battles of the civil war, with 40,000 Nationalist and over 60,000 republican casualties. In just a few weeks, Teruel went from being the republicans' biggest success, loudly trumpeted in their propaganda, to 'the biggest republican disaster in the whole war', because 'the Republic had set out to seize a city of no strategic value, which it could never have hoped to hold, all at a catastrophic cost in lives and equipment'.[23]

The disaster widened the breach between the communists and Indalecio Prieto, the Minister of Defence, who became the target of all their criticism, although General Vicente Rojo also began to be held responsible for the defeats in the reports that some of the Comintern delegates in Spain sent to Moscow. But Rojo was quite firm in his view that little could be done with 'the lack of materiel, the poor morale of our units, their incomplete organisation, and the

Battle of Teruel, December 1937–January 1938
(Archivo General de la Administración, Alcalá de Henares, Madrid)

ineptitude or incompetence of many of the commanders'. As he wrote to Prieto in his report of 26 February 1938, a few days after the withdrawal of the troops from Teruel: 'So far, we have only an outline (. . .), an embryonic organisation'. He also complained about the lack of discipline and how long it took to prepare the recruits that were joining the ranks.[24]

On the very morning that Teruel fell, Rojo presented his resignation to Prieto. Negrín, the Prime Minister, replied to him the following day that, the army of the Republic was in good hands with him, that he did not know of anybody who 'comes near you for your professional skill, composure, clear vision (. . .) precision and sense of organisation in your acts' and, as if that were not enough, 'above all these qualities', what he most admired about him was 'your human character'. As far as Negrín was concerned, blame for the defeats of the republican army could not be ascribed to the strategy of its top commander.

Leaving aside the overwhelming material superiority of the

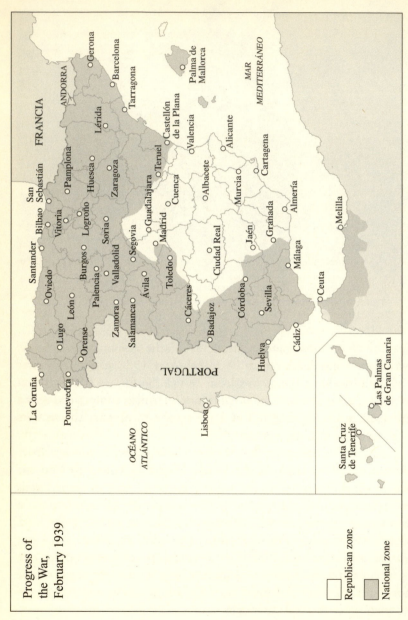

Spain: Republican and Nationalist territory, February 1939

Progress of
the War,
February 1939

Republican zone

National zone

OCÉANO
ATLÁNTICO

FRANCIA

ANDORRA

MAR
MEDITERRÁNEO

PORTUGAL

Lisboa

La Coruña
Pontevedra
Lugo
Orense
Oviedo
León
Santander
San
Sebastián
Bilbao
Vitoria
Pamplona
Logroño
Burgos
Palencia
Valladolid
Zamora
Salamanca
Ávila
Segovia
Soria
Zaragoza
Huesca
Lérida
Gerona
Barcelona
Tarragona
Teruel
Guadalajara
Madrid
Cuenca
Castellón
de la Plana
Valencia
Alicante
Albacete
Murcia
Cartagena
Toledo
Ciudad Real
Cáceres
Badajoz
Córdoba
Sevilla
Huelva
Cádiz
Jaén
Granada
Almería
Málaga
Ceuta
Melilla
Palma de
Mallorca

Santa Cruz
de Tenerife
Las Palmas
de Gran Canaria

Nationalist army, it was true that the state of the republican troops following the Teruel disaster was worrying, and this was shown just one month later in the major offensive that the Nationalists mounted through Aragón and Castellón to the sea. There was no let-up after so much attrition and Franco exploited the fact that he had more men in place there than the republicans, with higher morale and more equipment, in order to defeat the Aragón front and capture a vast expanse of territory.

On 9 March 1938, almost 200,000 men, backed up by hundreds of artillery pieces and air cover from the Condor Legion and the *Aviazione Legionaria*, attacked a front measuring over a hundred kilometres defended by 40,000 republicans. In barely two weeks they conquered the whole of the eastern half of Aragón, after extensive bombing on the population of various localities. On 17 March they entered Caspe, which had been the headquarters of the Council of Aragon and was now that of the republican authority that replaced it, the governor-general José Ignacio Mantecón. On 3 April, Yagüe's Morocco Corps entered Lérida, the first Catalonian capital to fall to the Nationalist troops, and they also occupied the power stations that supplied electricity to Barcelona. The campaign ended on 15 April on the Mediterranean coast. 'The victorious sword of Franco' said the Seville daily, *ABC,* the following day, 'has split the Spain still held by the reds into two'.

Air superiority was crucial for this swift conquest of a very broad front. Between 9 and 31 March, the rebel aircraft carried out 285 bombing raids, as against the republicans' 8. These events were the setting for the debut of the German Stuka aircraft, which subsequently made its mark in the Second World War. Trench warfare, which was chronicled on the same front by George Orwell during the early months of the war, with rifles and hardly any artillery, gave way to the lightning war of 1938, with the use of all the Italian and Condor Legion artillery and tanks. The bombing affected a large number of towns and villages, the heaviest of which was carried out by the Italians on Alcañiz, in the province of Teruel, on 3 March 1938, leaving over 250 dead amid the rubble.[25]

Split into two, and undergoing a serious economic crisis with its morale shattered, the Republic was languishing. Indalecio Prieto, who was quite open about his defeatism, resigned ('was driven out' as he put it) from the government of the Republic, which he had served both in peace and war. Outside Spain, things were no better because, on 20 February, Anthony Eden, the only minister in Neville Chamberlain's government who had not openly expressed any hostility towards the Republic, resigned as Foreign Secretary. On 16 April his successor in the Foreign Office, Lord Halifax, signed an agreement with Italy in which once again the British turned a blind eye to the Fascist intervention in Franco's camp. In France, after a short-lived government led by the socialist, Léon Blum, which lasted only thirty days, the radical Édouard Daladier took over that same month, and in June he once more closed the border with Spain. This was the grim situation that the Republic found itself in, and the government began to reform the Army of the East with all the units that had withdrawn to Catalonia. It needed to defend itself, resist, and at least prevent a swift collapse that would almost certainly be accompanied by an unconditional victory for Franco, while all the time hoping for a change in attitude towards the Republic on the international front.

The military rebels' advance through Catalonia seemed to be inevitable, it being the nearest and best objective given the state of the republican troops after the collapse of the Aragón front. But instead of launching a lightning attack on Barcelona, as he had been asked to do by his German and Italian allies, Franco ordered his men to advance from Teruel to Castellón, Sagunto and Valencia. They took Castellón on 13 June, although the offensive on Valencia, the main objective of this campaign, initiated a few days later, came up against an effective republican defence and the Nationalist army was held up less than fifty kilometres from what, for one year, had been the capital of the Republic.

Franco insisted on the idea of a long drawn-out war of attrition, in which he would conclusively crush the Republic. He had a vast army and his strategy was always at the service of his political ambitions, to consolidate power among his brothers in arms. His strategy destroyed the enemy, but also 'it cost the lives of thousands of his own troops and prolonged the suffering of the civilian population of his zone'. As far as he was concerned, casualties and suffering were 'inevitable issues in war'.[26]

The decision to attack Valencia instead of advancing on Barcelona kept Catalonia out of danger for a while and enabled the republican army to reorganise at the end of spring and beginning of summer 1938, with the mobilising of new drafts, among them one of young people born in 1920 and 1921, known as 'the feeding-bottle draft'. With all these new reorganised troops, General Rojo drew up a plan to unite the Levante with Catalonia once more, with an offensive along the River Ebro. On the night of 24 to 25 July, several units of the republican army, under the command of the communist Juan Modesto, crossed the river in boats. Thus began the Battle of the Ebro, the longest and harshest of the whole war.

Almost all the commanders in this ad hoc Army of the Ebro were communists. The commander-in-chief was Lieutenant-Colonel Juan Modesto, and on his staff were Enrique Lister, who commanded the 5th Army Corps and Lieutenant-Colonel Manuel Tagüeña, a physics and mathematics student who had begun the war in the ranks and ended up commanding the 15th Army Corps. They crossed the river at various locations, from Fayón in the north to Miravete in the south. The initial advance, as was normal in these republican actions, was considerable, but it was quickly halted, as also was normal. And Franco acted as he had done on previous occasions, in Brunete, Belchite and Teruel and began to regain the lost ground.

At first the battle looked like a tactical victory for the republicans, as they had succeeded in putting a brake on the Nationalist offensive on Valencia, but almost throughout it was a defensive battle whose aim was to tire the adversary and force them to negotiate a victory that was less unconditional, rather than to defeat them, which was impossible. 250,000 men fought for nearly four months, until 16 November. The Nationalists lost over thirty thousand men (dead and wounded) and the republicans double that number, although leading military historians disagree over the exact number of dead, some 13,000 in total, spread almost equally between the two sides. The Republic had lost the best of its army and soon afterwards the whole of Catalonia.

The Republic by now seemed to have been defeated, particularly because the Munich Pact, signed at the end of September, enabling Hitler to advance freely on Czechoslovakia, broke Negrín's resist-

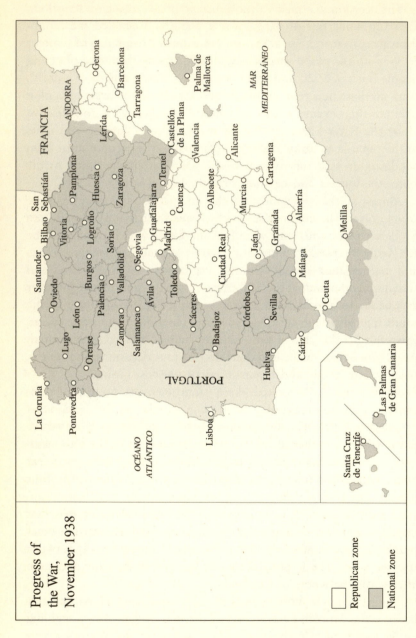

Progress of
the War,
November 1938

Republican zone

National zone

Spain: Republican and Nationalist territory, November 1938

ance strategy and showed that the democracies had no intention of changing their policy of appeasement of the Fascist powers. On 7 November, Franco told the vice-president of *United Press*, James Miller, something that he had repeatedly insisted on throughout that year: 'There will be no negotiated peace. There will be no negotiated peace because the criminals and their victims cannot live side by side'.[27]

Rojo's opinion after the defeat in Teruel was still the same after the Battle of the Ebro: all they had was an 'outline' of an army, 'an organisation in its embryonic state'. Policy and military strategy did not always coincide in the republican camp. And there was more conflict and disunity than in the nationalist camp. Hunger created dissatisfaction and protests as the war went on, and one defeat after another ended up by demoralising large sectors of the population that abandoned their commitment to the values and material interests they were fighting for.

The civil war in the republican camp began with a revolution and ended with a desperate attempt by Negrín to introduce a democratic and disciplined alternative which would bring about a change in French and British policy, and which many people, particularly anarchists and the socialist left, saw as a communist dictatorship, because of the Republic's dependence on the Soviet Union for military equipment and for the rise of communist militants in the republican army.

The military rebels, despite the disparity of their coalition forces, never had any problems of that type. Aid from the Fascist powers was more readily available and the military authorities, under the sole command of Franco, exercised firm control on the home front. Those who shared their values were enjoying the renaissance of a new Spain because their army always won its battles and so loss of morale was never an issue. But for those who did not support them, a savage violence awaited them, starting from the very day of the uprising, a violence that did not cease until many years after the end of the war.

DEFEAT

The end of the Republic had already been a foregone conclusion since the Munich Pact and defeat in the Battle of the Ebro, but its last three months were particularly painful. The whole of Catalonia fell to Franco's troops in barely a month, in the midst of patriotic and religious fervour. They entered Tarragona in the middle of January 1939 and Barcelona on 26 January. Three days later, Sunday 29 January, a multitudinous open-air mass was celebrated in the Plaza de Cataluña, presided over by General Juan Yagüe.

The republican troops retreated in a rabble to the French border. According to Manuel Azaña's description, 'the horde just kept on growing to immeasurable proportions. A crazed mob jammed the roads, and spilled onto shortcuts, looking for the frontier. It was one solid mass of humanity stretching fifteen kilometres along the road. Some women had miscarriages at the roadside. There were children who died from the cold or were trampled to death'.[28] Large numbers of people were either killed or injured by bombing and machine gun fire from Nationalist aircraft.

With the fall of Barcelona and the conquest of Catalonia, the Republic was in its death throes. The governments of Great Britain and France finally officially recognised Franco's government and on 27 February 1939 Manuel Azaña, who had crossed over into France three weeks previously, resigned as president of the Republic. Before that, on 1 February, in the last of the Cortes sessions, Juan Negrín asked that, as a condition for surrender, there would be no persecutions or reprisals, an impossible request in the plans of Franco and his brothers in arms. On 6 March, following the coup led by Colonel Segismundo Casado against his government to negotiate the surrender of arms and men to Franco, Negrín abandoned Spain.

Casado's coup was not only the culmination of a political conflict but also 'the rebellion of the officers' against the republican government, whose legitimacy they no longer recognised. It also substantialised their idea that 'it would be easier to settle the war through an understanding between officers'.[29] It was the beginning of a desperate, fratricidal struggle in this dying Republic, with offshoots in other parts of the central zone and Cartagena, which

'"The war is over", said the last official report issued by Franco's GHQ on 1 April 1939'.

achieved not an 'honourable peace' but an unconditional surrender, something which Franco, the officers, the civil authorities and the Catholic Church never tired of announcing – in other words, the annihilation of the republican regime and its supporters.

Still to come was the drama of Alicante. Some 15,000 people, consisting of senior officers, republican politicians, combatants and civilians had been assembling in the port since 29 March. At dawn the following day, Italian troops of the Vittorio Division, commanded by General Gastone Gambara, arrived in the city before most of this assemblage was able to board French and British ships. Many of those captured were executed on the spot. Others preferred to kill themselves before becoming victims of Nationalist repression. Among these was the anarchist schoolteacher, Evaristo Viñuales, ex-councillor for Information and Propaganda in the Council of Aragón. He committed suicide with his fellow-anarchist, Máximo Franco, head of the 127th Mixed Brigade of the 28th Division.

'Today, with the red Army captured and disarmed, our victorious troops have achieved their final military objectives. The war is over', said the the last official report issued by Franco's GHQ on 1 April 1939, read by the broadcaster and actor, Fernando Fernández de Córdoba.

Catholicism and the Fatherland had coalesced, liberated by the redeeming power of the cross. The war had been necessary and inevitable because 'Spain could not be saved by conventional means', wrote Leopoldo Eijo y Garay, Bishop of Madrid, in his pastoral letter '*La hora presente*', issued on 28 March, the day of the 'liberation' of the capital. It was 'the moment for settling mankind's account with the political philosophy of the French Revolution'.[30]

Almost a thousand days of war had left long-lasting scars on Spanish society in its wake. The total number of dead, according to historians, was nearly 600,000, of whom 100,000 were due to the repression unleashed by the military rebels, and 55,000 due to the violence in the republican zone. Half a million people were crowded in prisons and concentration camps.

Although in the First World War, one could already see the vast potential of the development of air warfare for modern armies, the Spanish Civil War was the first twentieth-century wars in which aviation was used deliberately in bombing raids behind the lines. Italian S-81s and S-79s, German He-111s and Russian *Katiuskas* turned Spain into a test bench for the major world war that was on the horizon. Madrid, Durango, Guernica, Alcañiz, Lérida, Barcelona, Valencia, Alicante and Cartagena were among the cities whose defenceless populations became military targets.

Bombing by the Nationalist, Italian and German planes accounted for over 11,000 lives, over 2,500 of which were in Barcelona, while deaths caused by republican and Soviet aircraft, according to the official figures given by the victors, numbered 1,088 up to May 1938. The intervention of Italian and German air power was a decisive factor in hastening the Nationalist victory. The sole objective of the majority of bombing raids was to terrorise and spread panic among the population, and many of them occurred in Catalonian and Levantine cities from the end of 1938, by which time the result of the war was in little doubt.[31]

The officers who rose up in July 1936 won the war because they had the best trained troops in the Spanish army, they had economic power, they were more united than the republican camp and the winds of international sympathy blew their way. After the First World War and the triumph of the revolution in Russia, no civil war could be said to be exclusively 'internal' any more. When the Spanish Civil War began, the democratic powers were attempting to 'appease' the Fascist powers at all costs, especially Nazi Germany, instead of opposing those who were really threatening the balance of power. Thus the Republic found itself at an enormous disadvantage in having to wage war on a group of military rebels who from the very start were the beneficiaries of this international situation that was so favourable to their interests.

The Republic was not short of money or armaments. In fact, losing the war cost the Republic almost as much as Franco spent in winning it, some six hundred million dollars on each side, but the war materiel the Republic acquired using Bank of Spain gold reserves was inferior, both in quantity and quality, to that which the Fascist powers supplied to the military rebels. And the most important factor was that Franco received this aid constantly, while the Soviet aid depended, among other things, on the entente between Moscow and the western democratic powers.

Because the arms came to republican Spain by sea and depended on the policies of Stalin, naval monitoring by the Non-Intervention Committee and the fluctuations of French politics as to whether to allow the shipments to go through or not, 'there were constant ups and downs in the supply line, and they could find themselves without arms or munition at the most vital or critical moment'.[32] Thus, at the end of 1937 and in 1938 shipments were either interrupted or blocked at the French border. The expanionist policies of the Fascist powers and 'appeasement', defended by Great Britain and supported by France, played a major role in the development and outcome of the Spanish Civil War.

The two sides in Spain were so different from the point of view of ideas, of how they wanted to organise the State and society, and they were so committed to the objectives that led them to take up arms, that it was hard to come to an agreement. And the international context did not allow for negotiations either. Thus, the war ended with one side obliterating the other, a victory thereafter associated with the killings and atrocities that were then spreading throughout almost every country in Europe.

Dictatorships dominated by totalitarian governments of just one man and one party were at that time replacing democracy in many countries of Europe, and except for the Soviet Union, all of these dictatorships rested on the ideas of order and authority of the extreme right. Six of the most solid democracies on the continent were invaded by the Nazis during the year following the end of the civil war. Thus Spain was no exception, nor was it the only country in which the ideas of order and extreme Nationalism replaced those of democracy and revolution. The victory of Franco was also a victory for Hitler and Mussolini. And the defeat of the Republic was also a defeat for the democracies.

Epilogue

AN UNCIVIL PEACE

After the official conclusion of the civil war on 1 April 1939, the destruction of the vanquished became an absolute priority. There began a new period of mass executions, prison and torture for thousands of men and women. The collapse of the republican army in the spring of 1939 meant that hundreds of thousands of prisoners were sent to prisons and improvised concentration camps. In late 1939 and throughout 1940, there were over 270,000 prisoners, according to official sources, a figure that constantly fell in the following two years because of the numerous executions and thousands of deaths from illness and starvation. At least 50,000 people were executed between 1939 and 1946.

The invasion of France by the German troops, which began on 10 May 1940, brought about the capture of thousands of Spanish republicans who had fled to French territory after the conquest of Catalonia by Franco's troops and the end of the civil war. Many of them were exterminated in Nazi concentration camps. Some of the more prominent of these republicans were wanted by the Interior Ministry and were handed over to the Nationalist authorities by the Gestapo and the Vichy regime.[1]

On 21 October, a summary trial condemned several of them to death. Among them was Julián Zugazagoitia, Minister of the Interior during the Republic, who was executed on 9 November. A few days earlier, on 15 October, Lluís Companys, president of the

Generalitat, faced the firing squad, accused of 'military rebellion'. Also handed over around this time was Joan Peiró, the anarchist Minister for Industry in Largo Caballero's government, whose date with the firing squad came in July 1942. All three had systematically denounced the brutal violence of the summer of 1936 in the republican zone and had helped to save the lives of a good many right-wing politicians and members of the clergy.

The political culture of violence and division between victors and vanquished, 'patriots and traitors' or 'nationalists and reds', prevailed in Spanish society for at least two decades following the end of the civil war. The vanquished who managed to survive had to adapt to the norms of coexistence imposed by the victors. Many lost their jobs; others, particularly in rural areas, were forced to move to new cities or villages. Accused and denounced, it was the militants of republican political parties and trade unions who came off worst. For those who were not so firmly committed, many of them illiterate, Francoism imposed silence in order for them to survive, forcing them to erase their own identity.

There were those who showed resistance to the dictatorship, the so-called *maquis* or guerrillas. Their origins lay in the '*huidos*' (fugitives), those who in order to escape repression by the military rebels had taken refuge at various stages of the civil war in the mountains of Andalusia, Asturias, León and Galicia, in the knowledge that they could not return if they wanted to stay alive. Early resistance by these fugitives, and all those who refused to bow to the victors, gradually gave way to a more organised armed struggle that emulated the characteristics of the anti-fascist resistance which had been tried out in France against the Nazis. Although many socialists and anarchists fought in the guerrilla bands, only the PCE gave full support to this armed response. In the 1940s, some 7,000 maquis took part in armed activities in the various mountain areas that covered Spanish soil, and some 70,000 contacts or collaborators ended up in prison for giving their support. If Civil Guard sources are to be believed, 2,713 guerrillas and 300 members of the armed forces died in clashes.

The exodus that began at the end of January 1939, with the fall of Barcelona, also left its mark. Never, in her long history of exiles, had Spain known one of such a type, for its dimension and duration, nor had France ever received on her soil such a massive and sudden exodus as the arrival of the Spanish republicans in 1939. This despite the fact that the history of Spain, since the '*afrancesados*' (a perjorative term to denote those who adopted French ideas and customs) and liberals of 1814, was a history of political exile, and in the 1920s and 30s France saw the mass influx of foreigners that made her the world's leading country for immigration: workers (Polish and Italian) and refugees (Russian, Armenian, Jews from eastern Europe and Italian, German and Austrian anti-fascists).

'The withdrawal', as this great exile of 1939 was known, saw some 450,000 refugees fleeing to France in the first three months of that year, of whom 170,000 were women, children and the elderly. Some 200,000 returned in the following months, to continue their living hell in the Francoist dictatorship gaols. Another 15,000 managed to sail from the ports of the Levante to northern Africa, where the French authorities received them with the same hostility as in France. The three prime ministers of the Republic during the war died in exile: José Giral in Mexico in 1962; Francisco Largo Caballero in Paris, in 1946, having passed through the Nazi concentration camp of Orianenburg; and in the same city, Juan Negrín died in 1956. Manuel Azaña, the president of the Republic and Spain's most important politician of the 1930s, died in Montauban, France, on 3 November 1940.

France was not expecting this massive influx of refugees and Édouard Daladier's government of centre-right 'concentration', which had been unsympathetic to the republican cause during the civil war, was firmly pressurised by the most reactionary right-wing groups, Fascists and xenophobes, and by the media, to avoid the 'invasion' of this 'Marxist army in retreat'. In just over three weeks, 450,000 refugees arrived in the département of Pyrénées-Orientales, which had barely a quarter of a million inhabitants. Once there, most of them, particularly civilian men and former republican army combatants, were transferred to internment or concentration camps, on the beach at Argelès and Saint-Cyprien, Vallespir and Cerdanya. The 275,000 interns in camps in March 1939 gradually decreased in

Exiled Spanish Republicans on the French border
(Ministerio de Cultura)

number, until there were only a few thousand one year later, when the Nazis invaded France.

From then on, some 40,000 Spanish republicans were transferred to Germany to work in war industries, and many of them ended up in concentration camps, especially in Mathausen, where 5,000 of the 7,000 interned there died. In Vichy France, Germany and Algeria during the Second World War, the Spanish republicans were treated as 'reds' who had no right to live. It marked the prolongation of the murders, persecutions and humiliations for the vanquished, their children and their children's children. 'Here only death grants freedom' said Major Caboche on receiving the Spanish survivors of the Durruti Column in Djelfa camp in Algeria (where the writer Max Aub was held from November 1941 to October 1942).[2]

The unconditional victory of General Francisco Franco's troops on 1 April 1939 saw the beginning of the last of the dictatorships to be established in Europe before the Second World War. Franco's dictatorship, like that of Hitler, Mussolini or other right-wing dictators of those years, was based on the rejection of liberal democracy and revolution by large sectors of society who asked instead for an authoritarian solution that would maintain order and fortify the State.

A few hours after announcing the defeat of the red army, the *Generalísimo* received a telegram from Pius XII, the former Cardinal Pacelli, who had been elected Pope on 2 March that year, after the unexpected death of his predecessor Pius XI on 10 February: 'With heart uplifted to the Lord, we sincerely give thanks, along with Your Excellency, for this long-desired Catholic victory in Spain. It is our express wish that this beloved country, now that peace has been attained, adopts with new vigour its former Christian traditions that made her so great'.

Such a victory deserved an apostolic blessing. And Franco was extremely grateful: 'Intense emotion at paternal telegram from Your Holiness on occasion of total victory of our arms, which in heroic Crusade have fought against enemies of Religion, the Fatherland and Christian civilisation. The long-suffering Spanish people, along with Your Holiness, also lifts its heart to the Lord, who granted it His mercy, and asks for His protection for the work to come'.[3]

Things returned to normal. Franco's victory in the war represented the absolute triumph of Catholic Spain. Catholicism once more became the official State religion. All the republican measures that the right and the Church had cursed were repealed. The Church recovered all its institutional privileges, some of them all at once, others gradually. And the Catholic Church enjoyed a long period of prosperity, with a regime that protected it, heaped privileges upon it, defended its doctrines and squashed its enemies.[4]

From April 1939 onwards, Spain experienced the peace of Franco, the consequences of the war and of those that caused it. Spain was left divided between victors and vanquished. From before the ending of the war, the churches were filled with plaques commemorating those who had 'fallen in the service of God and the Fatherland'. On the other hand, thousands of Spaniards killed by the violence initiated by the military rebels in July 1936 were never registered nor even had an insignificant tombstone to remember them by, and their families are still searching for their remains today. The reformist discourse of the Republic and all that that form of government meant was swept up and scattered over the graves of thousands of citizens; and the workers' movement, its organisations and its culture was systematically eliminated in a process that was more violent than that suffered by other anti-Fascist movements in Europe. This was the 'surgical operation on the social body of Spain', so vehemently demanded by the military rebels, the land-owning classes and the Catholic Church.

The climate of order, *patria* and religion overrode that of democracy, the Republic and revolution. In short, in Franco's long and cruel dictatorship lies the exceptional nature of Spain's twentieth-century history if it is compared to that of other western capitalist countries. It was the only dictatorship, apart from that of Antonio de Oliveira Salazar in Portugal, set up in inter-war Europe to survive the Second World War. With Hitler and Mussolini dead, Franco continued for thirty years more. The darkest side of this European civil war, this time of hate, that ended in 1945, was to live on in Spain for a long time yet.

Notes

Introduction: The Roots of the Conflict

1   Edward H. Carr, *The Twenty Years' Crisis. An Introduction to the Study of International Relations*, published in 1939, although the edition I have used is the one published by Harper & Row, New York, 1964.

2   A word derived from *cacique*, the name denoting an Indian chief in the Spanish Empire. In the nineteenth century, and up to the Republic, it referred to the common organisation of social and political control, whereby the *cacique* controlled the elections and handed out favours to his political cronies. 340).

3   Manuel Tuñón de Lara, who died in 1997, used 'power block' as an analytical category in a large proportion of his work, beginning with *Historia y realidad del poder. El poder y las elites en el primer tercio de la España del siglo XX,* Edicusa, Madrid, 1967.

4   An analysis of this Republic, its achievements and limitations, as well as the hounding it received, from above and below, may be found in my book *The Spanish Republic and Civil War,* Cambridge University Press, Cambridge, 2010, pp. 7–149.

5   José María Gil Robles, *No fue posible la paz,* Ariel, Barcelona, 1968, p. 32

6   The best study on the agricultural reform is still the one by Edward Malefakis, *Agrarian Reform and Peasant Revolution in Spain*, Yale University Press, New Haven, 1971.

7   Up until the formation of the CNT, anarchism, which had come to Spain in the 1870s, had had a limited foothold. But it emerged as a mass movement towards the end of the first decade of the twentieth century and its overwhelming acceptance in Barcelona, the most modern and indistrialised city in Spain, turned it into something exceptional,

atypical, among the countries of western Europe. A synthesis of the methods of protest, groups and insurrections by the anarchists during the Second Republic may be found in my book, *Anarchism, The Republic and Civil War in Spain 1931–1939*, Routledge, London, 2004.

8 A police force, under military organisation and discipline, set up in 1844 to maintain order in the rural environment. While it was feared by workers and farm labourers for its repressive methods, for others, particularly the landowners, the Civil Guard was the symbol of authority and guarantee of order, and it remained as such during the Republic.

9 Mark Mazower, *Dark Continent: Europe's Twentieth Century*, Penguin Books, London, 1999, p. 23.

10 After the proclamation of the Republic, Ramiro Ledesma Ramos, a young intellectual, and Onésimo Redondo, an extreme Catholic lawyer, sponsored the *Juntas de Ofensiva Nacional Sindicalista* (JONS). At the beginning of 1934, the Falangists merged with the JONS to form the *Falange Española de las JONS*, remaining until the spring of 1936 as a minority organisation with just a few thousand affiliates. The Falange failed to win a seat in February 1936 elections.

11 'Copy of the documents furnished by Lieutenant-Colonel Emilio Fernández Cordón, concerning the preparation and running of the National Uprising' (75 pages), kept in the Military History Service in Madrid.

12 On July 4 1936, the wealthy businessman, Juan March, who had previously financed Sanjurjo's coup in 1932, as well as other monarchist conspiracies against the Republic, provided the money to obtain the aircraft that was to take Franco from the Canary Islands to Morocco. The aircraft, a De Havilland Dragon Rapide, was chartered two days later in England with the £2,000 provided by March, by Luis Bolín, the London correspondent of the newspaper *ABC*.

1. Spain Split In Half

1 Santiago Casares Quiroga (1884), a left-wing republican lawyer, had been Interior Minister in the republican-socialist coalition government led by Manuel Azaña between October 1931 and September 1933. After the February 1936 elections, Azaña appointed him a minister again, this time in Public Works. In April of that year, Niceto Alcalá Zamora was dismissed as president of the Republic by the Cortes and on 10 May Manuel Azaña became the new Head of State. He appointed Casares Quiroga, one of his most faithful collaborators, as Prime Minister, and he in turn took on the Ministry of War as well. This government, made up of left-wing republicans only, since the socialists refused to take part, has passed into history as the weak government that permitted

conflicts and political violence, instead of repressing them, and which was unable to stop the military coup, the blame for which has tended to be placed on Casares Quiroga's shoulders.

2 Gabriel Cardona, *Historia militar de una guerra civil. Estrategias y tácticas de la guerra de España,* Flor del Viento, Barcelona, 2006, p. 33.

3 Paul Preston, *Franco. A Biography*, HarperCollinsPublishers, London, 1993, pp. 144–170.

4 Paul Preston, *A Concise History of the Spanish Civil War*, Fontana Press, London, 1996, p. 87.

5 Pablo Martín Aceña, *El oro de Moscú y el oro de Berlín,* Taurus, Madrid, 2001.

6 *Rapport fait au nom de la Commission chargée d'enquêter sur les événements survenus en France du 1933 à 1945*, Imprimerie de l'Assemblée Nationale, 1951, reproduced in Enrique Moradiellos, *El reñidero de Europa. Las dimensiones internacionales de la guerra civil española,* Península, Barcelona, 2001, pp. 268–271. Léon Blum had been appointed Prime Minister of France in June 1936, after the previous month's elections won by the Popular Front coalition. The government was made up of socialists and the Radical Party. In Spain, following the *Frente Popular*'s victory in the February 1936 elections, only the left-wing republicans took part in government. Subsequent references to this matter come from Blum's *Rapport*.

7 Quoted in Enrique Moradiellos, *El reñidero de Europa*, p. 79.

8 *Ibidem*, p. 87 and 81 for Baldwin's directive to Eden.

9 The 'confidential instructions' signed by General Mola as 'The Director' are reproduced in 'Copy of the documents furnished by Lieutenant-Colonel Emilio Fernández Cordón, concerning the preparation and running of the National Uprising' (75 pages), kept in the Military History Service in Madrid.

10 The Carlists, officially known as *Comunión Tradicionalista*, and with a paramilitary branch, the *requetés*, were monarchists, heirs of the political and social movement originating in the 1830s around the *Infante* Carlos, the brother of Fernando VII, who was in dispute with Isabel, the latter's daughter, and the Bourbon dynasty that reigned in Spain until 1931. During the Second Republic, their positions became radicalised, although their penetration remained restricted to the traditional hubs of the provinces of Álava and Navarre. Their doctrines and practices during the Republic and civil war are fully analysed in Martin Blinkhorn, *Carlism and Crisis in Spain 1931–1939,* Cambridge University Press, Cambridge, 1975.

11 George Orwell, *Homage to Catalonia,* Secker and Warburg, London, 1938, pp. 4–5

12 Francisco Lacruz, *El Alzamiento, la revolución y el terror en Barcelona,* Librería Arysel, Barcelona, 1943, p. 129.

13   Juan García Oliver, *El eco de los pasos,* Ruedo Ibérico, Madrid, 1978, p. 347. The anarchists, traditional defenders of anti-politics and non-intervention in politics, and radical critics of governments and States, took on four ministries for six months in the government led by the socialist Francisco Largo Caballero, a unique event in world history. The *paseo* (a walk) was the euphemism used to describe the murder of thousands of people in the two zones that divided Spain following the military coup, particularly during 1936. *Dar el paseo* (to take a walk) meant to seize the victim, murder him and leave him in a ditch, well, mineshaft or common grave.

14   '*Saca*' (removal): a term used in the civil war to denote the operation of removing prisoners from gaol to murder them in the countryside, usually at night. There were *sacas* on both home fronts, but a great many of them occurred in November 1936 in the Madrid gaols, from where tens of thousands of officers and right-winger were 'removed' and taken to Paracuellos del Jarama to be murdered.

15   Ian Gibson, *Federico García Lorca: A Life*, Faber and Faber, London, 1989. Ian Gibson maintains elsewhere that, in view of García Lorca's reputation, Major Valdés made an enquiry about the poet to General Gonzalo Queipo de Llano, the leader of the rebels in Andalusia. Apparently he answered him with the by now famous phrase 'give him coffee, plenty of coffee': *Queipo de Llano. Sevilla, verano de 1936*, Grijalbo, Barcelona, 1986, p. 106.

16   This marked the beginning of the legend of the Falangist martyr, cleverly cultivated by Franco. Throughout the dictatorship, solemn memorial services were held to honour José Antonio on the anniversary of his execution, and fate, or medicine, saw to it that Franco was to die on 20 November as well (1975). After the civil war, José Antonio Primo de Rivera's remains were taken from Alicante to the monastery of El Escorial, remaining there two decades, afforded the honours of a king, intricately united to the Spanish imperial past. When the *Valle de los Caídos* (Valley of the Fallen) was opened on 1 April 1959, two decades after Franco planned to build it as 'the magnificent temple (. . .) of those who fell for God and the Fatherland', José Antonio's remains were transferred there, to rest beside those of Franco.

17   One of the first accounts about everything that was known about his death sixty years later may be found in Santos Juliá (coordinator), Julián Casanova, Josep María Solé i Sabaté, Joan Villarroya & Francisco Moreno, *Víctimas de la guerra civil*, Temas de Hoy, Madrid, 1999. Since then, there has been a wealth of studies on the Francoist repression both during and after the war. The most ambitious and exhaustive analysis is Paul Preston's recently published *El holocausto español. Odio y exterminio en la Guerra Civil y después*, Debate, Barcelona, 2011 (English edition: *The Spanish Holocaust. Inquisition and*

Extermination in Twentieth Century Spain, Harper Collins, London; W. W. Norton, New York, 2012.

18 On the night of 22 to 23 August, a group of militiamen selected several out of the almost two thousand inmates who were at the time crowded into the Modelo prison. In that self-same spot they murdered several officers, right-wingers and politicians. Among them were the Falangists Fernando Primo de Rivera and Julio Ruiz de Alda; the founder of the *Partido Nacionalista* José Albiñana, several ministers in the republican governments of 1934–1935 and the elderly political expert, Melquíades Álvarez, aged seventy-two, and champion of reformism in Spain during the first third of the twentieth century. Manuel Azaña, who was still President of the Republic, recalled a year later his 'consternation, sadness and desolation at the murder of these well-known people': *El cuaderno de la Pobleta,* published in 1937, to be found in Manuel Azaña, *Memorias políticas y de guerra,* Crítica, Barcelona, 1981, vol. II, pp. 282–283.

19 Concerning the 'complex structure of popular justice', see Glicerio Sánchez Recio, *Justicia y guerra en España: Los Tribunales Populares (1936–1939),* Instituto de Cultura "Juan Gil-Albert", Alicante, 1991.

20 Juan García Oliver, *El eco de los pasos,* p. 347.

21 The information on Emili Darder comes from Jean Schalekamp, *Mallorca, any 1936. D'una illa hom no en pot fugir,* Prensa Universitaria, Palma de Mallorca, 1937, p. 125.

22 Georges Bernanos, *Los grandes cementerios bajo la luna,* Alianza Ed., Madrid, 1986. In this book Bernanos, a deeply religious writer, denounced the complicity of the clergy and the Bishop, José Miralles, with the violence of the rebels, particularly in the killing that took place in the cemetery at Manacor, where two hundred citizens were killed and then burnt in a heap. The bishop had sent there 'one of his priests who, with his shoes steeped in blood, gave absolution in the midst of the shots' (p. 84).

23 Manuel Azaña, *Los españoles en guerra,* Crítica, Barcelona, 1982, p. 19.

24 Ibidem, pp. 74–75.

2. Holy War and Anticlerical Hatred

1 Joan Connelly Ullman, 'The Warp and Woof of Parliamentary Politics in Spain, 1808–1939: Anticlericalism versus "Neo-Catholicism"', *European Studies Review,* vol. 13, 2 (1983), p. 155.

2 Feliciano Montero, *El primer catolicismo social y la 'Rerum Novarum' en España, 1899–1902,* CSIC, Madrid, 1983, p. 401, in which he gives a good account of the 'retardation' of Spanish, as opposed to

European, social Catholicism during those years.

3 Cited by Hilari Raguer, 'La cuestión religiosa', in Santos Juliá, ed., 'Política en la Segunda Republica', *Ayer,* 20 (1995), p. 232.

4 The significance of Azaña's sentence, from his historic speech in the Cortes on 13 October 1931, is included in Santos Juliá, *Manuel Azaña, una biografía política. Del Ateneo al Palacio Nacional,* Alianza Editorial, Madrid, 1990, pp. 132–133.

5 Santos Juliá, *Manuel Azaña,* pp. 242–243.

6 Quoted in Domingo Benavides, 'Maximiliano Arboleya y su interpretación de la revolución de octubre', in Gabriel Jackson *et al.,* *Octubre 1934. Ciencuenta años para la reflexión,* Siglo XXI, Madrid, 1985, p. 262.

7 Borja de Riquer, *El último Cambó 1936–1947. La tentación autoritaria*, Grijalbo, Barcelona, 1997, p. 31.

8 Bruce Lincoln, 'Revolutionary Exhumations in Spain, July 1936', *Comparative Studies in Society and History,* vol. 27, 2 (1985), pp. 241–260.

9 Quoted in Hilari Raguer, *La Espada y la Cruz (La Iglesia, 1936–1939),* Bruguera, Barcelona, 1977, p. 27.

10 'Thy kingdom come'. See Martin Blinkhorn, *Carlismo y contrarrevolución en España,* pp. 319–347.

11 'Report on the civil-military uprising in Spain in July 1936' signed at the Belascoin spa resort (Navarre) on 13 August 1936, reproduced in *Archivo Gomá. Documentos de la Guerra Civil. 1: Julio-Diciembre 1936* in the edition by José Andrés-Gallego and Antón M. Pazos, CSIC, Madrid, 2001, pp. 80–89 (hereafter referred to as *Archivo Gomá*). For the link established during the war between Gomá, the Holy See and General Franco, see María Luisa Rodríguez Aisa, *El cardenal Gomá y la guerra de España. Aspectos de la gestión pública del Primado 1936–1939,* CSIC, Madrid, 1981. The argument that the military rebellion was carried out to prevent a Communist uprising organised from Moscow was one of the great lies propagated by the military rebels and later by the victors, shot down several years ago by Herbert Rutledge Southworth in *El mito de la cruzada de Franco*, Ruedo Ibérico, Paris, 1963.

12 *Carta colectiva de los Obispos españoles a los de todo el mundo con motivo de la Guerra de España* (Collective letter from the Spanish Bishops to the bishops in the rest of the world on the occasion of the War in Spain), signed on 1 July 1937, reproduced in the *Boletín Eclesiástico del Arzobispado de Burgos*, 31 August 1937, pp. 180–213, which is the copy I use in this book. With a slightly different title it is reproduced, along with other important episcopal and pontifical documents, in Antonio Montero Moreno, *Historia de la persecución religiosa en España 1936–1939*, BAC, Madrid, 1999 edition (first edition 1961),

pp. 726–741. Gomá, primate of the Spanish bishops, died on 22 August 1940. Pla y Deniel, only seven years younger than Gomá, took his place in 1941. When he died in 1968, shortly before his ninety-second birthday, one of the ecclesiatical artifacts of the crusade and Franco perished with him.

13 Enrique Pla y Deniel, 'Las dos ciudades' (The Two Cities), 30–IX-1936, reproduced in Antonio Montero Moreno, *Historia de la persecución religiosa en España*, pp. 688–708.

14 Alfonso Álvarez Bolado, *Para ganar la guerra, para ganar la paz. Iglesia y Guerra Civil: 1936–1939*, Universidad Pontificia de Comillas, Madrid, 1995, pp. 50–53, the fundamental book for discovering, with the aid of first-hand official documents, how 'the Church was involved and involved itself' (p. 22) in the military uprising and civil war.

15 Quoted in *ibidem*, p. 54.

16 'Informe acerca del levantamiento militar', p. 87.

17 Alfonso Álvarez Bolado, *Para ganar la guerra, para ganar la paz*, pp. 55–56.

18 Quoted in Ronald Fraser, *Recuérdalo tú y recuérdalo a otros,* vol. I, pp. 209–210.

19 Fernando Díaz-Plaja, *La guerra de España en sus documentos,* Plaza y Janés, Barcelona, 1973, p. 87.

20 'Report from Cardinal Gomá to the Secretariat of State. Third general report on the situation in Spain on the occasion of the civil-military uprising of July 1936' (24 October 1936), in *Archivo Gomá*, pp. 245–252.

21 *Ibidem*. Paul Preston's account in *Franco*, p. 188.

22 'Letter from Cardinal Gomá to Cardinal Pacelli', 9 November 1936, *Archivo Gomá, pp. 289–293.*

23 I follow here the account by Paul Preston, *Franco*, pp. 243–47.

24 For the background of the collective letter, see Hilari Raguer in *La Espada y la Cruz*, pp. 102–119. I have also followed the documented summary by María Luisa Rodríguez Aisa, 'La Carta del Episcopado' in 'La Guerra Civil', *Historia 16*, vol. 13 (1986), pp. 56–63. The archbishop of Tarragona, Francesc Vidal i Barraquer, ended up in Italy, having managed to escape the revolutionary outbreak in Catalonia in the summer of 1936. He maintained a permanent critical position with regard to the close link between the rebel officers and the Catholic Church and did not return to Spain after Franco's victory.

25 See note 12 of this chapter.

26 Alfonso Álvarez Bolado, *Para ganar la guerra, para ganar la paz*, p. 159. He examines the international repercussion of the Collective Letter on pp. 207–09.

27 Gumersindo de Estella wrote some chilling memoirs on this violence and, atypically, from within the Church, denounced 'the political abuse

of religion'. His memoirs remained unpublished for a time and have recently been published under the title *Fusilados en Zaragoza, 1936–1939. Tres años de asistencia espiritual a los reos,* Mira Editores, Zaragoza, 2003.

28 The Jesuit priest Eduardo Fernández Regatillo, one of the most famous canon law experts and moralists at the time, went so far as to prescribe the best moment to give extreme unction: 'after the first shot and before the *coup de grâce*'. Quoted in Hilari Raguer, 'Caídos por Dios y por España', *La aventura de la Historia*, 17 (March 2000), pp. 14–18.

29 'The communists and anarchists are the sons of Cain, killers of their brothers, jealous of those who make worship a virtue, and this is why they kill them and martyr them; and unable to be done with God or Christ, they discharge their hatred on His images, His temples and His ministers, and they take delight in killing, in looting, destruction and fire-raising' (Enrique Pla y Deniel, 'Las dos ciudades', 30 September 1936).

30 Pelai Pagés, *La presó Model de Barcelona. Història d'un centre penitenciari en temps de guerra (1936–1939)*, Publicacions de l'Abadia de Montserrat, Barcelona, 1996, pp. 306–307.

31 *La Vanguardia,* 2 August 1936.

32 Anarchism as a 'cultural constant' of the Spanish left from the liberal revolution to the civil war is one of the theories that José Álvarez Junco develops in *El emperador del Paralelo. Lerroux y la demagogia populista*, Alianza

33 Ronald Fraser, *Recuérdalo tú y recuérdalo a otros*, vol. I, p. 207. Gerald Brenan, *The Spanish Labyrinth: An Account of the Social and Political Background of the Spanish Civil War*, Cambridge University Press, Cambridge, 1943.

34 José Álvarez Junco, *El emperador del Paralelo*, p. 401.

35 Antonio Montero Moreno, *Historia de la persecución religiosa en España*, p. 392.

36 José Álvarez Junco, 'El anticlericalismo en el movimiento obrero', in Gabriel Jackson and others, *Octubre 1934*, pp. 283–300.

37 Frances Lannon's interpretation in 'Los cuerpos de las mujeres y el cuerpo político católico: autoridades e identidades en conflicto en España durante las décadas de 1920 y 1930', *Historia Social*, 35 (1999), pp. 72–75.

38 Antonio Montero Moreno, *Historia de la persecución religiosa,* p. 430 & 495–514 for the account of the mass killing of nuns.

39 The arguments regarding the respect for nuns are developed from reading Frances Lannon, *Privilegio, persecución y profecía*, pp. 82–86 and Joan Connelly Ullman, 'The Warp and Woof of Parliamentary Politics in Spain, 1808–1939', pp. 145–176.

40 Antonio Bermúdez, *República y guerra civil. Manzanares (1931–1939)*, Diputación de Ciudad Real, Ciudad Real, 1992, pp. 62–76.

41 For Aragón see Pilar Salomón, *Anticlericalismo en Aragón. Protesta popular y movilización política (1900–1939)*, Prensas Universitarias de Zaragoza, Zaragoza, 2002. The Susan Harding quote comes from *Remaking Ibieca. Rural life in Aragon under Franco*, University of North Carolina Press, Chapell Hill, 1984, p. 63.

42 Antonio Montero Moreno, *Historia de la persecución religiosa en España*, p. 627.

43 Bruce Lincoln, 'Revolutionary Exhumations in Spain, July 1936', *Comparative Studies in Society and History*, 27, 2 (1985), pp. 255–256.

44 Mary Low & Juan Brea, *Red Spanish Notebook. The First Six Months of the Revolution and Civil War*, Martin Secker and Warbug, London, 1937, pp. 75–77.

45 Eduardo Barriobero, *Memorias de un tribunal revolucionario*, Hacer, Barcelona, 1986, p. 70. A thorough assessment of anticlericalism during those years in Julio de la Cueva, 'El anticlericalismo en la Segunda República y la Guerra Civil', in Emilio La Parra López & Manuel Suárez Cortina (eds.), *El anticlericalismo español contemporáneo*, Biblioteca Nueva, Madrid, 1998, pp. 211–301. Information on the *Causa General* in Ciudad Real comes from Francisco Alía, *La guerra civil en retaguardia. Conflicto y revolución en la provincia de Ciudad Real (1936–1939)*, Diputación Provincial, Ciudad Real, 1994, p. 229.

46 Frances Lannon, *Privilegio, persecución y profecía*, p. 127.

47 Bishops who managed to save their lives in Antonio Montero Moreno, *Historia de la persecución religiosa en España*, pp. 83–91. Also in Nicolau Pons i Llinas, *Jesuites Mallorquins víctimes de la guerra civil*, Lleonard Muntaner, Palma de Mallorca, 1994, pp. 11–12.

48 After the Nationalist occupation of the province of Guipuzcoa, in the Basque Country, in September 1936, sixteen Basque nationalist priests were shot, giving rise to a protest from Cardinal Gomá to Franco, who assured him there would be no further shooting of clergy in his zone. A few more priests were killed in other provinces, for being suspected republicans or for not complying with the principles of the *Falange Española*, but this type of persecution was fairly rare in the Nationalist zone. I have examined this

49 Bruce Lincoln, 'Revolutionary Exhumations in Spain, July 1936', pp. 241–260.

50 *Heraldo de Aragón*, 11 August 1936.

3. An International War on Spanish Soil

1 Piers Brendon, *The Dark Valley. A Panorama of the 1930s,* Vintage Books, New York, 2002, p. 354.

2 The concerns and prejudices of British and North American diplomacy towards the Republic were first examined by Douglas Little, *Malevolent Neutrality. The United States, Great Britain and the Origins of the Spanish Civil War,* Cornell University Press, Ithaca, N.Y., 1985. After Little's book, the most detailed analysis is that of Enrique Moradiellos, *La pérfida Albion. El gobierno británico la guerra civil española*, Madrid, Siglo XXI, 1996, and Tom Buchanan, *Britain and the Spanish Civil War*, Cambridge University Press, Cambridge, 1997.

3 Enrique Moradiellos, *El reñidero de Europa. Las dimensiones internacionales de la guerra civil española*, Península, Barcelona, 2001, p. 56.

4 Ángel Viñas, *Franco, Hitler y el estallido de la guerra civil*, Alianza Ed., Madrid, 2001, p. 518.

5 Jean-François Berdah, *La democracia asesinada. La República española y las grandes potencias*, Crítica, Barcelona, 2002, pp. 204–205.

6 Anthony Beevor, *The Battle for Spain*, Phoenix, London, 2006, p. 150.

7 Quoted in Enrique Moradiellos, *La pérfida Albión,* p. 61.

8 Kenneth Williams Watkins, *Britain Divided: the Effects of the Spanish Civil War on British Political Opinion,* Thomas Nelson, & Sons, London, 1963, p. 70.

9 Antonio Marquina Barrio, 'Estados Unidos y la guerra de España', in 'La Guerra Civil', *Historia 16,* n° 18, 1986, p. 81.

10 Reproduced in Enrique Moradiellos, *El reñidero de Europa*, pp. 98–99.

11 Detailed figures for Italian and German aid to Franco may be found in, respectively, John Coverdale, *Italian Intevention in the Spanish Civil War,* Princeton University Press, Princeton, NJ, 1977, and R. L. Proctor, *Hitler's Luftwaffe in the Spanish Civil War,* Greenwood Press, Westport, Connecticut, 1983.

12 Quoted in Enrique Moradiellos, *El reñidero de Europa*, p. 101.

13 The aircraft that France sold to the Republic had to be paid for in cash, at high prices, and not on credit like those from Italy and Germany, and they were delivered without armament or pilots. The most detailed analysis of all the shipments to Spain may be found in Gerald Howson, *Arms for Spain. The Untold Story of the Spanish Civil War,* St. Martin's Press, New York, 1999.

14 Quoted in Walther L. Bernecker, *Guerra en España, 1936–1939*, Síntesis, Madrid, 1996, pp. 49–50. The ground-breaking work by Ángel Viñas was *La Alemania nazi y el 18 de julio*, Alianza Ed., Madrid, 1977.

15 Enrique Moradiellos, 'El mundo ante el avispero español: intervención

y no intervención extranjera en la guerra civil', in Santos Juliá (ed.), *Historia de España Menéndez Pidal*, vol. XL, Espasa Calpe, Madrid, 2004, pp. 247–248.

16 Ibidem, p. 253.

17 Quoted in Antonio Elorza & Marta Bizcarrondo, *Queridos camaradas. La Internacional Comunista y España, 1919–1939*, Planeta, Barcelona, 1999, p. 460.

18 Daniel Kowalsky, *Stalin and the Spanish Civil War*, Columbia University Press, New York, 2004.

19 Pablo Martín Aceña, *El oro de Moscú y el oro de Berlín*, Taurus, Madrid, 2001, pp. 23–25.

20 Some 40 tonnes had previously been sent to Paris at the end of July 1936, by order of the republican government, to obtain money, some 507 million francs, which was used to buy arms and munitions before the Non-Intervention Treaty came into force.

21 Pablo Martín Aceña, *El oro de Moscú y el oro de Berlín*, p.64.

22 The Paul Preston quote is taken from *The Spanish Civil War. Reaction, Revolution and Revenge,* Harper Collins, London, 2006, pp. 191–192. Pablo Martín Aceña's argument in *El oro de Moscú y el oro de Berlín*, pp. 160–161. What is considered to be the most exhaustive study that opened the way to research on this matter was by Ángel Viñas, *El oro de Moscú. Alfa y omega de un mito franquista*, Grijalbo, Barcelona, 1979, later summarised in *Guerra, dinero y dictadura*, Crítica, Barcelona, 1984, from where I have taken the information that I use here (pp. 168–204).

23 Gerald Howson, *Arms for Spain: The Untold Story of the Spanish Civil War,* pp. 28–29.

24 Robert Whealey, 'How Franco financed his war –reconsidered', in Martin Blinkhorn (ed.), *Spain in Conflict 1931–1939: Democracy and Its Enemies,* Sage Publications, London, 1986, pp. 244–263, developed in more detail in his *Hitler and Spain: The Nazi Role in the Spanish Civil War,* Unviersity Press of Kentucky, Lexington, 1989.

25 Eduardo González Calleja, 'El ex rey', in Javier Moreno Luzón (ed.), *Alfonso XIII. Un político en el trono,* Marcial Pons, Madrid, 2003, p. 426.

26 Ricardo de la Cierva, *Historia del Franquismo. Orígenes y configuración (1939–1945),* Planeta, Barcelona, 1975, p. 80. A prime example of this type of historiography, represented by de la Cierva, Ramón and Jesús Salas Larrazábal, may be found in the collective work, *Síntesis histórica de la Guerra de Liberación, 1936–1939,* Servicio Histórico Militar, Madrid, 1968. Currently Pío Moa is the most successful in indiscriminately promoting these theories and passing it off as his own groundbreaking research: *Los mitos de la guerra civil,* La Esfera de los Libros, Madrid, 2003.

27 Quoted in Walther L. Bernecker, *Guerra en España 1936–1939*, Sintesis, Madrid, 1996, p. 45.

28 Report dated 19 February 1939, included in the collection *Documents on German Foreign Policy 1918–1945,* series D, vol. 3, *Germany and the Spanish Civil War,* London, HMSO, 1951, document 740, p. 844. Quoted in Enrique Moradiellos, 'La intervención extranjera en la guerra civil: un ejercicio de crítica historiográfica', in Enrique Moradiellos ed., 'Dossier. La Guerra Civil', *Ayer, 50* (2003), p. 231. See also H. R. Trevor-Roper (ed.), *Hitler's Secret Conversations 1941–1944. With an introductory essay on the mind of Adolf Hitler,* New York, 1953, p. 558.

29 Report by Major E. C. Richards, 25 November 1938, reproduced in Enrique Moradiellos, *La pérfida Albión. El gobierno británico y la guerra civil española,* p. 257.

30 Jason Gurney, *Crusade in Spain,* Faber, 1974, p. 18.

31 The idea of universal battles in Piers Brendon, *The Dark Valley. A Panorama of the 1930s,* Vintage Books, New York, 2002, p. 359.

32 Michel Lefebre and Rémi Skoutelelsky, *Brigadas Internacionales. Imágenes recuperadas,* Lunwerg Editores, Barcelona, 2003.

33 Kenneth William Watkins, *Britain Divided,* p. 170.

34 This information and the quote by Eoin O'Duffy, from his *Crusade in Spain,* 1938, are taken from Paul Preston, *A Concise History of the Spanish Civil War,* pp. 125–126.

35 Raymond L. Proctor, *Hitler's Luftwaffe in the Spanish Civil War,* Greenwood Press, Westport, C.T., 1983.

36 John F. Coverdale, *Italian Intervention in the Spanish Civil War,* Princeton University Press, Princeton, N.J., 1977.

37 Quoted in Hugh Thomas, *The Spanish Civil War,* Hamish Hamilton, London, 1986, p. 853.

38 Jason Gurney, *Crusade in Spain,* p. 188.

39 George Orwell, *Homage to Catalonia,* Harmondsworth, 1966, p. 221 (first published in English in 1938).

4. The Republic at War

1 There are two documentaries that sum up the extent of this revolution perfectly: '*Reportaje del movimiento revolucionario en Barcelona*', directed by Mateo Santos, Information and Propaganda Bureau of the CNT-FAI, 1936; and '*Barcelona trabaja para el frente*', also directed by Santos and produced by the Information and Propaganda Bureau of the CNT-FAI, 1936 Both documentaries may be found in '*La guerra filmada*', Spanish Film Library, Ministry of Culture, 2009.

2 An extensive, expiatory biography has been written by the anarchist

militant Abel Paz, *Durruti en la Revolución española*, La Esfera de los Libros, Madrid, 2004 (English version, *Durruti in the Spanish Revolution,* AK Press, 2007). An exact and updated brief outline may be found in José Luis Ledesma, '20 personajes clave de la historia del anarquismo español', in Julián Casanova (coord.), *Tierra y Libertad. Cien años de anarquismo en España,* Crítica, Barcelona, 2010, pp. 256–260.

3 *Solidaridad Obrera,* the influential anarchist newspaper with the highest circulation, 14 August 1936. On 12 September the same newspaper declared: 'We are not after medals or sashes. We do not want Provincial Councils or Ministries. When we triumph, we shall go back to the factories and workshops we came from, distancing ourselves from the safe deposit boxes that we have fought so hard to abolish. It is in the factories, the fields and the mines that the true defending army of Spain will be set up'.

4 I have analysed this process in depth in *Anarchism, the Republic and Civil War in Spain,* pp. 101–145. The Regional Plenum of the Anarchist Groups of Catalonia, held in Barcelona on 21 August 1936, the first written record on this theme, discussed and approved 'the requisition and collectivisation of all establishments abandoned by their owners . . . workers' control of banking businesses until the banks are nationalised . . . and workers' union control of any industry that is still being run as a private company'.

5 I am following here the research by Mary Nash, *Defying Male Civilization: Women in the Spanish Civil War*, Arden Press, Denver, 1995, pp. 101–102; she had previously presented a brief outline of the theme in 'Milicianas and Homefront Heroines: Images of Women in War and Revolution 1936–1939', *History of European Ideas,* 11 (1989).

6 'Materials for discussion, in the IWA Plenary Session, 11 June 1937', an unpublished document, one of the most thorough reflections there has been on the changes that the anarchist movement had to undergo during the war. Part of these discussions was made public in *El anarcosindicalismo en la Revolución Española,* Comité Nacional de la CNT, Barcelona, 1938.

7 Raymond Carr, *The Spanish Tragedy. Civil War in Perspective*, Weidenfeld & Nicholson, London, 1977, p. 118.

8 Julián Zugazagoitia, *Guerra y vicisitudes de los españoles*, Tusquets, Barcelona, 2001, p. 134. Zugazagoitia, a socialist deputy in 1936, minister of the interior in Juan Negrín's first government during the war, was exiled to France, arrested by the Gestapo in July 1940, handed over to the Nationalist authorities and shot in the East Cemetery in Madrid on 9 November that year. The advance of the rebel troops through Extremadura and the massacre of Badajoz in Francisco Espinosa, *La columna de la muerte. El avance del ejército franquista de Sevilla a Badajoz,* Crítica, Barcelona, 2007. A more recent account of the

massacre of Badajoz in Paul Preston, *The Spanish Holocaust,* pp. 321–323.

9 John Whitaker, 'Prelude to World War: A Witness from Spain', *Foreign Affairs*, Vol. 21, no 1, October 1942, pp. 104–106.

10 The quote by Aragquistain and the reference to the resignation of Giral come from Santos Juliá, 'El Frente Popular y la política de la República en guerra', in Santos Juliá (ed.), *Historia de España de Menéndez Pidal, República y guerra civil*, Espasa Calpe, Madrid, 2004, vol. XL, p. 126.

11 Indalecio Prieto, Largo's great rival in the Socialist Party, said to Mijail Koltsov, the *Pravda* correspondent, that Largo Caballero was 'a frozen bureaucrat . . . capable of ruining everything', although he also admitted that he was 'the only man . . . suitable for heading a new government'. And Negrín accepted after calling this government 'absurd': 'Are they really trying to lose the war? Is this a challenge to Europe?' Quotes in Ricardo Miralles, *Juan Negrín. La República en guerra,* Temas de Hoy, Madrid, 2003, pp. 79–80.

12 Francisco Largo Caballero, *Mis recuerdos*, Ediciones Unidas, Mexico, 1976, pp. 175–176, which mentions the term 'haggling'. Manuel Azaña, the president of the Republic refused to sign the decree at first 'because he found the presence of four anarchists in the government repellent': Indeed, months later Azaña wrote 'it was not only contrary to my opinion but also with my most bitter protestations, that the government reshuffle of November was imposed, with the entry of the CNT and the anarchists' (in 'Cuadernos de la Pobleta', annotation of 20 May 1937, in *Memorias políticas y de guerra*, II, p. 43). An account of the negotiation of the anarchists' entry into the government of the Republic may be found in my book *Anarchism, the Republic and Civil War in Spain,* pp. 116–121.

13 The anarchist newspaper *Solidaridad Obrera* for 10 November supported the transfer of the government. However, a few days later, a CNT National Assembly witnessed the indignation of some delegates over the way this unpopular measure had been supported. The scapegoat was the national secretary Horacio Martínez Prieto, who was held responsible for this abandonment. He was forced to resign and was replaced by Mariano R. Vázquez, the man who controlled the CNT in Catalonia and who was to be the leader of the organisation during the rest of the war.

14 Helen Graham, *The Spanish Civil War. A Very Short Introduction,* Oxford University Press, Oxford, 2005, p. 52. It is Helen Graham that we have to thank for the most thorough study on the political forces and their disputes in the republican zone: *The Spanish Republic at War 1936–1939*, Cambridge University Press, Cambridge, 2002.

15 Helmut Rudiger, *El anarcosindicalismo en la Revolución Española,* p. 49.

16 According to the report by the Bulgarian, Sotyan Mineevich ('Stepanov'), sent to Moscow on 17 March 1937, quoted in Antonio Elorza & Marta Bizcarrondo, *Queridos camaradas. La Internacional Comunista y España, 1919–1939*, Planeta, Barcelona, 1999, p. 340.

17 The origin of these disputes and an account of these conflicts and deaths in my book *Anarchism, the Republic and Civil War in Spain*, pp. 142–145.

18 Azaña's version in 'Teletypes between the President of the Republic in Barcelona and the central government in Valencia, on the situation in that capital', 4–6 May 1937, Servicio Histórico Militar (Madrid), cabinet 53, batch 461, file 1.

19 George Orwell's account, *Homage to Catalonia*, Secker & Warburg, London, 1971, pp. 160–192. That day, however, there were disturbances on the Aragón home front, with groups of armed men who attacked two military barracks, taking arms and munitions and killing a number of prisoners: Report from the Legal Service of the Aragón Front, Servicio Histórico Militar, cabinet 62, batch 788, file 1.

20 All the information on the handling of the crisis in the Civil War Archive, Salamanca, file 39 for Bilbao.

21 With his resignation, induced by the Communist Party and a sector of the PSOE executive, Largo Caballero, then 67, practically said goodbye to a long career devoted to trade union struggles, socialism and the Republic, although, by then in exile, he was yet to experience the hell of the Nazi concentration camp at Orianenburg. When it was liberated by the Soviet troops in April 1945, he returned to France and died in Paris on 23 March 1946. 'One way to regard the last stage of the Civil War', Raymond Carr writes, 'is to see it as the final triumph of the political parties over the trade unions. The defeated of May 1937 were Largo Caballero and the CNT. The victors were Prieto and the Executive Committee of the Socialist Party, the Communists and the Republicans' (*The Spanish Tragedy*, p. 199).

22 Manuel Azaña, 'El cuaderno de la Pobleta', p. 56.

23 This was the 'decisive reason' for his appointment, according to Santos Juliá, *Los socialistas en la política española, 1879–1982*, Taurus, Madrid, 1996, pp. 262–263. The quote on his 'effectiveness', in Ricardo Miralles, *Juan Negrín*, p. 129.

24 After the Republic's defeat, Negrín spent the first few months of exile in France. Afterwards, during the Second World War, he was in England, where he led the republican government in exile, a post that was never recognised by Winston Churchill. When the Second World War finished, he returned to Paris, where he died on 12 November 1956. Although he was despised by his enemies and some of his alleged friends, his political life and activity is better known today thanks to studies by authors such as the aforementioned Ricardo Miralles, *Juan Negrín*;

Enrique Moradiellos, *Negrín*, Península, Barcelona, 2006; and Gabriel Jackson, *Juan Negrín. Médico, socialista y jefe de Gobierno de la II República española*, Crítica, Barcelona, 2008.

25 Paul Preston, *The Spanish Civil War. Reaction, Revolution and Revenge*, HarperCollins, London, 2006, pp. 253–5 and Julián Casanova, *Anarchism, the Republic and Civil War in Spain*, p. 153.

26 Speech given on 16 November 1937, reproduced in J. M. Cuenca Toribio, *La oratoria parlamentaria española*, Centro de Estudios Políticos, Madrid, 2002, p. 944.

27 Enrique Moradiellos, *1936. Los mitos de la Guerra Civil*, Península, Barcelona, 2004, p. 131.

28 Helen Graham, *The Spanish Civil War: A very Short Introduction*, p. 101.

29 Helen Graham, *The Spanish Republic at War*, p. 383.

30 The two reports are in Ricardo Miralles, *Juan Negrín*, pp. 297–298.

31 Dispatch from R.S. Stevenson, 25 November 1938, quoted in Enrique Moradiellos, *El reñidero de España*, p. 235.

32 Cipriano Rivas Cheriff, *Retrato de un desconocido. Vida de Manuel Azaña*, Grijalbo, Barcelona, 1979, p. 437.

5. The New Order

1 Enrique Moradiellos, *1936. Los mitos de la Guerra Civil*, Península, Barcelona, 2004, p. 197–198. The 'direct relationship between the militarisation of public order and the politicisation of the military sectors', which was heightened during the republican years, had already been remarked upon some time previously by Manuel Ballbé, *Orden público y militarismo en la España constitucional (1812–1983)*, Alianza Ed., Madrid, 1985, pp. 317–319.

2 Isamel Saz, 'Política en zona nacionalista: la configuración de un régimen', in Enrique Moradiellos, ed., 'La guerra civil', *Ayer*, 50 (2003), p. 59.

3 Paul Preston, *Franco*, p. 177.

4 Quoted by his son Guillermo Cabanellas, *La guerra de los mil días*, Grijalbo, Barcelona, 1973, p. 652, vol. 1. General Cabanellas was demoted to the post of Inspector General of Military Hospitals and died, with few honours, in Málaga in May 1938.

5 In his first speech, Franco was already revealing his intentions: 'You have placed Spain in my hands. My hand will be steady, my grip steady and I shall strive to lift Spain to her rightful position as befits her history, the position she occupied in earlier times' (quoted in Enrique Moradiellos, *1936. Los mitos de la Guerra Civil*, p. 208).

6 'The making of a Caudillo' is fully examined by Paul Preston, *Franco*, pp. 171–198. See also Juan Pablo Fusi, *Franco. Autoritarismo y poder personal*, Taurus, Madrid, 1995, pp. 61–62.

7   'Report from Cardinal Gomá to the Secretary of State. Third general report on the situation in Spain on the occasion of the civil-military uprising of July 1936' (24 October 1936), reproduced in *Archivo Gomá*, pp. 245–252. *Documentos de la Guerra Civil. 1: Julio-Diciembre de 1936*, edición de José Andrés Gallego y Antonio M. Pazos, CSIC, Madrid, 2001, pp. 245–252.

8   Juan Pablo Fusi, *Franco*, p. 65

9   Quoted sentences, threats and exaggerations in Ian Gibson, *Queipo de Llano. Sevilla, verano de 1936*, Grijalbo, Barcelona, 1986, p. 72, 224, 256.

10 Carlism was an extreme right monarchist popular movement born a century before the Second Republic, in the 1830s, amid a dynastic dispute. Held back and weakened by the presence of the Alfonsine monarchy during the first third of the twentieth century, the Carlists gained great benefit from the fall of Alfonso XIII and the establishment of a republican regime in Spain. Its anti-republican ideology was accompanied in the 1930s by the active reconstruction of the *Requeté,* the military force formed by its most belligerent youth members, a modern paramilitary unit that was trained and in perfect readiness to assist in the *coup d'état* in July 1936. See Martin Blinkhorn, *Carlism and Crisis in Spain, 1931–1939*, Cambridge University Press, Cambridge, 1975. The information on Fal Conde in Paul Preston, *Franco*, pp. 208–9.

11 Quoted in Javier Tusell, *Franco en la Guerra Civil. Una biografía política*, Tusquets, Barcelona, 1992, pp. 91–92.

12 Ibidem, p. 112.

13 Joan Maria Thomàs, *Lo que fue la Falange*, Plaza & Janés, Barcelona, 1999, p. 145.

14 The process of unification is efficiently described in Paul Preston, *Franco*, pp. 248–274.

15 Hedilla asked Franco for 'mercy and magnanimity' and Pilar Primo de Rivera, José Antonio's sister, and Serrano Suñer also intervened to retract the sentence, while the German ambassador, General Wilhelm von Faupel, advised that 'with the times being as they are, it is very dangerous to create martyrs'. See Javier Tusell, *Franco en la guerra civil*, pp. 130–1, 301.

16 Paul Preston, *Franco*, p. 279.

17 Juan Pablo Fusi, *Franco*, p. 76.

18 The Jesuit Father, Constantino Bayle, 'El espíritu de Falange española', ¿es católico?, *Razón y Fe*, 112 (1937), p. 236.

19 Eloy Montero, *Los estados modernos y la nueva España* (1939), quoted in Alfonso Botti, *Cielo y dinero. El nacionalcatolicismo en España (1881–1975)*, Alianza Ed., Madrid, 1992, pp. 102–3. The seamless fusion between Catholic tradition and the new Fascist ideology since

the early days of the civil war is also recounted in detail with significant quotes in Santos Juliá, *Historia de las dos Españas*, Taurus, Madrid, 2004, pp. 298–99; also Helen Graham, *The Spanish Civil War*, pp. 83–84.

20 As time went by, and well into the Second World War, when the Axis powers saw defeat looming, the dictatorship was forced to abandon its Fascist leanings and emphasise its Catholic roots, the identification between Catholicism and Spanish tradition. The regime that came out of the civil war had nothing in common with fascism, said Franco in an interview with *United Press* in November 1944, because fascism did not include Catholicism as a basic principle.

21 Detailed information on this government in Paul Preston, *Franco*, 295–298; and Javier Tusell, *Franco en la Guerra Civil española*, pp. 228–246. As soon as this government was formed, Cardinal Gomá sent a report to Cardinal Pacelli expressing his conviction that Spain was on the eve of 'legal renovation in matters relating to the Church in its different aspects' ('Report from the Primate to Cardinal Pacelli', 2 February 1938, in María Luisa Rodríguez Aisa, *El cardenal Gomá y la guerra de España. Aspectos de la gestión pública del Primado 1936–1939*, CSIC, Madrid, 1981, pp. 295–296.

22 Published in the Official State Gazette of 10 March and included in the publication of the *FET y de las JONS, Doctrina e Historia de la Revolución Nacional Española*, 1939.

23 Quoted in Alfonso Álvarez Bolado, *Para ganar la guerra, para ganar la paz. Iglesia y guerra civil: 1936–1939*, Universidad Pontificia de Comillas, Madrid, 1995, p. 254.

24 Pastoral letter from Enrique Pla y Deniel, 'Los delitos del pensamiento y los falso ídolos intelectuales' (*The crimes of thought and false intellectual idols*), quoted in Alfonso Álvarez Bolado, *Para ganar la guerra, para ganar la paz,* p. 292. The idea of 'involving God and his works in everything' was written by Cardinal Gomá in *La España heroica. Ascética de nuestra guerra*, Gráficas Bercausa, Pamplona, 1937, pp. 37–38.

25 Report of the Technical Advisory Board on education in Barcelona, dated 16 January 1939 (Franco's troops entered Barcelona on 26 January). Sainz Rodríguez's circular is taken from the *Archbishopric of Burgos Ecclesiastical Gazette*, 22 March 1938.

26 Ángela Cenarro (quoting Martínez de Bedoya), *La sonrisa de Falange. Auxilio social en la guerra civil y en la posguerra*, Crítica, Barcelona, 2006, pp. 1–13.

27 Jaume Claret, *El atroz desmoche. La destrucción de la Universidad española por el franquismo, 1936–1945*, Crítica, Barcelona, 2006; and Mercedes del Amo, *Salvador Vila: el rector fusilado en Víznar*, Universidad de Granada, Granada, 2005.

28 Santos Juliá, *Historia de las dos Españas*, p. 318.
29 Ibidem, pp. 303–304 and 318.
30 Alfonso Álvarez Bolado, *Para ganar la guerra, para ganar la paz*, pp. 324 and 348.
31 Aniceto de Castro Albarrán, *Guerra Santa. El sentido católico del Movimiento Nacional Español*, Editorial Española, Burgos, 1938, p. 33.
32 Helen Graham believes that after May 1937 and with the arrival of Juan Negrín to the government of the Republic and the creation of a regular army, 'disunity in republican Spain had rather less to do with ideology and internal politics than it did with the cumulatively negative material and psychological impact of Non-Intervention [and] military defeat' (*The Spanish Civil War*, p. 68).
33 Pablo Martín Aceña, 'La economía española de los años treinta', in Santos Juliá (ed.), *Historia de España de Menéndez Pidal. República y guerra civil*, (42 vols.), España Calpe, Madrid, 2004, Vol XL, p. 403.
34 The efforts to mitigate the repression of Basque nationalist priests in María Luisa Rodríguez Aísa, *El cardinal Gomá y la guerra de España*, pp. 222–223. Franco was 'magnanimous' on p. 229; and Franco's comment to Gomá on 'unconditional surrender' on p. 170. The occupation of Guipúzcoa by the military rebels in September 1936 was accompanied by a blood-soaked repression of left-wingers, but sixteen Basque priests were shot in October 1936, by the very people who supported this 'holy, just war', and this caused a protest from Cardinal Gomá to Franco, who was unaware of the event and gave him his 'assurance that this will stop immediately' ('Letter from Cardinal Gomá to Cardinal Pacelli. Report of the shooting of priests by the military authorities of the national government', 8 November 1936, *Archivo Gomá*, pp. 283–286). I have written about these events and others involving priests killed by the military rebels in *La Iglesia de Franco*, Crítica, Barcelona, 2005, pp. 160–170.
35 Quoted by Alfonso Álvarez Bolado, *Para ganar la guerra, para ganar la paz*, pp. 318–319.
36 Ibidem, p. 319. The Sánchez-Juliá quote in José Ángel Tello, *Ideología política. La Iglesia católica española, 1936–1959*, Pórtico, Zaragoza, 1984, p. 85
37 Ibidem, p. 86; Georges Bernanos, *Los grandes cementerios bajo la luna*, Alianza Ed., Madrid, 1986; Antonio Ruiz Vilaplana, *Doy fe . . . un año de actuación en la España nacionalista*, París, n.d., 1938.
38 Manuel Azaña, 'Speech at the University of Valencia', 18 July 1937, in *Los españoles en guerra*, Crítica, Barcelona, 1977, pp. 74–75, although the reference to the 'terrible war . . .' is from the Speech in the Valencia City Hall', 21 January 1937 (p. 19).
39 The discordant voices in Juan María Laboa, 'La reacción católica

mundial', in 'La guerra civil', *Historia 16,* vol. 13, 1986, pp. 111–112.
The 'advisability' of the Holy See not collaborating in the mediation
to put an end to the war was communicated by Gomá to Monsignor
Pizzardo on 25 May 1937, in a letter quoted by María Luisa Rodríguez
Aísa, *El cardenal Gomá y la guerra de España,* p. 167.

6. A Long War

1 The argument and quoted phrases are taken from Gabriel Cardona,
*Historia militar de una guerra civil. Estrategias y tácticas de la guerra
de España,* Flor del Viento, Barcelona, 2006, pp. 21 and 45.
2 Ibidem, p. 24.
3 José Martínez Bande, *La invasión de Aragón y el desembarco en Mallorca,*
San Martín, Madrid, 1970, p. 75 and Ramón Salas Larrazábal, *Historia
del Ejército Popular de la República,* Editora Nacional, Madrid, 1973,
pp. 330–332, vol. I. Figures from the anarchist viewpoint in Juan
García Oliver, *El eco de los pasos,* Ruedo Ibérico, Barcelona, 1978,
pp. 198–199, and Rudolf Rocker, *The truth about Spain,* Frei Abeiter,
Stimme, New York, undated, p. 3.
4 The 'political benefits' in Paul Preston, *Franco,* p. 175. According to
Gabriel Cardona, diverting to Toledo instead of advancing on Madrid
was 'the first of many strategic follies committed by Franco during the
war' (*Historia militar de una guerra civil,* p. 79).
5 'Within range of our artillery', said the Nationalist army report for
6 November, quoted by Jorge M. Reverte, *La batalla de Madrid,* Crítica,
Barcelona, 2004, a day-by-day detailed account of the attack and defence
of the capital.
6 Gabriel Cardona, *Historia militar de una guerra civil,* p. 96.
7 Julio Aróstegui, "La defensa de Madrid y el comienzo de la guerra
larga", in Edward Malefakis (ed.), *La guerra de España (1936–1939),*
Taurus, Madrid, 1996, p. 151.
8 Quoted in José Andrés Rojo, *Vicente Rojo. Retrato de un general repub-
licano,* Tusquets, Barcelona, 2006, pp. 102–104.
9 A good many examples of this propaganda work can be seen in the
1936 documentary, *Defensa de Madrid,* directed by Ángel Villatoro and
produced by the International Red Aid, in 'La guerra filmada', Filmoteca
Española, Ministry of Culture, 2009.
10 José Andrés Rojo, *Vicente Rojo,* p. 76.
11 Gabriel Cardona, 'Entre la revolución y la disciplina. Ensayo sobre la
dimensión militar de la guerra civil', in Enrique Moradiellos, ed., 'La
Guerra Civil', *Ayer,* 50 (2003), pp. 41–51.
12 Ibidem.
13 According to Jorge M. Reverte (*La batalla de Madrid,* p. 209), 'the

difference between the *paseos* or indiscriminate killings of August is clear: in the November actions there was a direct intervention of republican authorities, of people in official posts'. See also Javier Cervera, *Madrid en guerra. La ciudad clandestina*, Alianza Ed., Madrid, 2006. For a recent detailed and meticulous analysis, see Paul Preston, *The Spanish Holocaust*, pp. 341–380, in which he notes the difficulties in ascertaining the 'collective responsibility' for those crimes. The political debate, stirred up by the Francoist far right, has always revolved around Santiago Carrillo, secretary general of the Communist Party of Spain for almost thirty years (1956–1985) and a significant politician during the transition from dictatorship to democracy at the end of the 1970s.

14 A good example is to be found in 'Prisoners prove intervention in Spain' (1938), produced by the Progressive Films Institute, and directed by Ivor Montagu, in which the Italian sub-lieutenant Gino Poggi, brought down when he was crewing a Savoia 79, acknowledges that he had taken part in the Abyssinia campain and that he was a member of the Italian army (included in 'La guerra filmada', Filmoteca Española, Ministry of Culture, 2009).

15 One person, for example, who doubted his 'competence' to direct the war was General Wilhelm von Faupel, the first German ambassador in rebel Spain, who said as much in a secret dispatch to the Nazi authorities on 10 December 1936 (quoted in Enrique Moradiellos, *Francisco Franco. Crónica de un Caudillo casi olvidado*, Biblioteca Nueva, Madrid, 2002, p. 85). The theory that Franco wanted a long war to exterminate the enemy was thoroughly analysed by Paul Preston in his biography *Franco*, an interpretation which has been backed up by others including Enrique Moradilellos and, from a military historian's viewpoint, Gabriel Cardona, the source of the 'taming the generals' reference (*Historia militar de una guerra civil*, p. 147). Francoist officers refute this theory and praise Franco's strategy (for example Rafael Casas de la Vega, *Franco militar*, Fénix, Madrid, 1995), but others, who had little time for him, such as Carlos Blanco Escolá, confirm, as the title of one of his books indicates, *La incompetencia militar de Franco*, [Franco's military incompetence] (Alianza, Madrid, 2000).

16 The two quotes in Paul Preston, *Franco*, the first on p. 222 and the second on p. 242.

17 Ibidem, p. 239.

18 Gabriel Cardona, *Historia militar de una guerra civil*, p. 150. In English, the military aspects of this war of attrition, from Madrid to the final victory of the Nationalists, are fully discussed in Antony Beevor, *The Battle for Spain. The Spanish Civil War 1936–1939*, Weidenfeld & Nicolson, London, 2006.

19 Quoted in Gonzalo Redondo, *Historia de la Iglesia en España 1931–1939. Vol. II. La guerra civil 1936–1939,* Rialp, Madrid, 1993, p. 288.

20 Michael Alpert, "La historia militar", in Stanley Payne & Javier Tusell (dir.), *La guerra civil. Una nueva visión del conflicto que dividió a España,* Temas de Hoy, Madrid, 1996, p. 163.

21 This strrategy, according to Gabriel Cardona, met with success in the early days, but soon afterwards, since the republican army lacked 'reserves able to take over and continue the offensive', Franco was able to transport fresh troops to the battle and short-lived victory became defeat: 'Entre la revolución y la disciplina. Ensayo sobre la dimensión militar de la guerra civil', in Enrique Moradiellos (ed.), 'La guerra civil', *Ayer,* 50 (2003), p. 49.

22 As well as Rey d'Harcourt, the Augustine friar Anselmo Polanco, the Bishop of Teruel, was arrested and they were taken, along with many other prisoners, to Valencia and then to Barcelona. On 16 January 1939, a few days before Barcelona fell into the hands of Franco's troops, they were taken out of the convent that was their prison and taken to the frontier, although they were machine-gunned down before crossing it, on 7 February. Among the victims were Bishop Polanco, Colonel Rey d'Harcourt and the vicar general of the diocese of Teruel, Felipe Ripoll Morata. I have recounted these events in *La Iglesia de Franco,* pp. 207–209.

23 Antony Beevor, *La guerra civil española,* p. 476.

24 José Andrés Rojo, *Vicente Rojo,* pp. 190–96, also the source for Negrin's reply quoted in the following paragraph.

25 A thorough analysis of the more than 2,000 bombing raids on Aragonese territory throughout the war (of which 71% were carried out by the Nationalist air force) in José María Maldonado, *Aragón bajo las bombas,* Government of Aragón, Zaragoza, 2011. This domination in the air and of Nationalist army tanks contrasted with the situation that the republican army found itself in on this front, according to the opinion that the investigating judge, General Carlos Masquelet, delivered on 2 April 1938 to the minister of Defence regarding the 'collapse' of the eastern front: 'deficient units, unarmed units (...) elementary fortifications (...) miserable means of transport and above all, a huge disproportion between our resources and those of the enemy, with advantage to the former' ('The collapse of the eastern front in March 1938', report of the examining magistrate, 2 April 1938, Servicio Histórico Militar, cabinet 46, batch 768, file 1).

26 Gabriel Cardona, *Historia militar de una guerra civil,* p. 242. Paul Preston also explains this decision not to attack Catalonia due to his strategy of eliminating his enemies and not worrying about the lives of his men: *Franco,* pp. 304–316.

27 Paul Preston, *Franco,* p. 316.

28 Manuel Azaña, 'Carta a Ángel Osorio', in *Obras Completas III*, edited by Juan Marichal, Oasis, México, 1967, p. 539.
29 A detailed analysis of Casado's coup and its consequences in Ángel Bahamonde & Javier Cervera, *Así terminó la guerra de España*, Marcial Pons, Madrid, 2000, pp. 349–404.
30 Quoted in Gonzalo Redondo, *Historia de la Iglesia en España*, pp. 603–605.
31 Josep Maria Solí i Sabaté & Joan Villarroya, *España en llamas. La guerra civil desde el aire*, Temas de Hoy, Madrid, 2003, pp. 9–10 and 313–316.
32 Gabriel Cardona, 'Entre la revolución y la disciplina. Ensayo sobre la dimensión militar de la guerra civil española', pp. 41–51.

Epilogue: An Uncivil Peace

1 On 16 October 1940, Franco appointed his brother-in-law, Ramón Serrano Súñer, who had occupied the Interior Ministry since January 1938, minister of Foreign Affairs. On 20 October 1940, to mark his triumphant debut in the new post, Serrano Súñer received in Madrid, with all the honours and Fascist paraphernalia, Heinrich Himmler, the architect of the SS and head of the Nazi police structure, to prepare the security measures for the historic meeting between Hitler and Franco which was to take place in Hendaye, on the Franco-Spanish border, three days later. As Paul Preston has related, this meeting between Himmler and Serrano Súñer also served to improve cooperation between the Gestapo and the Francoist police (Paul Preston, *Franco. A Biography*, HarperCollinsPublishers, London, 1993, 392).
2 For the concentration camps and exile in France the best analysis is by Geneviève Dreyfus-Armand, *L'exil des républicains espagnols en France. De la Guerre civile à la mort de Franco*, Albin Michel, Paris, 1999.
3 The exchange of telegrams between Pius XII and Franco may be seen in Gonzalo Redondo, *Historia de la Iglesia en España 1931–1939. Tomo II. La Guerra Civil 1936–1929*, Rialp, Madrid, 1993, pp. 607–608.
4 I have analysed the relations between the Church and Franco's dictatorship and the extent to which the Church and Catholicism condoned the persecution of the adversary, particularly during the first few decades of the dictatorship, in my book *La Iglesia de Franco*.

Bibliographic commentary

It was foreign historians, particularly British and North American, who were the first to challenge the version of history told by the victors of the civil war. And they did so with general syntheses that were finely crafted and elegantly written that are still useful today. The best examples are Gabriel Jackson, *The Spanish Republic and the Civil War*, Princeton University Press, 1965; Hugh Thomas, *The Spanish Civil War*, Eyre & Spottiswoode Ltd., 1961; and Raymond Carr, *Spanish Tragedy. Civil War in Perspective*, Weidenfeld & Nicholson, London, 1977.

The thought and constant search for accuracy that marked these early works are still the distinguishing features of these British and North American hispanists. Paul Preston is currently the bridging point between this first generation and the new British historians, to whom his research is usually directed. Chief among his extensive output are *Franco. A Biography*, HarperCollinsPublishers, London, 1993 and the revised and expanded version of *The Spanish Civil War*, Harper Perennial, 2006, which also includes a comprehensive bibliographic chapter. Preston's book and the work by Antony Beevor, *The Battle for Spain: The Spanish Civil War 1936–1939*, Weidenfeld & Nicolson, London, 2006, are the two most complete and updated syntheses of the war, although one should not forget the still valuable contribution, for its highly imaginative approach, of the work by Ronald Fraser, *The Blood of Spain: Experience of the Civil War*, Viking, 1979.

Concise, although evocative, is the work by Helen Graham, *The Spanish Civil War: A Very Short Introduction*, Oxford University Press, 2005. Also useful Francisco J. Romero Salvadó, *The Spanish Civil War*, Palgrave McMillan, New York. 2005. Significant is the work by Burnett Bolloten, *The Spanish Civil War: Revolution and Counterrevolution*, University of North Carolina Press, 1991. My recent contribution on the whole period in *The Spanish Republic and Civil War*, Cambridge University Press, Cambridge, 2010

The destruction of the adversary and different expressions of political violence have been synthesised, based on a large number of local, provincial and regional monographs on the subject, by Paul Preston in his exhaustive *The Spanish Holocaust. Inquisition and Extermination in Twentieth Century Spain*, Harper Collins, London, 2012.

A wealth of information on the dark world of arms trafficking in Gerald Howson, *Arms for Spain: The Untold Story of the Spanish Civil War*, St Martins Press, 1999.

A synthesis about the international dimension of the war in Michael Alpert, *A New International History of the Spanish Civil War*, Palgrave Macmillan, London, 2003. A good compilation of articles on the topic in Paul Preston & A. Mackenzie (eds.), *The Republic Besieged: Civil War in Spain 1936–1939*, Edinburgh University Press, Edinburgh, 1996. For the Republic at war, the most meticulous and detailed study is Helen Graham, *The Spanish Republic at War 1936–1939*, Cambridge University Press, 2002. I analysed the positions and practice of anarchism in *Anarchism, the Republic and Civil War in Spain: 1931–1939*, Routledge, London, 2005. For communism, see Stanley G. Payne, *The Spanish Civil War, The Soviet Union, and Communism*, Yale University Press, 2004. For socialism, Helen Graham, *Socialism And War: The Spanish Socialist Party In Power And Crisis, 1936–1939*, Cambridge University Press, 1991.

For Nationalist Spain, there is a wealth of well-organised information in Paul Preston, *Franco*. For the home fronts, Paul Preston has also made insightful contributions in *Doves of War: Four Women of the Spanish Civil War*, Harper Collins, 2003. The best synthesis on women on the republican home front is by Mary Nash, *Defying Male Civilization: Women in the Spanish Civil War*, Arden Press,

Denver, 1995. A social history, which places emphasis on the personal aspect and internal affairs of the civil war, while giving less importance to international influence, is the work by Michael Seidman, *Republic of Egos: A History of the Spanish Civil War*, University of Wisconsin Press, 2002. Significant works reflecting a new approach to the civil war in Chris Ealham & Michael Richards, *The Splintering of Spain. Cultural History and the Spanish Civil War, 1936–1939*, Cambridge University Press, Cambridge, 2005.

Index

Illustrations are indicated by italic references.
Endnotes are indicated by n.